1972

The Prince & the Genie

The Prince &
the Genie

A Study of Rimbaud's Influence

on Claudel

JOHN MacCOMBIE

THE UNIVERSITY OF MASSACHUSETTS PRESS 1972

For David and Theresa,
in memory of Jacqueline

Acknowledgments

I wish to express my deep gratitude to all those who were instrumental in preparing this book. Special thanks are due to Henri Peyre, for his initial encouragement in writing the PhD thesis for Yale University from which the present work evolved, for his continued generous interest in the project, and for his suggestions for revising the original manuscript; to my father, for his insights into various theological problems and clarification of Biblical texts; to my mother, for her encouragement and immeasurable patience during the incubation period of the book; to David Buskey, for his help in preparing the bibliography and reference notes of the original manuscript; to Marie-Odette Bullion-Barthouil, for her help on the reference notes of the present work; to Pierre Claudel and Renée Nantet, for allowing me access to certain of Claudel's manuscripts; to the late Henri Mondor, for suggestions on the method to apply to the analysis of Rimbaud's and Claudel's works; to Claude-Arthur, for his faithful companionship during the final months of preparation of the manuscript.

I am particularly indebted to Theresa de Kerpely, without whose discriminating editorial eye and infinite patience with an obdurate author, the present volume could not have been written.

John MacCombie

"Sandridge," September 26, 1971

Contents

Introduction

Jean-Arthur Rimbaud and Paul Claudel, born fifteen years apart—
in 1854 and 1868, respectively—were contemporaries in the broad
sense of the word. Greatly influenced by the turmoil of mid-nineteenth-century France, both poets were subject to the aftermath of
the Industrial Revolution which brought with it the materialistic
philosophies of expanding empires and colonialism, the pragmatism
of evolving socialistic doctrines, the impact of agnostic scientific
viewpoints perpetuated by adherents to the theories of Darwinism
and late-nineteenth-century skepticism, the revolutionary fervor
of republicanism coming into its own. While participating in such
expansion, each of these poets, in his own way, reacted violently against it. Each presented to the world a poetry of "revolt."
Rimbaud evoked a questioning revolt, which he sought to express
in a transcendental poetry that, more than positing vain hopes for
an unattainable ideal expressed in terms of concrete reality, explored the mystical possibilities of the imagination stimulated by
excessive wallowing in exotic existence; he sought to draw from
such experience essences and a new truth that would transcend the
rational realities of a scientific age. Claudel proposed an awareness
of religious spiritual mysteries to be recognized through a profound
sensitiviy to God's Creation in a deeply personal revolt against materialism. Both envisioned recognition of the broad cosmic implications of the universe as a means of reaction against materialism's
subjugation of the individual and its destruction of spiritual realities.

In the purely literary circles of the period, the Parnassians had
made a sterile attempt to impose their concept of *l'art pour l'art,*
art for art's sake, on poetry. Baudelaire, in response to Sweden-
borg, Balzac, even Gauthier, had brought a concept of "correspondences" into focus, and, under his tutelage, poets were beginning
an attempt to give a more personally essential meaning to their
works and to express what Rimbaud was to call "quintessences,"
which the poet distinguished in Baudelaire's "forest of symbols."

With Rimbaud's highly personalized approach and hermeticism, came the symbolism that was the backdrop for much of French literature—including the prose works of men like André Gide, as well as poetry—from the 1880s on. And Claudel, in the aura of Mallarmé's white sterility and under the influence of the era's poetic upheaval—its *révoltés, visionnaires,* and *décadents*—was to be what might well be called the last of the symbolist poets, bringing to poetry the concepts that Rimbaud had outlined, and giving to them some finite place in an infinite world, the expression of what he called an "inexhaustible" mystery.

Viewed in a more intimate light, Rimbaud and Claudel have strikingly similar personal backgrounds. Both were born in provincial France, into middle-class families struggling to make some mark on bourgeois society. Both grew up in a countryside that left them imbued with a love of nature which, by its very essence, alienated them spiritually from the "civilization" of the modern world, forcing them to seek refuge in "another time," "another setting," in a re-creation of mystery. Each had the same kind of Odyssean imagination that compelled him to undertake long voyages, both figuratively and literally. Consequently, even though they never met, there existed between them a priori a spiritual affinity, which made it possible for Paul Claudel to recognize in Arthur Rimbaud an *âme sœur.*

By the time Claudel became acquainted with Rimbaud's works in the spring and summer of 1886, Rimbaud was already in Africa and had long since turned his back on the literary world. In fact, he had so completely cut himself off from the poets whom he frequented from 1871 through 1874, that an editor published his *Œuvres Complètes* in 1888 as the works of "the late Arthur Rimbaud," presuming him dead, since Rimbaud had not answered letters concerning the publication of his works. But in a literary sense, Rimbaud was coming into his own as an acknowledged literary figure and as a precursor of the symbolist movement that was sweeping Parisian literary circles. Other poets were taking up his torch—at least as the flame seemed to burn for them—even though Rimbaud himself was no longer concerned with it. And Paul Claudel was catapulted into a life-long spiritual association with Rimbaud, from his first reading of *Une Saison en Enfer* and *Les Illuminations.* It was a relationship that had many ramifications in Claudel's life and that has caused a great deal of speculation by literary critics, from Jacques Rivière who, as early as 1908, "felt in *Connaissance de l'Est* certain recollections of Rimbaud,"[1] to W. M. Frohock who finds that "Paul Claudel's discovery of a source of spiritual sustenance in *Une Saison* is hardly more surprising than that the Surrealists should have claimed Rimbaud as their precursor."[2] Some of these critics have accepted Claudel's assertions concerning his spiritual intimacy with Rimbaud without question and even with enthusiastic approbation of Claudel's position; others have expressed the opinion that the extent of Rimbaud's influence must be qualified, that Claudel's hyperbolic praises of Rimbaud obscure and exaggerate the reality of his Rimbaldian experience; still others have found Claudel's affirmations quite preposterous. Few have gone any further than to recognize Claudel's deep reverence for Rimbaud and to state that it does or does not seem valid.[3] Nor has Claudel himself given us many insights into the nature of the influence which he repeatedly stated Rimbaud had on him, both personally and poetically.

The object of this study, then, is to reveal some insights into and an understanding of the nature of that influence, and to demonstrate that Claudel's affirmation was more than a vague impressionistic judgment based on some mystical and indefinable personal cult of Rimbaud. However, the process of examination of this influence cannot be based on a precise, scientifically analytical method, which follows some well-defined pattern of chronological development in order to establish specific and readily discernible stylistic or aesthetic borrowings. It cannot be said of Claudel's works—as it can of a sonnet by Marot, which may indicate the direct influence of a particular aspect of Italian Renaissance poetry—that certain poetic forms demonstrate a specific development along lines previously proposed by another poet, in Claudel's case, by Rimbaud. Rather, just as Claudel himself read and interpreted Rimbaud's works, we must examine closely and interpret Claudel's own works and attempt to arrive at some conclusions concerning the influence that he said involved his "principles, thought and even form." We must try to discover those elements that reflect the nature of a mys-

1. *Correspondance: Jacques Rivière et Paul Claudel*, 1907-1914 (Paris: Librairie Plon, 1926), p. 137.
2. W. M. Frohock, *Rimbaud's Poetic Practice* (Cambridge, Mass.: Harvard University Press, 1963), p. 3.
3. Two notable exceptions are Ernest Friche, *Etudes Claudéliennes* (cf. pp. 76-150), and F. Petralia, "*Le Rimbaud de Claudel*," Langues Vivantes, No. 49 (Brussels, 1956).

tical union between Rimbaud and Claudel. And even if it is actually impossible to point to a specific influence on form—though certain elements of Claudel's works do evoke what he referred to as "the modulation" of Rimbaud's phrases—nevertheless, an examination of his works does point to the subtleties of technique, an approach to aesthetic doctrine, various kinds of imagery and the symbolic values that Claudel associates with them, which reflect an understanding and assimilation of many of Rimbaud's ideas. They also reflect an interpretation of Rimbaud that is singularly Claudelian.

As a poet, dramatist, and Biblical exegete, Claudel was enormously prolific, especially considering his time-consuming duties in the French diplomatic service in China, Belgium, Brazil, the United States, and other countries. Despite his varied professional activities as a statesman, he found time to produce works which so far have been compiled into twenty-six volumes in the Gallimard editions, exclusive of the recent publication of the *Journal* (Tome I, 1968; Tome II, 1969) that Claudel kept from August 1904 until his death, in which there are reflections about literature, about personalities and events, about his own family, and also about Rimbaud. All of these works are to a certain extent autobiographical, as Claudel himself wrote to André Gide. However, in our study of Claudel's texts, we have refrained from repeating the extensive material which can be found by consulting Louis Chaigne's biography of Claudel, *Vie de Paul Claudel;* nor have we indulged in a discussion of Rimbaud's biography, which can be found in excellent works like Enid Starkie's *Arthur Rimbaud.* Rather, we have chosen to refer only to those biographical data that have some bearing on the nature of Claudel's quasi-mystical feeling for Rimbaud. Similarly, our study does not include a broad outline and analysis of the whole of the themes in Claudel's works, nor even necessarily of those usually associated with Claudel. Other critics—Wallace Fowlie, Henri Guillemin, Jacques Madaule, Henri Mondor, to mention only a few—have delineated those themes, and it is not our purpose simply to repeat what has been so often demonstrated elsewhere. Rather, our study is limited to those themes that—even more than any stylistic approach—indicate the enormous influence of Rimbaud on Claudel's works. Man's place in the universe, his search for spiritual truths, the Nietzschean-Rimbaldian willful hero attempting to establish his place in the sun, woman as a deterrent to man's perfection, the role of nature as a setting for man's realization of his goal, the possession of truth "in one soul and one body," the cosmic implications of man's unity with the Creation: all of these themes—in the proportionate importance Claudel places on them, in the language he uses to develop them, in the kind of comparisons he makes between them and Rimbaud's poetry—give evidence of Rimbaud's presence.

These thematic parallels have often been underlined by Claudel himself. At various points in his works he mentions aspects of Rimbaud's biography, as in *Partage de Midi,* or he makes specific quotations from Rimbaud's works, which he uses as parallels for his Biblical exegeses, as at the beginning of *Le Livre d'Esther.* Following Claudel's precedent, we have brought attention to various poems and images in Rimbaud's works, which Claudel has not mentioned, but which embody the very themes that Claudel includes and amplifies in his own works. This may at first give the impression of a certain artificiality, of a certain context imposed a priori on the texts under consideration. However, the method is suggested by Claudel himself, when—in discussing Biblical texts, for example—he compares them to Rimbaldian texts that seem to have little to do with Claudel's point, but that, when analyzed, point to the context into which Claudel placed Rimbaud.

These allusions seldom have any kind of chronological implications. Consequently, in our study of Rimbaud and Claudel, we have avoided discussing the texts in any chronological order, choosing, rather, to show how their themes relate to each other regardless of chronology, and how they relate to a whole and thus fit into a pattern that reflects Claudel's concept of Rimbaud and his understanding of him as a cosmic poet. In this way, the reasons for Claudel's quasi-mystical, quasi-religious cult of Rimbaud, his reasons for clinging desperately to his myth of Rimbaud become apparent. It also becomes apparent why he could not accept the image of Rimbaud as a *voyou,* as a homosexual, as a sordid, sadistic, iconoclastic *enfant terrible,* for this image has little to do with the essential beauty of Rimbaud's works and in no way reflects the basic Rimbaud-Claudel unity. Certainly, more than an image of the scandalizer of Parisian cafés is needed to understand in what way Claudel's works are really a continuation of symbolist concepts of poetry; but, more precisely, how they first of all stem directly from Rimbaud and then in turn reflect the ideas of other symbolist poets like Verlaine (on the somber quality of musicality) and Mallarmé (on the poetic suggestiveness of white).

One may readily accept the idea of Rimbaud's influence on Claudel—accept it even as extensive—and yet question Claudel's hyperbolic assertions as to the nature of Rimbaud's implications in his conversion. To such a question, the only possible answer is that, interesting as speculations may be about Claudel's reasons for saying or writing what he did and about the psychodynamics of influence in general, it is futile and somewhat specious in terms of literary criticism to attempt to find reasons or long explanations for his conversion and for the Claudelian form of faith. Claudel himself certainly never gave an explanation of the phenomenon. Was it a true conversion? Are there not young men who lose their faith at a particular moment, only to find it again? Was not the Rimbaldian experience essentially only coincidental with that conversion? These are pointless speculations. Claudel's faith and his association of it with Rimbaud cannot really be understood by those who have not experienced this same kind of faith. For that reason, it is better to take the advice that Claudel gave to a critic who reproached him for writing "incomprehensible works": "If he does not understand, he should keep quiet." The critic can do no more than bring to a work his knowledge about the author and about the historic background involved, his personal philosophy, his cultural background; but, above all, his sensitivity, which will in some way, great or small, influence his understanding of the work. From there, he must try to sort out as impartially as possible the significant details of the work itself, which throw light onto various aspects of it. For an understanding of Claudel's personal cult of Rimbaud, this means putting their works into the perspective suggested by Henri Guillemin:

> . . . *comme on comprend que Claudel, qui, le 10 novembre 1913—ce jour-là, il y avait vingt-deux ans juste qu'Arthur Rimbaud était mort—faisait dire une messe pour lui à Hambourg, comme on comprend que l'an dernier (1954), aux misérables cérémonies officielles du centenaire, il eût préféré, dans l'église de Charleville, la nudité d'une messe, oui, pour de bon, encore une fois, la messe là-bas.*

> [. . . how well one understands that Claudel, who, on November 10, 1913—on that day, just twenty-two years earlier, Arthur Rimbaud had died—had a Mass said for him in Hamburg; how well one understands that last year (1954), rather than the paltry official ceremonies for the centenary, he would have preferred, in the church at Charleville, the simplicity of a Mass, yes, in earnest, once more, the Mass over there.] [4]

4. Henri Guillemin, *"Claudel et Rimbaud"* in *Le Monde*, 14-20 juillet 1955. Guillemin's final phrase refers to the title of one of Claudel's literary texts: *La Messe là-bas* (cf. *Œuvres Complètes*, Vol. 2).

Finally, it is with hopes of bringing some further understanding to the "hymen" Claudel-Rimbaud, without profaning it, that we shall act in accordance with a suggestion from Etiemble about the works of Rimbaud—"What should be done? Pay less attention to biographies. Come back to the text, to its meaning. *Read Rimbaud.*"[5] —and apply that principle to Claudel.

5. Etiemble, *Le Mythe de Rimbaud* (Paris: Gallimard, 1952), p. 444.

Conte

Un Prince était vexé de ne s'être employé jamais qu'à la perfection des générosités vulgaires. Il prévoyait d'étonnantes révolutions de l'amour, et soupçonnait ses femmes de pouvoir mieux que cette complaisance agrémentée de ciel et de luxe. Il voulait voir la vérité, l'heure du désir et de la satisfaction essentiels. Que ce fût ou non une aberration de piété, il voulut. Il possédait au moins un assez large pouvoir humain.

Toutes les femmes qui l'avaient connu furent assassinées. Quel saccage du jardin de la beauté! Sous le sabre, elles le bénirent. Il n'en commanda point de nouvelles.—Les femmes réapparurent.

Il tua tous ceux qui le suivaient, après la chasse ou les libations.— Tous le suivaient.

Il s'amusa à égorger les bêtes de luxe. Il fit flamber les palais. Il se ruait sur les gens et les taillait en pièces.—La foule, les toits d'or, les belles bêtes existaient encore.

Peut-on s'extasier dans la destruction, se rajeunir par la cruauté! Le peuple ne murmura pas. Personne n'offrit le concours de ses vues.

Un soir il galopait fièrement. Un Génie apparut, d'une beauté ineffable, inavouable même. De sa physionomie et de son maintien ressortait la promesse d'un amour multiple et complexe! d'un bonheur indicible, insupportable même! Le Prince et le Génie s'anéantirent probablement dans la santé essentielle. Comment n'auraient-ils pas pu en mourir? Ensemble donc ils moururent.

Mais ce Prince décéda, dans son palais, à un âge ordinaire. Le Prince était le Génie. Le Génie était le Prince.

La musique savante manque à notre désir.

(Rimbaud, *Les Illuminations*)

Tale

[A Prince was vexed for never having occupied himself with anything more than perfecting trite munificence. He anticipated
astonishing revolutions in love and suspected his women of being
capable of more than mere complaisance graced with canopy and
opulence. He wanted to see truth, the hour of essential desire
and satisfaction. Whether or not this was aberrant piety, he remained resolute. He did enjoy at least rather broad human
powers.
    All the women who had known him were put to death. Such
ravage in the garden of beauty! As the sword fell, they blessed
him. He gave no order for new ones.—The women came back.
    He killed all those who followed him, after hunting or libations.—
All followed him.
    He amused himself by slitting the throats of luxurious beasts.
He set the palaces ablaze. He threw himself onto people and cut
them to pieces.—The crowd, the golden roofs, and the beautiful
beasts continued to exist.
    May one be enraptured over destruction, rejuvenated through
cruelty! His subjects made no complaint. No one offered the help
of his views.
    One evening he was out galloping proudly! A Genie appeared,
of ineffable beauty, unspeakable even. From his features and bearing came the promise of a manifold and complex love! of happiness beyond words, unbearable even! The Prince and the Genie
annihilated each other probably in essential well-being. How could
they not have died of it? So together they died.
    But this Prince passed away, in his palace, at an ordinary age.
The Prince was the Genie. The Genie was the Prince.
    Sapient music falls short of our desire.]

(Rimbaud, *Les Illuminations*)

The Prince & the Genie

1.
A Claudelian Myth

In the year 1886, upon reading *Les Illuminations* and *Une Saison en Enfer,* Paul Claudel first encountered the poetry of Jean-Arthur Rimbaud. It was, for Claudel, a startling encounter, which gave him his "first glimpse of truth" just as he was going through an adolescent period of deep religious apathy and despair; an encounter all the more startling, for us, in that it was an incorrigible blasphemer who opened a "fissure" in Claudel's "materialistic prison" and led him to re-embrace the Catholic faith with the dogmatic fanaticism peculiar to the convert. At the same time, Claudel's reading of these particular works engendered in him a feeling of profound spiritual affinity with Rimbaud, which, if the depth of human feelings is to be measured as much by their duration as by their intensity, is truly unique; not only did Claudel feel intensely the impact of Rimbaud's poetry upon that first encounter, he retained his deep admiration for the *"mauvais garçon,"* the "bad boy" from Charleville, throughout his long life. And even though the two poets never met, the spiritual affinity alluded to so often by Claudel was comparable to another relationship unique in the annals of French literature: the bond that linked Montaigne to La Boétie. Just as Montaigne mentions "a certain unexplainable and inevitable force, the mediator for this union," Claudel tells us that he can never hear Rimbaud talked about without emotion, he has lived with him so much and feels so united with him by "the most secret fibers."[1]

Rimbaud's initial effect on the eighteen-year-old Claudel was to awaken him to a "living and almost physical awareness of the supernatural."[2] *Les Illuminations,* published by the symbolist review

---

1. *Correspondance: Paul Claudel et André Gide 1899-1926* (Paris: Gallimard, 1949), p. 187.
2. Paul Claudel, "Ma Conversion" in *Contacts et Circonstances,* Vol. 16 of *Œuvres Complètes* (Paris: Gallimard, 1959), p. 190.

La Vogue in biweekly installments from early May through late June of 1886, and *Une Saison en Enfer,* which appeared in the same review in September of that year, had been, in the words of Claudel's elder son Pierre, "the pistol shot that started my father's work along the way,"[3] the initiating spark for his poetic vitality. But even more than a literary "pistol shot," Rimbaud, in Claudel's own view, was virtually the single continuing influence on the development of his poetic concepts as well as the single writer, indeed, the single individual, to give a definite direction to the pattern of his whole life, if it is possible to separate a poet's work from his life. As Claudel indicated in a letter to Jacques Rivière, although others—Shakespeare, Aeschylus, Dante, Dostoyevsky—had shown him the secrets of his art, Rimbaud alone had upon him "a seminal and paternal action."[4] Moreover, as he wrote to André Gide, Rimbaud was the writer whose memory he honored the most and whom he considered his spiritual ascendant,[5] his *âme sœur.*

In awakening Claudel to an awareness of the supernatural, Rimbaud's works had been the catalyst for the dramatic revelation of Christian faith which he experienced on Christmas Day, 1886, when, during vespers at Notre Dame de Paris, "in an instant my heart was touched and *I believed,*" and which he recounts both in prose, as in *Ma Conversion* and letters to Byvanck and Frizeau, and in poetry, as in the *Magnificat* and the poem entitled *Le 25 décembre 1886* from *Visages Radieux*—the beginning of the conversion to Catholicism that was to take four years to accomplish. One may, of course, take exception to Claudel's assertions in these and other documents, and question whether he was actually leaning against the second pillar by the entrance to the choir of Notre Dame on that particular day, as commemorated by a plaque placed on the presumed spot; one may wonder whether the revelation was as sudden or as dramatic as Claudel would have us believe, whether this was really a conversion, given his youth, innocence, and apparent naïveté in matters of faith; nor would it be entirely inappropriate to ask why he went to vespers at Notre Dame at all, except that he points out that he was there for aesthetic reasons, to find in the Catholic ceremonies "an appropriate stimulant" for his "greater

3. Author's interview with Pierre Claudel on Wednesday, February 8, 1961.
4. *Correspondance: Jacques Rivière et Paul Claudel* (Paris: Librairie Plon, 1926), p. 142.
5. *Correspondance: Claudel et Gide . . . ,* p. 187.

than normal dilettantism" along with "material for a few decadent exercises" in poetry. In fact, the particulars of the moment itself are of little consequence in arriving at an understanding of Claudel's religious attitude; in no way do they change the psychological effect of the conversion on the boy and, later, the man—the poet and dramatist whose predilection for the dramatic cannot be overstated and to whom a certain poetic license must be allowed; nor do they alter the fact of that conversion. Even though Claudel came from a family that was Catholic by baptism, if not either particularly believing or practicing, his was a true conversion rather than simply a reaffirmation of faith: his fanaticism was that of a convert, with a militancy to match. Not only did this militancy mark his religious enthusiasm and convictions, it colored his over-all view of Christianity. He often emphasizes the militant facet of Christ, particularly in his exegeses of Biblical texts, in which he constantly refers to Matt. 10:34, "I have not come to bring peace, but a sword."

The importance of Claudel's reading of Rimbaud, this "capital event," and of its influence on the revelation and conversion becomes all the more evident when we consider that Claudel had previously felt strongly influenced by Renan's agnostic views and by the scientific concepts that were the result of theories of Darwinism as interpreted in nineteenth-century France, theories that Claudel later found both "absurd and contradictory in terms."[6] With the conversion came a deep-rooted hatred for Renan, who, presiding at the distribution of secondary school prizes in 1883, had given the fifteen-year-old Claudel a crown of imitation laurel in recognition of his having won first honor prize in *discours français,* and who now "glittered, resplendent in all the bourgeois virtues and all the sycophancy of fortune."[7] Despite his profound belief in Christianity and all its orthodox implications, Claudel often demonstrated a lack of Christian charity in his extremely biased opinions and hates, which are reflected in his intransigent opposition to the materialistic determinism and the positivism that he saw as the philosophy fundamental to such works as *Vie de Jésus,* "That filthy heap of infamies, perfidies and lies that some Jew publisher has been careful to multiply in cheap editions."[8] Erroneous as such an interpretation of Renan may seem, Claudel always associated him with Voltaire and with the materialists, an

6. *Positions et Propositions II,* Vol. 15 of *Œuvres Complètes* (1959), p. 231.
7. *Un Poète Regarde la Croix,* Vol. 19 of *Œuvres Complètes* (1962), p. 421.
8. Ibid.

association for which Renan was never forgiven: inability to for-
give was another of Claudel's failings, at least in his literary works.
His essays—in particular the exegetic works—his letters, and his
journals are filled with epithets about "that hideous, vile" Renan
and also about Voltaire whom he often mentions in connection
with Renan as though they had lived in the same age. One especially notable example of the bitter polemics Claudel indulged in
when discussing Renan is to be found in the seventh *cahier* of his
journal: "The two great hates that I have always kept in my heart
are Protestantism and the University. Add: Ernest Renan."[9] His
hate of Protestantism, which caused him to write that much to his
disgust he had been "once more obliged to be present at an Episco-
palian mummery occasioned by [Franklin D. Roosevelt's] inaugu-
ration"[10] (Claudel was the French ambassador to Washington at
the time), was, of course, a direct result of his convert's fanaticism;
as for the university, he was displeased most likely because he felt
that professors in France had either neglected to give him his proper due or had misunderstood his works. In the case of Renan, Claudel's philosophical and theological views, his belief that "each new
being is not the product of other beings, he asserts himself from
the outside, and the 'struggle for life' is only that inclination for
the infinite with which each one of us is animated,"[11] were diametrically opposed to determinism and positivism; moreover, Renan's
most cardinal of sins was that in *Vie de Jésus,* he had described a
Christ stripped of his divinity. But if Darwinism and Renan's "materialism" were the antithesis of Claudel's beliefs, Rimbaud's ideas
concerning the mystical and the supernatural with its cosmic implications seemed to him to embody the central theme of his life's
work and were a strong antidote against what he called nineteenth-
century *scientisme;* Rimbaud showed him, as Henri Guillemin points
out in *Le "Converti" Paul Claudel,* "the reality of the real," brought
him to realize that things are more than things, that they "bear witness," that they are "a manifestation," that they "both veil and reveal a Presence," that "nature is supernatural." It is this reaction
against nineteenth-century skepticism and atheism that permits a
first parallel between Claudel and Rimbaud to be drawn in a single

9. *Journal* (Paris: Bibliotèque de la Pléiade, Gallimard, 1969), Tome II, Cahier
7, April 1935, p. 89.
10. *Journal,* Tome II, Cahier 7, Sunday March 5 1933, p. 10.
11. *Correspondance: André Suarès et Paul Claudel* (Paris: Gallimard, 1951),
p. 106.

word: revolt; their common revolt against the materialism that was
personified for Claudel by Renan and symbolized for Rimbaud by
"*la bouche d'ombre*," "*la mother.*"[12] Claudel's conversion was
nothing if not the outward symbol of the inner revolt that established a first spiritual rapport with his lifelong idol.

As well as awakening an awareness of the supernatural, Rimbaud
had awakened in Claudel an awareness of the revolt within himself,
of the doubt, the questioning, the unrest of a tortured soul. Rimbaud is "a *prophet* on whom the Spirit has fallen; not as on David
but as on Saul."[13] He is a Saul struggling with the Philistines, just
as Claudel felt himself struggling with the doctrines of Renan. But
even if for Rimbaud it was a physical struggle in many ways—revolt
against his immediate family, against bourgeois society, even against
other poets—it was above all a spiritual struggle. Claudel could not
have numbered among those who consider Rimbaud a precursor of
modern existentialism, for he saw in him not so much a man of action as a meditator, one for whom meditation and contemplation
were a sublime and supreme occupation. In *Présence et Prophétie*
he mentions Rimbaud specifically in connection with the role of
contemplator:

> *Mais ce qui fascine le contemplateur, ce qui fait passer dans
> ses cheveux le frisson sacré, c'est la vie prodigieuse dont est
> animé ce rideau d'abeilles, cette prairie arithmétique! C'est le
> Voyant Rimbaud qui le premier a vu* les plages du Ciel toutes
> couvertes de ces blanches nations en joie.

> [But what fascinates the contemplator, what makes the sacred
> shudder pass through his hair, is the prodigious life with which
> is animated this curtain of bees, this arithmetic prairie. The
> Seer Rimbaud was the first to see *Sky beaches all covered
> with joyful white nations.*][14]

He makes the same point in the seventh *cahier* of his journal in
which he quotes a line from *Une Saison en Enfer:* "Action, says
Rimbaud, is a wasting of some force, debilitation.—And Plotinus,
quoted by Bergson: Every action, every fabrication is a weakening

---

12. *"La bouche d'ombre"* was Rimbaud's disrespectful name for his mother,
taken from a poem by Victor Hugo. He uses it in a letter to Paul Demeny on
17 April, 1871. See Arthur Rimbaud, *Œuvres Complètes* (Paris: Bibliotèque
de la Pléiade, Gallimard, 1954), p. 265.
13. *Journal.*
14. *Présence et Prophétie*, Vol. 20 of *Œuvres Complètes* (1963), p. 411.

of contemplation."[15] Elsewhere in the journal, Claudel repeats his assertion that "this is exactly what Rimbaud says: Action is not life."[16] Rather than in action, for Claudel life is to be found in the creation of poetry, in the expression of one's inner thoughts and visions through a poetic experience: "How sad, this child of our heart [poetry] whom no one welcomes and who does not communicate the life which we gave it."[17] If life is basically communication and interaction of individuals, and poetry essentially a form of speaking with others—and Claudel says it is: "No artist worthy of the name really works for himself, but for others, since one always writes to someone, since one really always speaks to a second person"[18]—then poetry is a very real form of life, and real adventure in life, as Pierre MacOrlan puts it, "is not the strangeness of stories lived in far countries. Adventure is to be found in words, in the joy of words, in their strange ability to transplant us where they please and when they please." It is a cerebral rather than a physical experience. The fact that Claudel singles out this concept of "action not being life" as one of the few Rimbaldian ideas to which he refers in his journal, the fact that he associates Rimbaud with the vocation of prophet, further underlines his conception of Rimbaud as a meditator rather than a man of action. Rimbaud's adventuresome adult life might seem at first to belie this point of view, except that his journeys and hardships in Africa and elsewhere bear a striking resemblance to the kind of spiritual anguish he expresses in his poetry; and inasmuch as this is so, these "adventures" are manifestations of inner reality, the "reality of the real," the things that are more than things in that they transcend appearances. In Claudel's terms, then, Rimbaud, whatever else he may have been or may have been associated with, was a mystic, a dreamer—in the sense of *voyant,* a seer—whose revolt was essentially a spiritual struggle within the boy himself, a struggle that was parallel to Claudel's own adolescent revolt.

C. A. Hackett's thesis characterizing Rimbaud as a poet essentially *enfant*—even if an *enfant terrible*—is of capital importance in understanding Claudel's *rapprochement* of himself with Rimbaud. For it is precisely that part of the child that is inherent in us all—

15. *Journal,* Tome II, Cahier 7, October 1943, p. 72.
16. *Journal* (Paris: Bibliotèque de la Pléiade, Gallimard, 1968), Tome I, Cahier 6, August 1932, p. 1008.
17. *Correspondance: Suarès et Claudel,* letter 75, written from Tientsin, 3 mai 1907, p. 100.
18. Ibid.

the revolt against gross injustices; the thirst for truth; the innocent, unsullied, unjaded awareness of what is immediate to existence; the capacity for spontaneous reactions, for strong convictions, and for constant renewal—and that is basic to Rimbaud's poetry, which makes Rimbaud's work a living thing and which made Claudel first aware of his own struggle. That struggle, his conversion from materialistic determinism to Christian and specifically Catholic mysticism, lasted four years. But the final solution was definite. And since this solution was Christianity—and in particular, Catholicism (Christianity meant Catholicism and only Catholicism for Claudel; he used the terms synonomously)—and since Claudel identified himself so closely with Rimbaud, it stands to reason that he would attribute this kind of innate faith to Rimbaud.

It is perhaps overstating the case to say, as does Enid Starkie, that Claudel tries to make of Rimbaud an orthodox Catholic, though it is certainly true that he does see in Rimbaud's poetry the expression of a relentlessly Christian religious feeling. In an unpublished letter to Claudine Chonez, Claudel writes that "Rimbaud is great only because he is a Christian, an untamed Christian" [*"Chrétien à l'état sauvage"*]. Curiously enough, Claudel himself wishes to be seen as an adolescent "sauvage," an untamed adolescent, as he clearly states in *L'Œil Écoute:* "all alone under the rain and perfectly happy to be alone, his heart full of a kind of untamed hurrah" [*hourra sauvage*]. A similar reference to Rimbaud as an "untamed mystic" [*"mystique à l'état sauvage"*] is repeated over and over as one of the leitmotifs of his interpretation of Rimbaud, in his letters as well as in the intimacy of his private journal where he writes simply and with no elaboration, as a self-evident truth, "*Arthur Rimbaud fut un mystique à l'état sauvage*" ["Arthur Rimbaud was an untamed mystic"].[19] His first statement in print of this point of view was made in the preface he wrote for Paterne Berrichon's edition of Rimbaud's works in 1912.

Arthur Rimbaud fut un mystique à l'état sauvage, *une source perdue qui ressort d'un sol saturé. Sa vie, un malentendu, la tentative en vain par la fuite d'échapper à cette voix qui le sollicite et le relance, et qu'il ne veut pas reconnaître: jusqu'à ce qu'enfin, réduit, la jambe tranchée, sur ce lit d'hôpital à Marseille, il sache!*

19. *Journal.*

[Arthur Rimbaud was a mystic *à l'état sauvage,* a lost fountain-head springing up from saturated ground. His life, a misunderstanding, a vain attempt—by running away—to escape that voice which kept calling out to him and starting him up again, and which he did not want to recognize: until finally, subdued, his leg cut off, on that hospital bed in Marseille, he knew!] [20]

This certainly does not make an orthodox Catholic out of Rimbaud, but it does underline an irresolvable religious struggle. Even the most objective critic cannot help but be aware of Rimbaud's religious sensitivity or at least of the torture of an irresolute soul well-versed in religious instruction. *Une Saison en Enfer,* for example, abounds in references to Christ, to the catechism, to the agonizing and torturous thirst for a Supreme Being, and to the fundamental religious theme of the interaction of the soul and body as expressed in the closing words of Rimbaud's long prose poem: ". . . and I shall be free to *possess truth in one soul and one body.*" Whether or not religious sensitivity or even mysticism makes a Christian out of an individual is, of course, quite another matter. Claudel apparently thought that it did—at least for Rimbaud (though he also found that Suarès was "sick with God" and, presumably, longing for Christianity)—which helps to explain his curious interchanging of "mystic" and "Christian" (compare "untamed Christian" of Miss Chonez's letter with "untamed mystic" in the journal). In recent years, critics have tried to show that Claudel had confused the matter and have even suggested that he eventually regretted having made the statement that Rimbaud was an "untamed mystic." Etiemble makes a point of it, as had le Père Blanchet before him. However, the real problem for Claudel is not that he sees Rimbaud differently in later years. If he regrets anything, it is that others have "sullied" ["*galvaudé*"] Rimbaud. His works, both early and late in his career, are too filled with references to Rimbaud as a mystic for us to really believe otherwise. Moreover, he invests Rimbaud with God's grace: "Theology gives a name to this mysterious gift [of prophecy]: Grace, and it makes a distinction between two kinds of grace, *gratia gratis data,* or charisma, which makes poets, Arthur Rimbaud, for example, and *gratia gratum faciens,* which makes saints."[21] Elsewhere, he refers to

20. Jean-Arthur Rimbaud, *Œuvres* (Paris: Mercure de France, 1949), pp. 7-8.
21. *Accompagnements,* Vol. 18 of *Œuvres Complètes* (1961), p. 19.

Rimbaud as *"cet illuminé"* ["this illuminato"].[22] And when he juxtaposes Rimbaud's words—quoted out of context—with those of Sainte Chantal, as he does in the preface to Berrichon's edition of Rimbaud's works, it is as though he were equating Rimbaud with the saints. With all of these points of reference taken into consideration, then, Claudel's position on the matter of Rimbaud's religious anxiety becomes clear: Rimbaud is an illumined mystical Christian.

It may seem at first that Rimbaud had been far too blasphemous to be considered among God's chosen few. But, as André Dhôtel rightly points out, "Rimbaud had blasphemed too much for religion to have been foreign to him." And if blasphemy can be further construed as indicative of grace, in that it may suggest a reaction against some deep awareness of God's will within oneself, then we can hardly contest Claudel's assertions. But, actually, whether Rimbaud's blasphemy was merely an adolescent's reaction not so much against God as against men, against society, the adolescent's wish to shock and to assert himself, is irrelevant, for in Claudel we are dealing with a man who has believed in Rimbaud, who has "taken him at his word, one of those who have trusted in him."[23] Isabelle Rimbaud's letters to her mother during her brother's death agony served to substantiate Claudel's attitude. In his preface to the Mercure edition of Rimbaud's *Oeuvres,* he makes a point of referring to one of these letters "which recounts her brother's last days in the Hospital of the Conception in Marseille. '. . . He looked at me . . . with heaven in his eyes . . . then he said to me: everything must be prepared in the room, everything arranged: the priest will be coming with the sacraments.' "[24] It was inconceivable to Claudel that Rimbaud should not have died a believer, and he had an almost pathological need to know and believe in Rimbaud's Catholic death. In a letter to Paterne Berrichon, in which Claudel pleads to know the circumstances of Rimbaud's last moments, there is a note tantamount to desperation for fear that Rimbaud had not embraced the Catholic faith on his deathbed: "I have heard it denied that Rimbaud died a Catholic, and this has troubled me a great deal . . . it would be hard for me to think that Rimbaud, to whom I owe my own faith, died without having found it himself."[25] Claudel was

22. *Un Poète Regarde la Croix,* p. 421.
23. Jean-Arthur Rimbaud, *Œuvres* (Paris: Mercure de France, 1949), Preface by Paul Claudel, p. 17.
24. Ibid.
25. Letter to Paterne Berrichon, Francfort, le 20 novembre 1911.

such an ardent convert, so certain of his faith (or, at least, so certain of his need for faith), so certain that outside the Catholic Church there is no salvation, that conversion of others was paramount to his thinking and preoccupied him much of the time. Years of correspondence were devoted to attempts to influence the religious convictions of others, among them: André Gide, who was undoubtedly the least successful of his attempts at conversion (it is said that Gide wrote a note to be read after his death, to the effect that "There is no Hell, tell Claudel!"—a story that is at least in keeping with Gide's impiousness); Francis Jammes, who finally did succumb, as it were, and whom Claudel included in that almost closed circle of the chosen few who really do believe ("If there are only two left, let's be those two!" Claudel is said to have remarked in one of his letters to Jammes); André Suarès, who was certain that Claudel had completely misinterpreted Rimbaud's intentions and that the Rimbaud of Claudel's preface to the Berrichon edition in 1912 was really the double of Claudel himself in the process of conversion, one of those characters in whom a playwright unconsciously projects the drama of his own life; and Jacques Rivière, who, as early as 1908, was one of the first to notice "in *Connaissance de l'Est* certain recollections of Rimbaud." As for Claudel's concern about Rimbaud's faith, Paterne Berrichon assured him that his brother-in-law had indeed died embracing Catholicism and showed him Isabelle's letters as proof. Mollified, Claudel went on not only to include Rimbaud among the converted and devout believers, one of the entries in his journal is tantamount to asserting that Rimbaud too was a proselytizer: "Rimbaud, Verlaine—and everything that has come out of it for the Church. Strange story. Eugénie Krantz says that Verlaine in his death throes fell from his bed, crying out for a priest."[26] Apparently intrigued by the possible implications of Verlaine's conversion after his association with Rimbaud and during his year and a half in prison, Claudel interprets Verlaine's sentimental religiosity—which is positively embarrassing at times or at least in bad taste—as an indication of the influence of Rimbaud's innate religious mysticism; his conviction in this regard is so strong that he includes the poem *Verlaine* in his collection of *Feuilles de Saints,* in which he makes numerous references to Rimbaud and to his mystical influence on Verlaine. Such a "canonization" of Verlaine would seem to indicate a humorously ironic intent, were Claudel not so serious about the matter. Without taking exception

26. *Journal,* Tome II, Cahier 7, March 1935, p. 84

even to Verlaine's *"musicalité,"* he insists that "Verlaine's originality . . . is that he was a Christian poet."[27] There can of course be no
other explanation for such an original idea than that it is a reflection
of Claudel's own Christian fervor. In his fervor, at least, Claudel
was more Gidian than he realized or admitted.

But for all the proselytizing, Claudel's ardor for Rimbaud remained profoundly personal; it did not allow him, for example, to
profane his image of Rimbaud by participating in public demonstrations in honor of his "fellow convert." Despite urgent letters from
Paterne Berrichon, he refused to become involved with the erection
of a monument to Rimbaud at Roche, in 1911. A public monument, with all the attendant ceremonies at its unveiling, seemed
virtually blasphemous against his idol, and his answer to Berrichon
is perhaps the most revealing document he ever wrote about his
spiritual involvement with Rimbaud:

> *Votre lettre me met dans un cruel embarras. Il n'y a pas*
> *d'homme, en effet, dont la mémoire me soit plus chère, à qui*
> *j'aie plus d'obligations et à qui j'aie voué un culte plus reli-*
> *gieux qu'Arthur Rimbaud. D'autres écrivains m'ont instruit,*
> *mais c'est Arthur Rimbaud seul qui m'a construit. Il a été*
> *pour moi le révélateur, dans un moment de profondes ténè-*
> *bres, l'illuminateur de tous les chemins de l'art, de la religion*
> *et de la vie; de sorte qu'il m'est impossible d'imaginer ce que*
> *j'aurais pu être sans la rencontre de cet esprit . . . Principe,*
> *pensée, forme même, je lui dois tout . . . Ce sont ces raisons*
> *qui m'empêchent de m'associer à l'hommage populaire qu'une*
> *piété bien naturelle vous engage à rendre au grand disparu.*
> *Je ne connais point de sculpteur dont l'œuvre, si intéressante*
> *qu'elle soit, toujours grossièrement matérielle, puisse être*
> *autre chose qu'injurieuse à une mémoire vénérée . . . Il ne me*
> *convient pas que ce grand évasif, enfin, s'il est là, ce soit pour*
> *faire l'ornement d'un lieu public, mais pour être à jamais la*
> *voix sans visage qui murmure au fond des esprits capables de*
> *le comprendre des paroles inoubliables.*

[Your letter puts me in a difficult position. There is, in fact,
no man whose memory is dearer to me, to whom I have more
obligations and to whom I have vowed a more religious cult
than Arthur Rimbaud. Other writers have instructed me, but
Arthur Rimbaud alone formed me. He was for me the revealer,

27. *Accompagnements*, p. 121.

in a moment of deep darkness, the illuminator of all the roads
of art, of religion and of life; so much so that it is impossible
for me to imagine what I might have been had I not encountered this spirit . . . Principle, thought, even form, I owe him
everything. These are the reasons that keep me from associating myself with a public homage that a quite natural affection
urges you to render to a great lost one. I know no sculptor
whose work, as interesting as it may be, but always clumsily
material, could be anything more than offensive to a venerated
memory . . . I cannot allow this great evader, if he is there,
to be the ornament of a public place; he should rather be forever the faceless voice that murmurs unforgettable words in the
depths of spirits capable of understanding him.]
(Letter to Paterne Berrichon, June 13, 1911)[28]

Nor was this feeling about Rimbaud simply a passing humor: more
than forty years later, Claudel was equally adamant and even more
blunt in refusing to participate in a centenary celebration of Rimbaud's birth:

*Je suis très sensible aux termes aimables dans lesquels vous
exprimez vos sentiments à mon égard, mais je ne puis vous
donner satisfaction. Arthur Rimbaud, je vous l'ai donné à
comprendre, se situe pour moi sur un tout autre plan que
celui de la littérature. Les célébrations vulgaires, avec orphé-
ons, pompiers, discours, récitations, inscriptions au coin d'une
rue, décorations et le banquet final, me paraissent entièrement
déplacées. Je n'ai aucune envie de m'y associer.*

[I am very touched by the friendly terms in which you express your feelings about me, but I cannot honor your request.
I have given you to understand that Arthur Rimbaud is for
me on quite another level than literature. The vulgar ceremonies with choral societies, firemen, speeches, recitations,
inscriptions on street corners, decorations and a final banquet
seem to me entirely out of place. I have no desire to become
involved with them.]

(Notes in *Accompagnements*)[29]

28. Letter to Paterne Berrichon, June 13, 1911. How ironic that Claudel's
own name is now "an ornament" on one of the prominent squares of Paris, at
the Théâtre de l'Odéon!
29. *Accompagnements*, notes on p. 451. Letter to Jean-Paul Vaillant, dated
April 17, 1953, and appearing in *Le Figaro Littéraire*, October 23, 1954.

Not only did he not wish to become involved with public demonstrations, he would not put himself in a position that might require him to express anything specific about this object of his intimate concern. When he was approached by Copeau and Gide to write an article on Rimbaud for the *Nouvelle Revue Française* (*NRF*) in 1912, he refused, though not without a certain *crise de conscience* which, in letters to Gide and Suarès, he expressed in terms appropriate to his religious cult of Rimbaud:

Depuis que Copeau et vous m'avez parlé de quelques lignes à écrire sur Rimbaud et que je vous ai refusées, je suis tracassé par une espèce de remords. Il me semble que je ne puis refuser un hommage public à un homme à qui je dois tout.

[Ever since Copeau and you asked me about writing a few lines on Rimbaud which I refused you, I have been bothered by a kind of remorse. It seems to me that I cannot refuse public homage to a man to whom I owe everything.] [30]
(Letter to André Gide, June 15, 1912)

Il y a deux mois, Copeau me demanda d'écrire pour la NRF un article sur Rimbaud. Je refusai, le sujet me paraissant supérieur à mes forces, comme divers essais me l'avaient montré. Cependant, je conservais un certain remords: il me semblait que je devais un hommage public au poëte qui avait eu la part prépondérante dans la formation de toutes mes idées.

[Two months ago, Copeau asked me to write an article on Rimbaud for the *NRF*. I refused, the subject seeming to me beyond my abilities, as various efforts have shown me. However, I have been feeling a certain remorse: it seems to me that I owe public homage to the poet who had a prominent place in the formation of all my ideas.] [31]
(Letter to André Suarès, August 2, 1912)

Even so, he did not write the article for the *NRF*, though he did finally agree to a preface to Paterne Berrichon's edition of Rimbaud's works that was published by Mercure in 1912. As the years went on, however, Claudel's feelings about Rimbaud became even more personal, to the point that he finally said in an inter-

30. *Correspondance: Claudel et Gide*, letter 136, Francfort, 15 juin 1912, p. 200.
31. *Correspondance: Suarès et Claudel*, letter 148, Francfort, 2 août 1912, p. 174.

view with Dominique Arban in 1947, that he preferred not to talk about Rimbaud, "he has been so sullied by others." He was "disgusted by what they have done with him."[32]

When one objectively considers the facts of Rimbaud's biography, the depravity and debauchery of which he was capable at times, one cannot help but wonder just how Claudel—so pious and so apparently imbued with middle-class morality, so prosaic—ever managed to evolve his religious cult of Rimbaud. At least part of the explanation of this strange paradox lies in Claudel's strong belief in the necessity of sin. He feels that sin has a definite place in the order of things, that "sin also serves."[33] One of the things for which he reproached Renan was that Renan had said that "sin does not exist."[34] This was tantamount to saying that God does not exist, since, for Claudel, sin is, in human terms, a means of becoming all the more aware of God. Consistent with this idea, Claudel associates Rimbaud with the prodigal son (so at least he is not unaware of Rimbaud's profligacy) and throughout the Biblical exegeses he constantly makes reference to the parable of the prodigal son, reminding his readers that "joy shall be in heaven over one sinner that repenteth, more than over ninety and nine just persons, which need no repentance" (Luke 15:7). In L'Otage, Coufontaine tells Sygne that sin is a sure way of discovering God's intentions, that "the only way for us to know [God's will] is to contradict it."[35] But this is not the whole of the matter.

A more compelling answer to the perplexing problem of Claudel's cult of Rimbaud lies precisely in the fact that this cult was essentially personal. Claudel's immediate admiration for Rimbaud upon that first encounter in 1886, his feeling for the supernatural, for the mysticism in Rimbaud, was the result of direct contact with the poetry itself, of his personal interpretation of it, and could not have been influenced by any extraneous knowledge about Rimbaud's intimate life. Certainly the erroneous reference to "the late Arthur Rimbaud" in the Vanier edition of Les Illuminations in 1886 (Rimbaud died at the Hôpital de la Conception in Marseille, on November 10, 1891) sheds no light on Rimbaud's biography. At most, Claudel might have heard vague stories about the young poète-voyou from Charleville who had scandalized the Parisian cafés on numerous occasions fifteen years earlier. What is more probable is that he cre-

32. Cf. Correspondance: Claudel et Gide, p. 248.
33. Le Soulier de Satin, Vol. 12 of Œuvres Complètes (1958), p. 190.
34. Du Sens Figuré de l'Ecriture, Vol. 21 of Œuvres Complètes (1963), p. 59.
35. L'Otage, Vol. 10 of Œuvres Complètes (1956), p. 21.

ated his own image of Rimbaud, endowing him with all the idealistic fantasies of which a young man is capable, identifying himself to an extreme with his new-found *poète-mystique* and evolving throughout the years a private version of Rimbaldian hagiography that is the projection of his own literary and religious ambitions.

Claudel did see the amoral aspects of Rimbaud's thinking. He wrote to Jacques Rivière that "the 'adolescent and amoral' side has been insufficiently touched upon. Likewise, the animal, the terrible, 'self-willed' poet (not a gelding) that Rimbaud was at seventeen."[36] But he was never capable of accepting the more sordid facts of Rimbaud's life. Any suggestion of sexual aberration, for instance, would have been incompatible with Claudel's Catholic convictions. His answer to Hackett's question, "Is a lily less beautiful for having been immersed in mud in order to live?"[37] is an emphatic "Yes!" Despite Claudel's concept of a universal unity where all things have their interrelationships, where even sin has its proper place, the thought of a homosexual, often quite sadistic, Rimbaud was totally unacceptable to him. The Rimbaud-Verlaine affair never had any more significance for Claudel than that of a superficial admiration for Rimbaud's poetry on the part of Verlaine: "What Verlaine liked were his lines of verse."[38] In their obscenities and sordid relationship, he claimed to see little more than the innocence of "two bad boys."[39] When, upon the publication of *Les Caves du Vatican* in 1912, he first became aware of Gide's admitted sexual preferences and was concerned and even alarmed by them, he asked in a letter to Jacques Rivière, "Is that why Gide wants so much to have the same mores attributed to Arthur Rimbaud, and probably to Whitman?"[40] His own innocence, in any case, could hardly be more apparent. The most he ever admitted to seeing in the relationship between Rimbaud and Verlaine was a poetic entente, with the possible exception of some religious inspiration for Verlaine, whose *Romances sans Paroles* he admired in particular, mostly for their "incomparable prestige of having been written directly under the influence of Rimbaud."[41]

36. *Correspondance: Rivière et Claudel*, p. 244.
37. C. A. Hackett, *Le Lyrisme de Rimbaud* (Paris: Librairie Nazet et Bastard, 1938), p. 17.
38. *Journal*, Tome I, Cahier 6, August 1932, p. 1008.
39. *Accompagnements*, p. 108.
40. Cf. in *Correspondance: Claudel et Gide*, letter from Claudel to Rivière, quoted on p. 216.
41. *Accompagnements*, p. 103.

Claudel's tendency to distort matters in order to fit them into his own purview of Christianity goes beyond his refusal to accept certain aspects of Rimbaud's life; it extends to the themes that he associates with Rimbaud—not to be confused with the Rimbaldian themes in Claudel's works, which we shall discuss in a later chapter—and that, while varied, are usually involved with Christian concepts. Scattered throughout his works are quotations drawn from *Une Saison en Enfer* and *Les Illuminations.* Although other writings by Rimbaud found their place in Claudel's works, they were not instrumental in bringing about his first *élan* towards Catholicism; rather, they later served to corroborate his first impressions. Claudel's application of these quotations vary, but they are used essentially to convey the image of a mystical Rimbaud, acquainted with Scripture and desirous to re-create a Biblical experience.

At the beginning of his discussion of the book of Esther, for example, in what is virtually an incantation to evoke Rimbaud, Claudel compares the colors of the hangings in the house of the Persian king Ahasuerus to those used by Rimbaud in the eleventh strophe of *Les Premières Communions:*

> *Le verset 9 nous décrit ces tentures azurées* (aerii coloris) *qui pendaient de toutes parts, les unes tirant sur le vert et les autres sur le violet* (carbasini, hyacinthini). *Cf. Arthur Rimbaud,* Les Premières Communions:
>
>> Adonaï! dans les terminaisons latines,
>> Des cieux moirés de vert baignent les fronts vermeils,
>> Et, tachés du sang pur des célestes poitrines,
>> De grands linges neigeux tombent sur les soleils.
>
> [Verse 9 describes for us these blue tapestries (*areii coloris*) hanging everywhere, some shading into green and others into violet (*carbasini, hyacinthini*). Cf. Arthur Rimbaud, *Les Premières Communions:*
>
>> *Adonaï! in the Latin endings,*
>> *Skies shimmering with green bathe the vermilion brows,*
>> *And, spotted with the pure blood of the heavenly breasts,*
>> *Great snowy linens fall over the suns.*][42]

Moreover, he states that the Persian sovereign's "hundred-and-eighty-day or half-year banquet . . . offered . . . in order to show the wealth of the glory of his reign, his grandeur, and the magnifi-

42. *Le Livre d'Esther* in *Les Aventures de Sophie,* Vol. 19 of *Œuvres Complètes* (1953), p. 20.

cence of his power" is "probably the one in which Rimbaud took part and of which he tried to recapture the taste" in his orgiastic bouts of absinth and hashish during his bohemian stays in the Latin Quarter of Paris. It would seem that Claudel needs to find some justification for Rimbaud's excesses through drawing Scriptural parallels; and, although he dismisses the amorality of his prophet by asserting that "the gift of prophecy is independent of the beneficiary's moral value,"[43] he apparently accepts Rimbaud's penchant for the exotic only insofar as he can discover some expression of it or something comparable to it in Biblical truths.

Of particular interest in the passage concerning the book of Esther, in addition to Claudel's allusions to color (one of the important stylistic similarities between his works and Rimbaud's), is the theme of glory through strength and power, the "sword" of Christ's message, and Claudel's application of it to Rimbaud's life and works. In the same way that it may be said that Rimbaud's journeys and hardships in Africa and elsewhere were an attempt to find a measure of material wealth and power—as is suggested by the banal letters he wrote to his family while in Africa—Claudel implies that Rimbaud's exotic excesses, artificially stimulated by absinth and hashish, were an attempt to find spiritual strength and power. He considers the youthful Rimbaud's actions to be manifestations of an inner struggle, which in turn is closely associated with a search for truth, a truth which, in Claudelian terms, is God. Just as Scripture is a figurative representation of spiritual truths—one of Claudel's exegetic texts is entitled *Du Sens Figuré de l'Ecriture*—Rimbaud's early life is, for Claudel, a figurative representation of the mystic's inner reality, and of his innate, even if unconscious, grace; its outward manifestations, his actions, are the essence of poetry, and an understanding of the essence of poetry is of primary importance in understanding Scripture: Claudel insists on the poetic aspects of Scripture. In Scripture, as well as in poetry, visual realities become spiritual or cerebral illusions which in turn are transformed into poetic allusions:

La réalité est devenue illusion et l'illusion est devenue allusion, allusion à je ne sais quelle ultériorité tantalisante dont le soleil demain ne nous livrera qu'une médiocre traduction. C'est cette attention au mystère ambiant, cette aptitude au rêve, cette capacité de transformation, cette lente sympathie avec l'invisible, qui donne leur accent poignant à telle de ces

43. *Accompagnements*, p. 19.

chansons populaires qui n'ont pu fleurir qu'entre l'Oise et l'Aisne, et dont les deux mauvais garçons, Verlaine et Rimbaud, ont emprunté la technique.

[Reality has become illusion and illusion has become allusion, allusion to some indefinable yet tantalizing remoteness of which the sun tomorrow will deliver to us only a mediocre translation. It is this attentiveness to the ambient mystery, this aptitude for dreams, this capacity for transformation, this slow, instinctive harmony with the invisible, that give their poignant tone to certain of those folk songs which have been able to flourish only between the Oise and the Aisne, and whose technique was borrowed by those two bad boys, Verlaine and Rimbaud.]

(*Accompagnements*)[44]

In this passage concerning reality and poetic allusions, one of the keys to a Claudelian understanding of *Une Saison en Enfer* lies in the "ambient mystery" and "this aptitude for dreams" which are inseparable from the "desire to escape from reality, an escape which would leave [reality] intact, but which would permit us to go beyond it with no difficulty, to infer meaning from a proposition, 'to go towards the spirit.' "[45] The words are Claudel's, at least the elaboration of them is; but the central theme comes directly from Rimbaud's *Délires:* "How many night hours I watched beside his dear sleeping body, seeking to understand why he so longed to escape reality." Just as the tortures in Dante's *Inferno*, taken from the medieval world in which the poet lived, were not a literal revelation of Hell but rather a poetic expression of the individual's spiritual anguish, Rimbaud's *Saison en Enfer* is, for Claudel, an expression of tortures of the soul, of a capacity for sin, and of the ineluctable retribution for sin through a terrestrial struggle:

C'était bien l'Enfer, l'ancien, celui dont le Fils de l'Homme a ouvert les portes (Arthur Rimbaud). *Car l'enfer n'est pas seulement hors de nous, il est en nous. Ce n'est pas seulement demain, mes bons messieurs et chers camarades, que nous y serons, c'est tout de suite, dès que le péché mortel a été commis, dès que la grâce a été perdue.*

[*It was really Hell, the old one, the one whose doors were opened by the Son of Man* (Arthur Rimbaud). For hell is not

44. *Accompagnements*, p. 108.
45. *Accompagnements*, p. 109.

only outside of us, it is in us. It is not just tomorrow, my
good sirs and comrades, that we will be there, it is right now,
as soon as mortal sin has been committed, as soon as grace
has been lost.] [46]

(Un Poète Regarde la Croix)

It is the expression of a state of mind, of a state of spiritual existence, of "hell on earth"—of hell "as definitive as this earth permits":

> *Le vagabond à longues enjambées qui commence,*
> *Rimbaud, et qui s'en va de place en place,*
>   *Avant qu'il ait trouvé là-bas son enfer aussi*
> *définitif que cette terre le lui permet . . .*

[The vagabond with long strides who begins,
Rimbaud, and who goes from place to place,
  Before he found down there his hell as definitive
as this earth permits him . . .]

(Verlaine in *Feuilles de Saints)* [47]

Above all, Rimbaud's *Saison en Enfer* is comparable to Christ's
harrowing of Hell:

> *C'est le pays* [*cette* Vallée de l'Ombre de la Mort] *qui s'est*
> *fait lui-même, et que chaque année, vomie des entrailles de*
> *l'Afrique, envahit une nouvelle provision de boue. Faut-il*
> *croire qu'il était nécessaire que la carrière du Christ s'ouvrît*
> *comme elle devait se clore par une* Saison en Enfer?

[It is the country [this *Valley of the Shadow of Death*]
which has made itself, and which is invaded each year by
a new provision of mud vomited from Africa's guts. Are
we to believe that Christ's career had to open, as it was to
close, by a *Season in Hell?*]

(L'Epée et le Miroir) [48]

And it admits of eventual salvation through an awareness of Christ's
presence, through a conscious cleansing of the soul and of one's
outer reality, one's terrestrial acts:

---

46. *Un Poète Regarde la Croix,* pp. 385-386.
47. *Verlaine* in *Feuilles de Saints,* Vol. 2 of *Œuvres Complètes,* p. 65.
48. *L'Epée et le Miroir,* Vol. 20 of *Œuvres Complètes* (1963), p. 25.

*De toutes parts autour de nous du fond des vallées fumantes
se poursuit une grande opération de lessive. Les gouffres sous
nos pieds et là-bas la vaste étendue de ces pays à hommes
approvisionnent notre buanderie. Il monte vers nous d'énor-
mes ballots de brume sale, d'atmosphère usée, résidu de la
respiration, exhalation de la terre, empreinte confuse de toute
cette âme sous nos pieds collective. Et de toutes parts sous
le soleil actif, à nous le nettoyage! parmi les provisions de
savon transparent qui fondent et les plaques d'écume, on a
mis à sécher ces* grands linges *dont parle Rimbaud, ces pans
de draps! Ce sont les nappes et les corporaux de cette vaste
messe que ne cessent de célébrer pontificalement les mon-
tagnes au-dessus de la terre.*

[All around us from the depth of the smoking valleys a
great washing operation is going on. The abysses under our
feet and over there the vast expanse of these men-filled countries supply our washhouse. Rising toward us are enormous
bundles of dirty mist, stale gases, refuse from breathing, ex-
halings from the earth, confused imprint of this collective
soul under our feet. And from everywhere under the active
sun, for us the cleansing! amidst the dissolving supplies of
transparent soap and the patches of lather, those *great
linens* that Rimbaud speaks of have been put out to dry,
those pieces of sheets! They are the cloths and the cor-
porales of that vast mass that does not cease to be cele-
brated pontifically by the mountains above the earth.]

(*L'Epée et le Miroir*)[49]

The way to avoid repetition of such suffering in Hell is through
recognition of a *sens supérieur,* a higher sense, an existence outside
of ourselves, different from our immediate experience, to which we
can aspire or at least turn our attention and which, being elusive
and beyond our immediate experience, retains a certain element of
mystery:

*Tout sens supérieur une fois refusé à l'existence, toute issue
condamnée et toute fenêtre du côté de l'idéal une fois bouchée,
il ne restait plus qu'une cohue misérable en proie à toutes les
formes de la souffrance et de la convoitise, une agitation hideuse
et ridicule d'individus embrouillés que se disputent des délires
grotesques (je cite l'expression de Rimbaud).*

49. *L'Epée et le Miroir,* pp. 101-102.

[Once existence has been denied a superior sense, every exit
closed off, and every window looking out on the ideal boarded
up, there remains nothing more than a wretched mob tormented by every kind of suffering and cupidity, a hideous
and ridiculous restlessness of confused individuals wrangled
by grotesque frenzy (I quote Rimbaud's expression).]

(*Accompagnements*)[50]

With this recognition comes an awareness of the unity of the universe and of the relation between the finitude of God's creation (in
that His creation is complete) and the infinity of His presence (in
that it is eternal):

*Et maintenant nous sommes arrivés sous l'alluvion à ce fonds,
à ce fonds qui chez un poëte constitue la justification essentielle, la chose pour quoi il est né, la nécessité qui lui a ouvert
la bouche. Vous vous rappelez le roman de Jules Verne où
deux explorateurs suivent jusqu'aux entrailles de la terre un
voyageur légendaire qui a laissé d'étape en étape les initiales
runiques de son nom, Arne Sakneesem. Eh bien! maintenant,
c'est tout un continent, c'est le monde de la beauté, de l'espé-
rance et de la joie (sur lequel le navigateur que vous avez con-
senti avec tant de patience à accompagner) émergé des flots
confus du nihilisme et du doute (a laissé la trace audacieuse de
ses cinq doigts). Ce monde n'est pas le sien, il est celui sur qui
règne depuis deux mille ans la croix de Jésus-Christ. "Elle est
retrouvée," s'écriait Arthur Rimbaud. "Quoi? l'Eternité."
Chesterton a écrit l'histoire du conquistador qui après bien
des aventures finit par atteindre un pays merveilleux, inouï,
supérieur à tous ses rêves, et ce pays n'est autre que celui de
sa naissance. Cette aventure est celle de tout homme qui par
la grâce de la foi a réussi à réunir les deux parties de la Création,
c'est-à-dire le monde des choses visibles et celui des choses
invisibles.*

[And now we have arrived under the alluvium, at this basic
concern which for a poet constitutes essential justification,
the thing for which he was born, the necessity which opened
his mouth. You remember Jules Verne's novel in which two
explorers follow right to the bowels of the earth a legendary
traveler who left in various places along the way the runic

50. *Accompagnements*, p. 145.

letters for his name, Arne Sakneesem. Well! now it is a whole
continent, it is the world of beauty, hope, and joy (on which
the navigator whom you consented to follow so patiently)
emerged from the confused waves of nihilism and doubt (has
left the bold trace of his five fingers). This world is not his,
it is the one over which the cross of Jesus Christ has reigned
for two thousand years. "It is recovered," shouted Arthur
Rimbaud. "What? Eternity." Chesterton wrote the story of
the conquistador who, after many adventures, ended up finding a marvelous country, unbelievable, superior to all his
dreams, and this country is none other than that of his birth.
This is the adventure of every man who through the grace
of faith has succeeded in uniting the two parts of the Creation, that is to say the world of things visible and the one of
things invisible.]

(*Accompagnements*)[51]

In attaining this dual awareness of the "world of invisible things"
and the "world of visible things," we have attained a concept of
something more essential than just the banal reality of the visible
creation, for, as Claudel says, "We are no longer in the middle of
the work of six days as if in that tormenting chaos that terrified
Pascal himself and that, after him, disconcerted so many weak
hearts"; we are no longer in the world, "we have learned again to
lend our ears, as Rimbaud says, to the reasonable song of the
angels."[52] We, with Rimbaud, have become aware of God's presence and have entered into communication with Him. We have
gone outside of ourselves, outside of our immediate physical existence, and it is our capacity for going "to the Spirit" that enables
us to transcend banal realities and make us "no longer of this
world." That is not to say that God is separate from His Creation;
on the contrary, the whole of nature—like the priest who "does
not just pray 'Thy Kingdom come'" but who "is there"—bears witness to His presence and is involved with it, is in fact an integral
part of it:

> L'Office qu'un prêtre dit, c'est le devoir
> de toute la nature . . .
>   Il ne prie pas seulement "Advienne Ton Règne!"
> il y est.

51. *Accompagnements*, p. 365.
52. *Discours et Remerciements*, Vol. 18 of *Œuvres Complètes*, p. 383.

[The Office which a priest says is the duty of the
whole of nature . . .
He not only prays "Thy Kingdom come!" he is there.]
(*La Messe là-bas*)[53]

This is a theme that, like Rimbaud's phrase *"nous ne sommes pas
au monde* ["we are not of this world"][54] is often repeated throughout Claudel's works; together, they form the basis for an understanding of Claudel's association of Rimbaud with a mystical awareness
of God. When he writes that "a Christian is not entirely of this
world,"[55] he obviously has Rimbaud in mind.

Yet, although Claudel believes that if we are Christian we belong
no longer to this world but to God, he says that we must at the same
time assume our place in the proper order of things terrestrial and be
essential:

> *Nos psychanalystes parlent de* refoulement. *Et c'est vrai qu'il
> y a refoulement, mais il ne se produit pas toujours du dehors au
> dedans. Plus puissant encore quand il s'exerce du dedans au
> dehors, quand la créature,* qui est soumise à la vanité, ne le
> voulant pas, *entend qu'on l'a appelée par son propre nom, et
> dans un coup d'indignation se débarrasse de ces liens de l'ani-
> malité et de l'habitude dont on essayait de la garrotter. Je ne
> suis pas au monde! Je ne demande pas qu'on me soutire mes
> forces! Je demande qu'on ait besoin de moi. Besoin de moi
> essentiellement.*

[Our psychoanalysts talk of *repressed desire.* And it is true
that there is repressed desire, but it is not always produced
from the outside in. It is even stronger when exerted from
the inside out, when the creature, *who is subject to vanity
and does not wish to be,* hears himself called by his own name,
and in sudden indignation gets rid of those bonds of animality

---

53. *La Messe là-bas,* Vol. 2 of *Œuvres Complètes* (1952), p. 59.
54. Arthur Rimbaud, *Délires* in *Une Saison en Enfer.* Claudel uses variations
of this phrase throughout his works; in one instance, when he writes, *"Je ne
suis pas au monde,"* in *J'Aime la Bible* (p. 417), he confuses it with another
phrase from *Nuit de l'Enfer* in *Une Saison en Enfer,* "*Je ne suis plus au monde.*"
It is in this same text that Rimbaud writes, *"nous sommes hors du monde."* In
fact, we find many of Rimbaud's phrases incorporated directly into Claudel's
texts, sometimes with slight variations, as seen above, with no reference to
Rimbaud's text. Cf. in particular, *L'Œil Ecoute,* p. 48: "*le* Fils du Soleil"
taken from Rimbaud's *Vagabonds.*
55. *Correspondance: Suarès et Claudel,* letter 61, from Tientsin, le 9 septembre 1906, p. 86.

and of habit that have been trying to strangle him. I am not
of this world. I do not ask that my strength be drawn off!
I ask to be needed. To be needed in an essential way.]

(*J'Aime la Bible*)[56]

But if he asks to be recognized, to be essential, to be associated
with the "sword" of Christ's presence, that is, to be heard, he is
also aware of a silence that bears witness to the fragility and tenderness of God's love made manifest through the presence of a small
child, the Son of Man. This too reminds him of Rimbaud, for just
as Rimbaud wrote, "It is raining gently on the town,"[57] Claudel
commands, "Silence! It is raining gently on Nazareth. We hear a
child crying and the voice of his mother chiding him."[58]

Associated with this "gentle rain," which in Claudel's terms may
be properly understood as "the gentleness of the holy child," is another key word: charity. *"La Charité est cette clef"* ["Charity is
that key"] is another of the leitmotifs in *Une Saison en Enfer,* and
Claudel refers to it often, but with an interpretation that is both
unique and surprising. For Rimbaud, charity designates the means
—love, understanding, empathy, sympathy of a very personal sort
since "each of us has his reason, scorn, charity"[59]—by which he may
return to "the ancient feast" and thereby discover the essence of his
soul; it is through charity that he may be "awakened" to the primordial human existence with which he feels a certain consanguinity,
the primitiveness that was really his "element," his escape from the
"barbarity" of contemporary Christian bourgeois civilization. For
Claudel, too, charity, though it is no longer to be found in the Rimbaldian context of a search for the ancient feast but in a realization
of the necessity of accepting one's place in the proper order of
things, is the key to the understanding of one's soul, the key to the
door through which one must pass in order to bring the soul's search
for sympathy and understanding to fulfillment:

*L'Evangile nous dit (Matt., 10, 39): Celui qui aura perdu et
comme oublié son âme à cause de moi, il la trouvera! C'est
d'abord une recherche suivant cette parole de l'Ecclésiaste*

56. *J'Aime la Bible,* Vol. 21 of *Œuvres Complètes* (1963), p. 417.
57. *Bribes* in *Œuvres Complètes,* p. 109. See also, in the same volume, *Phrases*
from *Les Illuminations,* p. 186: *"Avivant un agréable goût d'encre de Chine,
une poudre noire pleut doucement sur ma veillée."*
58. *La Rose et le Rosaire,* Vol. 21 of *Œuvres Complètes* (1963), p. 259.
59. *Mauvais Sang* in *Une Saison en Enfer,* p. 225.

(7: 28, 30): Voilà ce que j'ai trouvé, une chose et l'autre,
afin que je trouve la raison pour laquelle mon âme est encore
à la recherche. *Et puis c'est une possession, comme nous dit
le Cantique (3: 4):* J'ai trouvé Celui que cherche mon âme:
je l'ai trouvé et je ne lâcherai pas. *Ah! il y a fallu du temps et
de la peine! elle a exploré la cité de fond en comble, elle en
a fait le tour, elle a fiscalisé tous les lieux publics, les rues qui
ne servent qu'à passer, les places qu'à nous arrêter, les carre-
fours qu'à nous embrouiller, et je ne parle pas de ces impasses
exécrables. Et comment ne pas être décontenancé par cette
inscription péremptoire çà et là:* Sens unique? *(Cant., 3: 2.)
Et tout à coup elle a trouvé!* Ne savais-tu pas qu'en ces choses
qui sont de Mon Père il faut Moi être? *(Luc, 2: 49.)*
  Voici la clef. La clef de la porte et la clef de ce chiffre
dont parle Pascal. La charité est cette clef *(A. R.).*

[The gospel tells us (Matt. 10: 39): *He who has lost* and
seemingly forgotten *his soul for my sake will find it!* It is
first of all a search pursuant to these words from Ecclesiastes
(7: 28, 30): *Here is what I have found, one thing and another, so that I may find the reason why my soul is still
searching.* And then it is a possession, as the Song of Solomon tells us (3: 4): *I have found Him whom my soul is
searching for: I have found him and I will not let go.* Ah!
that took time and trouble! she explored every nook and
cranny of the city, she took a complete tour of it, she went
through all the public places, the streets that serve only to
let one pass through, the little squares that are only resting
places, the intersections whose only purpose is to confuse
us, and I won't mention those abominable dead ends. And
how not to be put out by this pre-emptive direction here and
there: *One-way* (Song of Sol. 3: 2). And suddenly she has
found! *Did you not know that I must be about my Father's
business?* (Luke 2: 49).
  Here is the key. The key to the door and the key to the
number that Pascal talks about. *Charity is that key* (A. R.).]
                                    (Du Sens Figuré de l'Ecriture)[60]

This in itself is not surprising, since this interpretation applies to
charity as it is used both in the Bible and by Rimbaud (though
Rimbaud retracts his statement that "charity is that key" by declar-

60. *Du Sens Figuré de l'Ecriture*, p. 19.

ing that "this inspiration proves that I have been dreaming!"—perhaps since "love must be reinvented"—a fact that Claudel conveniently neglects in his expropriation of the phrase). The startling aspect of Claudel's use of the word is the meaning he gives to it, for, contrary to the Biblical meaning of charity as well as to Rimbaud's, Claudel's "charity" does not include the concept of love. In his terms, love is unattainable except in a relationship with God; it can be obtained only through an *élan* toward Him and is forever beyond the grasp of mortals seeking it in each other; it is not a human relationship but a deistic one: man involved with God. Claudel's charity, then, refers to the mystical essence of poetry rather than to love; it means only "communication between men" and "endeavor in common":

> ... *le Cantique (2: 4) fait dire à la Créature que* Dieu a ordonné en elle la charité, *c'est-à-dire la possibilité entre tous les êtres de communier et de se faire du bien les uns aux autres, c'est-à-dire de s'aider réciproquement dans leur travail en vue d'une fin commune.*

> [... the Song of Solomon (2: 4) has the Creature say that *God has commanded charity in her,* that is to say the possibility for all beings to be in communion and to do good unto each other, that is to say to help each other reciprocally in their work with a view toward a common goal.]
>
> (*J'Aime la Bible*)[61]

And where there is no charity there is abject poverty, Claudel's word to describe ordinary men's misunderstanding and consequent "crucifixion" of the mystic-conqueror (as in "Christ-the-conqueror"):

> C' [la pauvreté] est vraiment cette perle de l'Evangile pour qui le spéculateur judicieux n'hésite pas à se défaire de tout ce qu'il a. Tels Rembrandt qui s'éloigne à mesure que la faveur des hommes cherche à le rejoindre et qui meurt enfin, saisi à la gorge par les huissiers, Christophe Colomb qui découvre un monde pour en ramener des chaînes, Napoléon qui conquiert l'Europe pour s'assurer la possession de ce rocher au milieu de l'Atlantique; Rimbaud dévoré par un cancer.

61. *J'Aime la Bible*, p. 410.

[Poverty is really that pearl of the Gospel for which the wise speculator does not hesitate to get rid of everything he has. This was the case with Rembrandt who withdraws proportionately as men's favor attempts to catch up with him and who finally dies, the bailiffs at his throat; Christopher Columbus who discovers a world only to bring back chains from it; Napoleon who conquers Europe only to guarantee possession of that rock in the middle of the Atlantic; Rimbaud devoured by a cancer.]

(Figures et Paraboles)[62]

In his role as *the prophet of charity* (that is, of poetic essence) *who has given us the revelation of Hell and made the supreme sacrifice, in poverty, in order that we may join in the paradise of God's love,* Rimbaud has become, for Claudel, no less than a *mystical Christ figure.*

Whatever the merits of such an interpretation of the life and works of Rimbaud, however peculiarly personal, however obscure Claudel's association of Rimbaud's violent, tortured, and even obstinate revolt with Christ's serene spiritual strength, it was nevertheless a viewpoint from which he never deviated once he arrived at it after Rimbaud's ideas had fermented in his mind during the four years it took to complete his conversion, a viewpoint that no amount of intellectual or spiritual persuasion could alter and with which he refused to make any compromise.

62. *Figures et Paraboles,* Vol. 5 of *Œuvres Complètes* (1953), p. 226.

2.
Kindred Spirits

Claudel was the perfect example of what the French refer to as *"un homme entier,"* "a whole man"—a self-willed man. His obstinacy, his headstrong refusal even to discuss the validity of any point of view concerning Rimbaud other than his own, was a source of contention for many people, and it colored his evaluations of other critics and authors. André Gide, for one, bitterly reproached him for his limited insight and for his refusal to accept about Rimbaud anything more than he wanted to. On one occasion, when Gide brought the conversation around to Rimbaud's relations with Verlaine, Claudel, "with a vacant look," rather than answering, simply "touched a rosary on the mantelpiece," a reaction that prompted Gide to comment that "in his eyes, any opinion other than his own has no *raison d'être* and almost no excuse."[1] In reacting to Claudel's hagiographic interpretation of Rimbaud in his preface to the works of Rimbaud published in 1912 by Paterne Berrichon (better designated by his nickname, Baderne Patachon), André Suarès—who in the same year had also written an article on Rimbaud that, being diametrically opposed to Claudel's opinions, would have resulted in his having "the whole holy family on my back" had it been published—ill-temperedly noted that "Claudel sees only what he wants to see."[2] His refusal to accept or even so much as to attempt to understand other men's opinions was perhaps best expressed—and humorously evaluated—by himself when he said in an interview that "incomprehension is one of my attributes." It is even questionable whether he ever really understood a great deal of what Rimbaud wrote, considering he believed that Paterne Berrichon, in his superficial commentaries on his brother-in-law's poetry and life, had

---

1. André Gide, *Journal—1889-1912* (Rio de Janeiro: Americo-Edit., 1943), p. 465.
2. Etiemble, *"D'André Suarès: La ténébreuse affaire Claudel-Rimbaud"* in *Le Monde,* 16 novembre 1968, p. v.

written about Rimbaud "all that is essential." In the light of contemporary criticism with its references to "Rimbaud=*enfant terrible*," "Rimbaud=*alchimiste*," "Rimbaud=*existentialiste*," "Rimbaud=*voyou*," "Rimbaud=*voyant*," and even sometimes "Rimbaud =*poète*"—but certainly not "Rimbaud=*saint*," Claudel's opinions seem even more distorted than they must have seemed to Gide and to Suarès in 1912. And it seems all the more ironic that Claudel should have felt that other men—in particular Verlaine and Mallarmé—had completely misunderstood or misinterpreted Rimbaud, or, rather, had not understood him at all. Upon reading that Verlaine had said that Rimbaud exerted upon him "a demoniac seduction" and "even now I dream about him every night," Claudel commented that it only proved that Verlaine "had never understood anything about Rimbaud's prose, no more than had Mallarmé."[3] And if he was certain that others did not understand Rimbaud, he was equally certain that they did not understand Claudel either. His colossal pride and certainty of the validity of his own opinions and of the merits of his own work becomes apparent when, in terms similar to those he used to express his rancor against university professors in his poem *Verlaine*,

> *L'argent, on n'en a pas de trop pour Messieurs*
> *les Professeurs,*
> *Qui plus tard feront des cours sur lui et qui*
> *sont tous décorés de la légion d'honneur . . .*

> [Money, they never have too much of it for the
> "honorable" Professors, [i.e., they can always find some]
> Who later will give courses on him and who are all
> decorated with the Legion of Honor . . .]

he writes of himself that he believes

> there are not many examples of a great poet so completely unappreciated and neglected in his time, thanks to the hatred of the members of the *Académie Française* and the professors, which has never ceased to accompany me. Why don't I write twelve-syllable lines of verse? If I hadn't some other profession, Léon Bloy's lot . . . would have been reserved for me.

3. *Journal*, Tome I, Cahier 6, August 1932, p. 1008. *"Verlaine raconte que Rimbaud exerçait sur lui 'une séduction démoniaque.' 'Encore maintenant je rêve de lui toutes les nuits.' Ce qu'il aimait, c'était ses vers. Ce qu'il dit prouve qu'il n'a jamais rien compris à sa prose, pas plus que Mallarmé."* The use of the verb *raconter* indicates that Claudel considers that Verlaine is "telling a tall story" as it were.

France really cherishes and appreciates only mediocrity. When I am dead, monuments will be raised in my honor and professors will be paid to write commentaries about me. Then critics will write books about me. Whereas in my lifetime, as in the case of other great poets who have preceded me, I have nothing.[4]

As for those who did not share his understanding of Rimbaud, Claudel was apparently convinced that they were not themselves worthy of very high critical esteem. In more than one instance, for example, he makes caustic remarks about Mallarmé. This is curious, particularly since the importance of Mallarmé in Claudel's own thinking is unmistakable. His mark is clearly discernible in pronouncements such as "one must resolutely shut the door to one's imagination and to dreams and learn to live fully and strongly in the immediate" in reference to the lines from *Toast Funèbre: "le poète pur a pour geste humble et large / De l'interdire au rêve, ennemi de sa charge,"*[5] or, concerning the essence of a poem, "white . . . is the very condition of its existence, of its life, and of its breathing."[6] In *L'Œil Ecoute*, Claudel makes numerous references to Mallarmé which seem to indicate his essential approval of Mallarmé's poetic position. Having attended at least two of the "Tuesday afternoons" held by Mallarmé in the dining room of his home at the rue de Rome in Paris, Claudel was acquainted with Mallarmé's literary circle and he particularly praised his "pedagogic" abilities: "Mallarmé gave us classes every Tuesday."[7] Yet, that the caustic reference to him in connection with Verlaine was not just a passing allusion to Claudel's unflattering private opinion of the author of *L'Après-midi d'un Faune*—as expressed in his journal—is borne out by his comment that "Mallarmé leaves 'the initiative to words.' Like a drunken man leaves the initiative to his legs. With the result that

4. *Journal*, Tome I, Cahier 6, October 1929, pp. 882-883.
5. *Positions et Propositions II*, p. 257.
6. *Positions et Propositions I*, p. 72.
7. *Journal*, Tome II, Cahier 8, February 1942, p. 389. One noteworthy example of Claudel's numerous references that seem to contradict his "private" opinion of Mallarmé, is to be found on page 46 of *L'Œil Ecoute: "Le liquide en équilibre dans le grand verre, n'est-ce pas la pensée à l'état de repos, ce niveau moyen qui sert de base à notre étiage psychique, tandis que ce svelte cornet plein d'un élixir rougeâtre qui s'enfonce dans la nuit et que souvent décèle seul un éclat furtif, un Mallarmé serait prêt à y voir, comme moi, une espèce de dédicace à l'ultérieur."*

you can well imagine.''[8] Vituperation of this kind abounds in Claudel's letters as well as in his journal and was apparently what he would have qualified as one of his "attributes." Few people escaped such diatribes. Yet, however caustic his comments about virtually everyone he knew, the Rimbaud family, and Arthur Rimbaud in particular, lived with impunity. Except for saying that Paterne Berrichon's "all that is essential" and his hagiographic interpretation of Rimbaud were expressed "in a style of which I cannot always approve,"[9] Claudel never showed anything but the deepest admiration for the Rimbaud-Berrichon clan.

Although the basis for this admiration was obviously Claudel's association of Rimbaud with his own conversion, it would be inaccurate to say that he saw in Rimbaud no more than mysticism, dormant Christianity and Catholicism. It would be a distortion of Claudel's position as a poet, of his poetic concepts, even of his *raison d'être,* of his human integrity, to minimize the other ramifications of the Rimbaud experience. Claudel's opinions of the importance of Rimbaud in his own poetic evolution as well as of Rimbaud's place in French poetry, as he has expressed them in his letters, in his mentions of Rimbaud in various prose texts and scattered throughout his journal, are multifarious. His views even appear sometimes contradictory; but contradiction is the inevitable pitfall of the man who expresses himself in extremes as Claudel did and as he himself must have realized when he said to Henri Guillemin, "Surely you don't take seriously everything I say!" But whether or not one always takes Claudel seriously, he did make certain observations about Rimbaud's influence on poetry that, with due regard for his mordant sense of humor, must be taken into account because they give us a more complete picture of his estimate of Rimbaud's worth as a poet, and because they divulge clues as to the precise nature of that influence on his own poetry.

Yet, some of Claudel's references to Rimbaud indicate quite explicitly that he did not consider Rimbaud to have had any literary influence on his own poetic career. Rather, he says, it was the

---

8. *Journal,* Tome II, Cahier 10, February 1950, p. 719.

9. *Correspondance: Claudel et Gide,* letter 135, 10 juin 1912, p. 199. *"Ecrire sur Rimbaud est une idée que j'ai longtemps nourrie, mais mes essais ne m'ont jamais satisfait: il est difficile de s'exprimer autrement qu'en 'paroles païennes'! Et puis il me semble que Paterne Berrichon a dit tout l'essentiel . . . dans un style que je ne puis toujours approuver."* The expression *"paroles païennes"* comes, of course, directly from the end of the second section of *Mauvais Sang* in *Une Saison en Enfer.*

spiritual and mystical aspects alone of Rimbaud's poetry that made a profound impression on his thinking: "Rimbaud alone had the influence of which you are aware, but, for me, he is not a writer, he is a seer and a prophet."[10] Again, in the eighth *cahier* of his journal, he writes that "Rimbaud is not a poet, he is not a man of letters. He is a prophet on whom the Spirit has fallen."[11] Elsewhere in the same *cahier,* he states an extreme and apparently quite opposite point of view when he says that he would not have to be pushed very much to say that "French poetry begins with Rimbaud."[12] In *Positions et Propositions I,* he refers to the phrases of Rimbaud's prose poems as *"ces oiseaux merveilleux"* ["those marvelous birds"] of French literature.[13] Furthermore, although Claudel has taken from Rimbaud what he feels are his "principles" and his "thoughts," it is also for "form even" that he says "I owe him everything." Confronted with such seemingly contradictory statements, we must assume that what he meant to say was that even more than a poet, Rimbaud was a prophet; we must conclude that it is precisely this quality of the prophet, of the mystic become poet—or of the poet become mystic (in any case, of the poet-mystic)—which Claudel saw for the first time in Rimbaud and which was essential to both of them, that brings Claudel to state such extremes. He himself realized that these were extremes, for he says that although he believes that "French poetry begins with Rimbaud," this is "one of those excessive and outrageous opinions that it is preferable to keep to oneself."[14] However, we have here a clear Claudelian definition of the essential role of the poet and of Rimbaud as a poet: it is, as Herman Van Hoorn puts it in his *Poésie et Mystique,* a case of a mystic looking for "the poetic word in order to divinize the earth." Rimbaud is, for Claudel, the prophet who has given back to French poetry "the inventiveness, the power, the passion, the eloquence, the dreams, the verve, the color, the spontaneous music and everything that has been thought of as essential in poetry since the time of Homer."[15] He is not only a spiritual but also a poetic mentor, a profound influence on what Claudel calls the "modulation" of his own phrases.

10. *Préface à Jacques Madaule* in *Accompagnements,* p. 329.
11. *Journal.*
12. *Journal.*
13. *Positions et Propositions I,* p. 55.
14. *Journal.*
15. *Positions et Propositions I,* pp. 54-55.

However, Claudel's interest in Rimbaud was not confined to a spiritual, intellectual, or even poetic realm. His self-identification with the young poet from "Charlestown" (as Rimbaud referred to his home town Charleville in letters to his boyhood friend Ernest Delahaye) generated in him an interest in the most insignificant details of Rimbaud's life and travels, insofar as they were compatible with his own concept of Rimbaud. Just as there were no questions, only answers implied in Claudel's poetic work, there was no questioning of Rimbaud's worth: it was a simple, forthright acceptance, as a child accepts "truths" unquestioningly. And just as there seems to be a childlike association between Rimbaud's adolescent crisis and Claudel's own spiritual doubts, Claudel's interest in Rimbaud is often childlike, bordering on the sort of admiration that adolescents entertain for a movie idol. When writing about his trip to the Rimbaud farm at Roche in 1912—which was virtually a pilgrimage to the countryside that, for Claudel, had inspired Rimbaud and fired his boyhood imagination—he recounts that he slept in "the very room where Rimbaud wrote the *Season in Hell,* in his own bed,"[16] rather in the spirit of the advertisements for wayside inns that entice tourists with signs proliferating the information that George Washington slept there. At various times, we find him collecting and disseminating photographs of Rimbaud. In letters to André Gide, both early and late in their correspondence, he mentions photographs that he had sent to Gide and others that Gide had sent to him. In his journal he pasted, without any commentaries, newspaper clippings showing photographs of Rimbaud. Also in the journal are scattered, without regard to order of any kind, entries made simply to note some new bit of information he had learned about Rimbaud. In connection with Rimbaud's return from Africa, he writes, "I read that A. R. at the end of his life, having returned to Roche, used to drink infusions of poppies that his sister would prepare for him in order to calm his horrible suffering, and sang about his sad life, accompanying himself on a guitar. His sister would also sing: was it *La Chanson de la plus haute tour?* or some of the other *Illuminations?*"[17] He refers to Rimbaud's boyhood dreams, plans, hopes, interests: "Rimbaud was chums at the little seminary in Charleville, with Paul Bande and the novelist Jules Mary. They plan a trip to Central Africa

16. *Correspondance: Claudel—Francis Jammes, Gabriel Frizeau* (Paris: Gallimard, 1952), p. 249.
17. *Journal,* Tome II, Cahier 10, March 1954, p. 857.

and so R. starts to study the Abyssinian language."[18] He even mentions inquiries that other people had made concerning Rimbaud's travels: "V. L. is taking up, with the means of a rich man, the mad search for Rimbaud, this time not only through geography but through the literatures of the whole of Europe."[19] In reference to Rimbaud's correspondence, but without specifying which letters he has in mind, Claudel states that it would be "impossible to imagine a more atrocious life—Hell!"[20] Obviously, he is equating the spiritual hell of *Une Saison en Enfer* with the physical hardships that Rimbaud suffered in the tropics of Africa and not with those of some other period of his life. He did not have access to much of Rimbaud's correspondence—certainly not to the correspondence with Verlaine, which, if we are to believe Enid Starkie, Mathilde Verlaine had burned many years earlier so that it would not fall into the hands of her young son Georges—and in no letters of the extant Rimbaud correspondence other than those from Africa, is any extensive mention made of Rimbaud's living conditions. Claudel's interest in the particulars of Rimbaud's life is mentioned for the last time near the end of the last *cahier* of his journal, in one simple, uncommented affirmation: "Arthur Rimbaud, born on October 20, 1854."[21] Perhaps this was Claudel's personal way of marking the centenary of Rimbaud's birth; the entry was made in 1954, at the time he refused to participate in any public celebrations of the event. In less than a year, Claudel was to complete the particulars of his own life in what may be called a final tribute to Rimbaud, for it was while reading Henri Mondor's book on Rimbaud that Claudel suffered a fatal heart attack on February 22, 1955.[22]

Besides these biographical references in the journal, Claudel makes notations about Rimbaud's calligraphy. In one remark about Rimbaud manuscripts, he draws attention to the formation of an R that is remarkably similar to the R of German Gothic script: (Commentary on a reproduction in *La Grive* of the manuscript of *Promontoire* from *Illuminations*) "Rimbaud. Notice the 𝔤 and the double 𝔯𝔯."[23] In all probability this is, for Claudel,

18. *Journal,* Tome II, Cahier 9, February 1943, p. 442.
19. *Journal,* Tome II, Cahier 9, March 1949, p. 677. V. L. refers to Valéry Larbaud.
20. *Journal.*
21. *Journal,* Tome II, Cahier 10, February 1954, p. 855.
22. In an interview with the author in March, 1961, Professor Mondor humorously noted: *"Je crois quand même ne pas lui avoir causé une crise cardiaque!* Even so I don't think I caused his heart attack!"
23. *Journal,* Tome II, Cahier 7, July 1933, p. 31.

evidence that the manuscript was written by Rimbaud in Germany, while he was studying German and living with a German family in Stuttgart. It certainly is apparent that he was interested in Rimbaldian manuscripts, perhaps simply out of affection for Rimbaud, since he expresses no interest in paleography as such. In the eighth *cahier* of the journal, he refers to the only extant, though incomplete, manuscript of *Une Saison en Enfer:* "This fragment of a draft for *Une Saison en Enfer* is the only known manuscript of this book by Rimbaud."[24] Once more, Claudel makes no commentary on the matter, just as he never commented publicly on anything to do with Rimbaud.

To be sure, none of these references sheds much light on Claudel's interpretation of Rimbaud's work; nowhere in them do we encounter anything that approaches an analysis either of Rimbaud or of his poetry. However, these constant mentions of Rimbaud underline the depth of the "fissure" in Claudel's thinking, both private and public, which was opened during the spring and summer of 1886. Throughout the journal, in which scathing and often bitter comments about many of Claudel's contemporaries indicate that he never meant it to be published, we are confronted with the disarming and often humorous intimacy of a man's personal reflections, reflections that often are not particularly profound but that reveal the human qualities—the faults, the humor, the private rages, the engaging sentimentality—of the man beneath the pompous exterior. And of paramount interest for our present study, we see that whether as an ambassador in Washington, in China, in Japan, in Belgium, or as an elderly gentleman living in retirement at Brangues or in Paris, Claudel remained profoundly faithful to his image of Rimbaud; thinking of him each day, as he said in his *Prière pour les miens* at the end of *Un Poète Regarde la Croix,* "with an inviolable fidelity, with infinite gratitude, with deep affection, as one would think of an older brother or a superior master."[25] Nor was a single prayer sufficient, for even had Claudel used the title *Messe Pour Un Des Miens,* it could hardly be clearer than the text makes it that *La Messe là-bas* was written in such a way that it serves not only as Claudel's apology for not having become a priest but also as his most eloquent literary tribute to his "spiritual ascendent."

24. *Journal.*
25. *Prière pour les miens* in *Un Poète Regarde la Croix,* p. 421.

Claudel's fidelity brought him into contact with the Rimbaud family, with whom he cultivated a lasting friendship. It was a friendship that began in a lengthy correspondence with Paterne Berrichon, as a prelude to Claudel's trip to Roche in the summer of 1912. And even though Claudel refused to participate in the erection of the monument to Rimbaud at Roche in 1911, the warmth of his relationship with Berrichon remained unaltered. Moreover, it extended as well to Rimbaud's sister Isabelle, a remarkable woman, he said, for whom he felt great admiration and in whose epistolary talents he found "a muffled echo of the fraternal instrument" which suggested to him that "perhaps the great writer [Rimbaud] had simply brought out into the open a certain tone that had been slowly developed and matured by a whole family."[26] The extreme closeness of Claudel's relationship with the Rimbaud family is further emphasized by the fact that when Isabelle Rimbaud Berrichon died in 1919, she willed the Rimbaud estate at Roche to Claudel. However, upon her husband's urgent request, Claudel elected to sign the property over to him. This was one aspect of the Rimbaldian "legacy" that Claudel did not accept.

An examination of Claudel's biography leads one to surmise that there were certain aspects of that legacy that Claudel himself either did not recognize or else left for others to observe and comment upon (perhaps the professors "who will be paid to write commentaries about me"). Claudel's celibacy in his youth, for example, is all but an established fact. It is unlikely that he had any kind of sexual contact with women until he met "Ysé" at age thirty-two, if we are to judge from the evidence in *Partage de Midi*. In this drama, which, in Claudel's words, is not a creation of the mind but which actually happened and which had a predominant influence on his existence for twenty years, Mesa, the poet-diplomat who obviously represents Claudel himself, says to Amalric at the beginning of the play, before his affair with Ysé, "You know that I know nothing about women." And later, when Ysé, intrigued with the idea of seducing a virgin, asks Mesa whether it is true that he has never had an affair with any woman, he answers quite simply, "That is true." With so public a confession to judge from, Claudel's abstinence from any early sexual relations with women is ascertained beyond reasonable doubt. And if we are to take his scandalized naïveté upon learning about Gide as any indication, it is even more unlikely that he had any kind of homosexual contacts. This suggests

26. *Positions et Propositions I*, p. 49.

that he may have applied Rimbaud's phrase, "debauch and the comradeship of women were forbidden me" (*Mauvais Sang*), to his own heterosexual moral code as an interdiction on sex. Such an idea is perhaps not as absurd as it may appear at first, considering how deeply affected Claudel was by *Une Saison en Enfer* and *Les Illuminations* in which there are few mentions of women that suggest any particular sympathy towards them on Rimbaud's part. On the contrary, towards the end of *Une Saison en Enfer* he says, "I have seen the hell of women back there." A passage from a letter to André Suarès sums up the attitude towards women that is found throughout Claudel's works:

> *Ce n'est pas tant Cressida que je n'ai pas comprise, ce sont les amants de cette demoiselle. Que d'affaires pour une péronnelle! Réellement, Suarès, croyez-vous que les femmes méritent qu'on leur attache tant d'importance? Ah, que les premiers souffles du soir sont rafraichissants, qui nous disent que nous allons être définitivement libérés d'un esclavage humiliant! Autant j'aime Tannhäuser qui lutte noblement contre un poison dont il sent à la fois la force et l'infamie, autant les braiements de ce grand âne de Tristan qui s'imagine trouver le paradis de Schopenhauer entre les bras de son gros édredon d'Isolde, me sont insupportables. Je sais que je vous scandalise. J'ai assisté plusieurs fois à la représentation de ce drame, mais, non, malgré moi, je ne peux pas, je me révolte, non, je ne peux pas accepter cela. La femme peut être dans la vie une aise momentanée, elle atteint une grandeur auguste, quand unie à nous par le sacrement, mère d'êtres vivants qu'elle fait sortir d'elle-même, elle nous est attachée par un serment sur qui la perte même de sa beauté n'a point de prise. Mais faire de la possession de ce corps tel quel l'objet principal de nos préoccupations, c'est une chose que je ne puis comprendre, et je souffre de vous voir philosopher là-dessus.*

[It is not so much Cressida whom I did not understand as that young lady's lovers. What a lot of bother for a hussy! Really, Suarès, do you think that women are worth attaching so much importance to? How refreshing are the first breaths of evening air, telling you that we are finally going to be freed of a humiliating slavery! As much as I like Tannhäuser struggling nobly against a poison of which he feels both the force and the infamy, I find unbearable the braying of that great ass Tristan who imagines that he has discovered Schopen-

hauer's paradise in the arms of his big eiderdown Isolda. I
know I'm shocking you. I've been to see several performances
of that drama, but, no, in spite of myself, I cannot, I am
revolted, no, I cannot accept that. Woman can be a momen-
tary comfort, she attains majestic grandeur when, united to
us by a sacrament, the mother of living beings which she has
produced from inside herself, she is attached to us by an oath
which has nothing to do with beauty. But to make the possession of that body the principal object of our preoccupations
is something which I cannot understand, and it pains me to
see you philosophizing about it.]

(September 16, 1913)[27]

And a somewhat less than ecstatically enthusiastic feeling for wom-
en is indicated by his penchant for the priesthood—a wish often expressed in his works: "I have not been allowed to be one of Your
priests"[28]—and by his feeling of having missed his vocation for not
having become a priest: "Why am I not a priest, as I probably
should have been."[29] In still another letter to Suarès, he expresses
a bitterness towards women which leaves one to wonder just how
he ever did manage to marry:

"*J'ai trouvé la femme plus amère que la mort . . . Ne livre
pas tes années à la cruelle, et ses pas mènent vers l'intérieur
de la mort . . ."* Ah, que j'ai compris, amèrement, profondé-
ment, tout ce que vous dites de la femme. Certains de ces
cris de torture, il me semblait qu'ils sortaient de mon cœur
même. Oui, la femme est forte, mais il y a encore quelque
chose de plus fort qu'elle, c'est la prière; la prière non pas
telle que nous l'inventons nous-même, mais la formule que
Dieu même a mise dans notre bouche, le "Notre Père."*

["I have found women more bitter than death . . . Don't
sacrifice your years to that cruel one, and her steps lead towards death's interior . . ." How well, how bitterly, how
deeply, I have understood everything you say about women.
Certain of those cries of torture seemed to be coming from
my own heart. Yes, women are strong, but there is still

27. *Correspondance: Suarès et Claudel,* letter 154, Francfort-sur-le-Mein,
16 septembre 1913, pp. 179-180.
28. *L'Epée et le Miroir,* p. 74.
29. *Correspondance: Suarès et Claudel,* letter 19, 2 septembre 1905, p. 45.

something stronger than they: prayer, not as we invent it ourselves, but the formula which God Himself has put in our mouths, the "Our Father."]

(January 3, 1906)[30]

What is all the more piquant is that two paragraphs later, in the same letter, Claudel mentions, in passing, that he has recently become engaged to be married. At no point in his life, not even several years after his marriage, does he indicate any especial warmth towards women.

An even more striking similarity in the psychological makeup of Rimbaud and Claudel, as manifested both in their literary and their personal lives, is their love of nature. Both had come from a harsh, forested countryside—Claudel was born in the Tardenois region, Rimbaud in the Ardennes—and, with what appears to be an innate love of the earth, were great walkers. Indeed, without making the same comparison, Claudel himself often made this point about Rimbaud. When discussing Verlaine in *Accompagnements,* he refers to Rimbaud as "that other fascinated fancier of the high road" whom destiny "seized by the leg"[31] (probably in reference to the amputation of Rimbaud's right leg at the Hôpital de la Conception in Marseille—perhaps also to Verlaine's game leg—as well as to his love of long walks; walking was Rimbaud's principal means of transportation in his youth, since, being kept on a strict allowance by his mother, he never had any money to pay for any other kind of transportation). And when describing walking and movement as "the instrument of perfection everywhere in the Bible," he says that Rimbaud—who had referred to the importance of *"le pied gauche"* ["the left leg"] in his prose poem *Antique*—spent his whole life trying to bring his "left leg, the organ for traveling, for transportation, and for walking" back to "the terrestrial Paradise" that Adam had spurned.[32] In his travels, his love of nature, his physical vigor, his restlessness, his wish for the eventual departure —"young people today want to *arrive. I* am never happier than when departing"[33]—Claudel is what André Blanchet refers to as "the new Rimbaud," the Rimbaud who calls for *"Départ dans l'affection et le bruit neufs"* ["Departure into new affection and sound"] (*Départ*).

30. *Correspondance: Suarès et Claudel,* letter 38, Paris, 3 janvier 1906, pp. 62-63.
31. *Accompagnements*, p. 112.
32. *L'Epée et le Miroir,* pp. 91-92.
33. *Journal,* Tome I, Cahier 6, May 1928, p. 815.

A further interesting point of comparison between Rimbaud and
Claudel is their decision at some point to abandon literature. The
decision was definitive for Rimbaud; except for banal letters from
Africa to his family, he wrote nothing after the *Illuminations*,[34]
whereas Claudel resumed his literary career after only a few
weeks' abortive attempt at life in a monastery. Noteworthy, however, are Claudel's reasons for his own decision to give up his diplomatic career and to cease writing poetry as compared to what he
believed was the cause for Rimbaud's literary silence. Claudel de-
cided to renounce poetry when, at the age of thirty-two in 1900,
he felt a call to the monastic life. He regarded this intention as a
sacrifice to God in the name of Catholicism, feeling that "there is
no convert who has not at some point wondered with deep anguish
whether God, who commanded him to take a first step, will not ask
him to take a second." This anguish was so profound in Claudel
that he finally asked to be allowed to enter the order of the Bene-
dictines at Ligugé as a novice, "having made the complete sacrifice
of a poetry which I believed to be useless in the service of God."[35]
Claudel thought that Rimbaud's silence was the sign of his renouncement of "pagan words," similar to his own renouncement
of poetry. He believed that Rimbaud, his blood "stirred up," his
duty accomplished, could only stop talking and listen, since "secrets are not confided to a forced heart,"[36] to a heart that has lost
its spontaneity. Yet, if he felt that Rimbaud's silence was due to
some indefinable mysticism, he was not satisfied that that was the
whole of the matter; he realized that human reasons were also part
of the explanation and was certain that Rimbaud's disappearance,
his "betrayal to the world," could not be explained without taking
into consideration "his sudden vision of reality, Verlaine's weakness
and ignominy, the gossip in the cafés . . . the profound suffering of
a young soul whose honor has been attacked."[37]

34. The romantically comfortable idea that *Une Saison en Enfer* marked an
abrupt stop to all of Rimbaud's poetry has been generally refuted by modern
critics, most of whom accept as a reasonable certainty that at least some, if
not most, of *Les Illuminations* were written *after* the *Saison*.
35. Claudel quoted by Louis Chaigne in *Vie de Paul Claudel* (Mame, 1961),
p. 86.
36. Jean-Arthur Rimbaud, *Œuvres* (Paris: Mercure de France, 1949), preface
by Paul Claudel, p. 9.
37. Unpublished letter from Claudel to Paterne Berrichon, Francfort, February
21, 1912, in the Doucet Library in Paris, France. *"L'explication mystique du
silence de R. ne me satisfait pas entièrement: il faut y ajouter les raisons hu-
maines qu'explique votre travail, c.à.d. la brusque vision de la réalité, la faiblesse*

Whether Claudel's attitude towards women and towards the revelation of the mystical through nature, his view of the cosmic fantasmagoria of the universe, his revolt against the materialistic preoccupations of scientific reality and bourgeois society, even, in part, his decision to renounce poetry were actually influenced by Rimbaud, whether his cult of Rimbaud penetrated this deeply into his psyche, can only be a matter for conjecture. To the observer who finds Freudian connotations in virtually every human thought and action, Claudel's obdurate defense of Rimbaud through constant repetition of a single viewpoint for which he gives no rational explanation (Gide called him *"un marteau,"* a hammer) his attraction to him to the point of adoration and his apparent self-identification with him may very well suggest that, without being consciously aware of it, Claudel was basically in love with Rimbaud. Of course, any evidence for this must remain purely hypothetic and circumstantial; Claudel himself certainly never commented upon it. However, in establishing psychological similarities between Rimbaud and Claudel, we gain a deeper insight into the nature of Claudel's reverence for Rimbaud, a greater understanding of his reasons for having seen in Rimbaud an *âme sœur.* Claudel's aloofness, his inability to establish a close and intimate friendship either with women or with men (Francis Jammes was an exception), his creation of barriers between himself and the rest of humanity, is remarkably similar to Rimbaud's introversion. These two men are of kindred temperaments.

---

et l'ignomonie de Verlaine, les racontars de café, etc. . . . la profonde souffrance d'une jeune âme atteinte dans son honneur. La disparition de R., sa 'trahison au monde' [these last words in quotation marks are from *Saison*], *ne s'expliquent pas sans cela."* The reference to Verlaine's "ignominy" should in all likelihood not be interpreted as meaning his pederastic tendencies. In this same letter, in a note at the end, Claudel asks, *"La sodomie de Verlaine peut-elle être affirmée hors de toute discussion?* Can Verlaine's sodomy be verified beyond all doubt?" Obviously, Claudel is not convinced about the veracity of the story. Besides, he refers to the *"racontars de café,"* suggesting that he does not believe the stories about Verlaine and Rimbaud were true.

3.
Claudel as a
Non-Christian Poet

Paul Claudel has long been treated by literary critics as the Catholic
poet par excellence, though it is ironic that his archconservatism
and orthodoxy—his belief that outside the Catholic Church there is
no salvation, for example—might well be considered heretical by the
Church today. Throughout his long career as diplomat and poet, in
lectures, essays, letters, private conversations, newspaper articles,
dramas, and poems he took advantage of every opportunity to pro-
claim his zealous faith. Even one of his severest critics, Pierre Lasserre, credited him with incomparable eloquence after listening to
one of his lectures in which "a few passages on morality, somewhat
all-inclusive but worded in everyday language, left me with the impression of having heard the first sermon by which I was not bored."[1]
Yet, although Claudel's works are considered essentially Christian in
theme and concept, there is much in his thought, in the structure of
his plays, in the lyricism of his poetry that defies analysis and understanding in Christian terms despite the overlay of scripture, liturgy,
and references to the Marian cult and to God's love. A complete
understanding of Claudel's literary and religious endeavors requires
an analytical approach that goes further than the pious acceptance
and repetition of what he himself said he felt or believed. By including in his works not only liturgical allusions but verbatim quotes
from the liturgy as well (as in the final scene of the second version
of *La Ville,* in which he incorporates a French translation of the
Credo), Claudel often creates the impression of forcing the issue of
his religious beliefs, of rationalizing in Christian terms acts and words
that might otherwise lie well outside the realm of Christian thought
and for which he desperately seeks some justification. His own basic
ferociousness and belligerence, for example, his closeness to nature
in a virtually paganistic way (quite apart from his allusions to my-

1. Pierre Lasserre, *Les Chapelles Littéraires* (Paris: Librairie Garnier Frères,
1920), pp. 44-45.

thology), his concept of man essentially alone in a personal struggle with other men and in a willful revolt against them—the kind of man whose forceful individuality and violent disdain of humanistically oriented society, owes much more to Rimbaud and Nietzsche than to God—all require a larger context than the limited scope of Catholicism or even of Christianity, despite Claudel's constant justifications of his viewpoint by saying that "Catholic" means "universal, all-embracing." His concept that in the sociological order and in the universe "everything has its place which cannot be any other,"[2] is not specifically Christian; it is Platonist in origin. Nor is his monotheism a concept limited to Christianity. Yet these are two of his fundamental claims to Catholicism. And his inability to submit to arbitrary authority, his lifelong revolt against it, certainly goes beyond the pale of Catholic hierarchy. Even the central themes of his best plays, adultery, pride (which, in *Tête d'Or,* is tantamount to *hubris* in its original Greek sense), Odyssean adventure, are not specifically Christian and would be equally as effective, perhaps even more so in the case of *Tête d'Or,* if their Christian trappings were removed. This is not to say that Claudel himself did not feel deeply religious, or that he was insincere in professing Catholicism, but, rather, that his works are Christian more by virtue of his witness than of their form. One might possibly consider his exegeses of Scripture an exception, though even these are sometimes infused with pagan sensuality.

Despite his apparent claim to orthodox Catholic thought which would allow him no questioning of the absolute and universal truth of Christian and specifically Catholic theology, Claudel seems unable to remain entirely within the confines of Christian reference; specific examples of this inability are to be found in his repeated evocations of mythology. At first they appear to be mere literary conceits in the tradition of certain Renaissance poets, but on closer examination they are seen as expressing the intensity of his themes more vividly than any of his Biblical metaphors. While Claudel cer-

2. *L'Otage,* p. 57. Examples of this theme, repeated often throughout Claudel's works, are to be found even in his earliest plays, such as the following from *La Ville* (first composed in 1890), p. 153:

> *Et, comme d'un nombre soumis aux opérations*
> *d'une éternelle arithmétique,*
> *Je sais qu'aucune part de cette somme qu'il*
> *est n'est inutile ou vaine;*
> *Et de même chaque être vivant a sa tâche*
> *prescrite avec sa provision d'énergie.*

tainly does not believe in mythological figures in a literal sense as the Greeks or Romans presumably did, nevertheless, they provide him in many cases with a frame of reference more imaginatively appealing than do his saints; for example, he evokes Zeus,

> *Or maintenant comme le chêne de Zeus qu'emplit le*
> *vent prophétique et qui ne peut quitter*
> *La terre qu'il embrasse de ses racines multipliées,*
> *Je ne bouge point du lieu, et mon bruit n'est pas*
> *entendu . . .*

> [So now like the oak of Zeus which the prophetic wind
> fills up and which cannot leave
> The earth it embraces with its multiple roots,
> I do not move from the place at all, and my sound
> is not heard . . .]

> (*La Ville*)[3]

Apollo,

> *Et je vois encore notre précanteur quand il*
> *montait au lutrin,*
> *Le sceptre au poing, ruisselant d'or, pareil*
> *au Dieu Apollon, et marchant dans sa majesté . . .*

> [And I still see our precentor as he ascended the
> lectern,
> The scepter in his fist, streaming with gold, like
> the God Apollo, and walking in his majesty . . .]

> (*L'Otage*)[4]

Pallas Athena,

> *Vous parlez comme Pallas elle-même, aux bons jours*
> *de cet oiseau sapient dont on la coiffe . . .*

> [You speak like Pallas herself, in the good days of
> that sapient bird with which her head is covered . . .]

> (*L'Otage*)[5]

---

3. *La Ville*, Vol. 7 of *Œuvres Complètes* (1954), p. 162.
4. *L'Otage*, pp. 49-50.
5. *L'Otage*, p. 55.

Jupiter,

> *Ainsi notre mariage auguste sera comme celui de*
> *Jupiter et de la Nymphe . . .*

[Thus our marriage will be like that of Jupiter and
the Nymph . . .]

(*La Ville*)[6]

and Pegasus,

> *C'est Pégase même tout à coup à grand bruit de ses ailes*
> *déployées qui a quitté le sol, et, la main au-dessus des yeux,*
> *je n'ai plus qu'à le suivre d'un regard appréciateur dans l'azur!*

[It is Pegasus himself suddenly with the great sound of his
spread wings who has left the ground, and, with my hand
shielding my eyes, I have now only to follow him with an ap-
preciative gaze into the azure!]

(*L'Œil Ecoute*)[7]

In another instance, one of his characters makes libations to the
moon, like a pagan appealing to the gods:

> *Ovation à la resplendissante Lune, œil de la*
> *gloire!*
> *Tu manifestes, sans le détruire, le mystère du*
> *Ciel avec son étendue.*
> *Car, comme le maître nouveau d'un palais qui le*
> *visite, un flambeau à la main,*
> *Tu marches en l'éclairant à travers la salle de*
> *la Nuit vide.*
> *Et bien que tu chérisses d'autres séjours, toute*
> *eau qui tombe, sauvage,*
> *Ou domestique sous les feuilles, moulin, scierie,*
> *qui se tient debout sous la roue mouvante;*
> *Et tu favorises de nouveaux amants, qui,*
> *s'embrassant,*
> *Ont perdu toute puissance de se séparer,*
> *Et le fleuve herbeux, cycnéen;*
> *—Aime*
> *Ce jardin parmi le lieu qui ne montre rien que*
> *d'aride, Diane!*

6. *La Ville*, p. 151.
7. *L'Œil Ecoute*, Vol. 17 of *Œuvres Complètes* (1960), p. 154.

Je te salue avec, ne t'offrant rien d'autre,
Cette libation de terre.
Les fleurs nouvelles te rendent, Lampe du Sommeil,
l'encens.

[Ovation to the resplendent Moon, eye of glory!
You reveal, without destroying it, the mystery of
the Sky with its expanse.
For, like the new master of a palace who is visiting
it, a torch in hand,
You walk across the empty room of the Night, light-
ing it up.
And even though you cherish other sojourns, every
water that falls, wild,
Or domestic under the leaves, mill, sawmill, which
remains erect under the moving wheel,
And you favor new lovers, who, embracing, have lost
all power to separate,
And the grassy river, *cycnéen;*
—Love
That garden in the place which shows only barrenness,
Diana!
I pay you tribute with, offering you nothing else,
This libation of earth.
The new flowers offer you, Lamp of Sleep, the
incense.]

(*La Ville*)[8]

The reference to incense does recall the Catholic Mass. Yet, whereas incense at Mass is used to purify the altar, here it becomes an
idolatrous sacrifice. Considering that it is Cœuvre who makes this
libation and sacrifice in *La Ville*—Cœuvre, who, upon becoming a
bishop, adopts ideas concerning mysteries and poetic aesthetics
that are extremely similar to Claudel's own "Christianity"—one begins to wonder to what degree his creator, Claudel, really was a
pagan at heart.

   In other instances, Claudel introduces into his works a symbolism
of numbers that have a Christian significance, such as three, seven,
or ten, yet that are imbued with paganistic overtones. In *La Cantate à Trois Voix,* for example, the three women bring to mind the
trinity; moreover, their names—Fausta, Læta, and Beata—are sug-

8. *La Ville*, p. 160.

gestive of liturgical terms. Yet their fiercely sensual evocations of their physical beings and their quasi-mystical invocations to nature identify them far more with pagan earth rites than with the spiritual aspects of Christianity. And it is the kind of individual characterized by these three women on whom Claudel is capable of bestowing a truly vibrant existence, in whom his lyric genius and all his poetic abilities find their most poetically convincing expression. Even in *La Muse qui est la Grâce* from the *Cinq Grandes Odes* which, according to Wallace Fowlie, fully express "Claudel's sense of vocation as a religious poet,"[9] the bark, having wrenched itself from its moorings and left port to embark on an adventure that will lead it to the discovery of a perfection and a new paradise, sees "God on his throne," only to recognize that the "legitimate son" will be not Christ but the poet.

It seems ironic that many of Claudel's most artistically successful creations—*Tête d'Or, Partage de Midi, L'Echange*—are essentially non-Christian or at least not dependent on his theme of Christianity for their poetic impact. Rather, they indicate a poetic fervor tantamount to the paganism that Claudel equated with one of his pet hates, materialism. One is led to consider seriously Claudine Chonez' suggestion that, more than anything, Christianity was "a spring for his poetic inspiration," that his poetry took precedence over Catholicism and not the other way around, that Christianity was really only incidental to his poetic spirit; in short, that Claudel was a poet regardless of his religious beliefs. Certainly it was through poetry, his interpretation of Rimbaud notwithstanding, that Claudel was awakened to a Christian awareness; and he was writing poetry long before his "discovery" of Rimbaud and his dramatic conversion.

One of the keys that open the door to a broader perspective of humanity than the restrictive view imposed by Claudel's understanding of Catholicism—one of those keys that, as Claudel writes in *Du Sens Figuré de l'Ecriture*, "are worth something because they open"[10]— is to be found at the beginning of *Le Soulier de Satin* where he describes "the setting of this drama" not only as Spain but, more broadly and, as a consequence, more inclusively, as "the world," a world in which he finds a place for virtually everyone and everything. Claudel's "view from the bridge" sees the world as an all-inclusive cosmos created and put into movement by God, a manifestation of

9. Wallace Fowlie, *Paul Claudel* (New York: Hillary House Inc., 1957), p. 39.
10. *Du Sens Figuré de l'Ecriture*, p. 61.

God and His munificence, and really identifiable with Him. This is
a monotheistic concept, to be sure, but it goes far beyond the limi-
tation of grace to those who believe in Christ; moreover, it is cosmic
in its inclusion of the celestial bodies and what appears to be their
astrological rapport with mankind, as suggested by the soliloquy of
the moon in *Le Soulier de Satin* and as specifically indicated in
L'Epée et le Miroir in which Claudel says that "it is this cosmic debt
which we have inherited and which makes us open our mouths both
to shout and to ask."[11] Curiously enough, Claudel was always an-
noyed by critics' references to him as a "cosmic poet," though the
source of his annoyance sometimes struck his sense of humor as well;
in one of the entries in the eighth *cahier* of his journal he mentions
his elation when he thought he had read as the title for an article,
"Claudel, the Great Comic Poet": "What a feeling of joy! Finally,
someone has understood me! Not at all! it really reads, 'the great
cosmic poet.' Let's get used to the idea, each morning, when I look
at myself in the mirror to shave, that I am 'cosmic.' So much for
cosmic!"[12] This helps to explain why Claudel's cosmic view of the
universe is really the broad backdrop for a theme much more important in his work than either Christianity or monotheism: name-
ly, humanism. Yet, if his works can be interpreted as being broadly
humanistic, they are at the same time, deeply personal. Like Rimbaud's works, Claudel's dramas are essentially an expression of himself, of his own personal experiences and intimate ideas—even his
humor. Certain critics have felt that Claudel's implacable seriousness—despite himself—has discouraged any sense of humor. Yet the
Soulier de Satin, the most "cosmic" and the most comprehensive of
his dramas, contains many scenes, such as the one with the Sentinel-
les or another between La Logeuse and Don Léopold, that are little
short of slapstick and that recapture to a certain degree the *esprit
de vaudeville* of plays at the end of the nineteenth century in
France, in particular, those of Feydeau. In the Pirandello-like beginning of *Le Soulier de Satin,* the comments of L'Annoncier are
not entirely serious at first, and his last words inform us that in this
play "it is what you do not find amusing that is the funniest." This
subtle sense of humor pervades much of the dialogue in Claudel's
plays. Even Mesa in *Partage de Midi,* who appears to be completely
humorless and whom Ysé describes as "that damned little bourgeois," displays signs of drollery in some of his observations, such as,

11. *L'Epée et le Miroir,* p. 151.
12. *Journal,* Tome II, Cahier 8, August 1941, p. 371.

*"Il a des mains agréables. (Car les choses sont comme une vache /
Qui sait bien ne pas se laisser traire quand elle veut, la vache!)"*
["He has nice hands. (For things are like a cow / Who knows perfectly well how not to let herself be milked when she wants, *la
vache!*)"].[13] (The expletive *"la vache!"*—literally, "the cow!"—is
roughly equivalent to "the bitch!" in colloquial English, and, used
as a jocular pun on the cow "who knows perfectly well how not to
let herself be milked when she wants," is the word revealing the
sense of humor here. Since this pun does not appear in the first
version of *Partage de Midi,* we are led to surmise that as Claudel
grew older—the stage version dates from 1948—his "implacable
seriousness" was very much tempered.) Claudel was capable of being equally humorous when discussing his most implacably serious
subject, religion: "The Curé d'Ars reveals to us that between the
railing of a bridge in Paris and the Seine there was, at least once,
time enough for an act of perfect contrition. From the top of the
Empire State Building to its base there is room for a complete examination of one's conscience!"[14] And apart from the humor in
his works, one is confronted with his pet peeves. He derides "the
University," referring scornfully to "a mind impregnated with the
facile training of our University."[15] And just as he had expressed
his rancor against professors in his poem *Verlaine,* he is critical of
"our solid Pedro, as we call him, the rampart of Salamanca, Professor Pedro de las Vegas, denser than mortar!"[16] His disdain for what
he referred to in his prose works as *"le scientisme"* (just another
"ism", like *"romantisme"*—which was one of his early hatreds), having been emphasized strongly in *La Ville* where Claudel wrote "there
is no garbage or filth that science cannot make use of,"[17] becomes
mockery in *Le Soulier de Satin:* "My poor Daibutsu, I see that you
are not familiar with modern science / Which tells you that everything
comes from nothing and that it is a hole which bit by bit makes a canon";[18] it shows a contempt for scientific "truths" similar to Rimbaud's
attitude in lines like, "and science is too slow" (*L'Eclair*). Here in
Le Soulier de Satin are also discussions of grammar and of Claudel's
idea that the poet has the right to take liberties with syntax and to

13. *Partage de Midi (version pour la scène),* Vol. 11 of *Œuvres Complètes* (1957),
p. 115.
14. *Sous le Signe du Dragon,* Vol. 4 of *Œuvres Complètes* (1952), pp. 141-42.
15. *Le Soulier de Satin,* p. 164.
16. *Le Soulier de Satin,* p. 160.
17. *La Ville,* p. 196.
18. *Le Soulier de Satin,* p. 254.

introduce neologisms into the vocabulary of a language, as seen in the following satirical passage in which Don Fernand expounds to Don Léopold about the "horrors" perpetrated by Spanish soldiers in the New World:

> *Chère grammaire, belle grammaire, délicieuse grammaire, fille, épouse, mère, maîtresse et gagne-pain des professeurs!*
>
> *Tous les jours je te trouve des charmes nouveaux! Il n'y a rien dont je ne sois capable pour toi!*
>
> *La volonté de tous les écolâtres d'Espagne m'a porté! Le scandale était trop grand! Je me suis jeté aux pieds du Roi.*
>
> *Qu'est-ce qui se passe là-bas? qu'est-ce qui arrive au castillan? Tous ces soldats à la brigande lâchés tous nus dans ce détestable Nouveau-Monde,*
>
> *Est-ce qu'ils vont nous faire une langue à leur usage et commodité sans l'aveu de ceux qui ont reçu patente et privilège de fournir à tout jamais les moyens d'expression?*
>
> *Une langue sans professeurs, c'est comme une justice sans juge, comme un contrat sans notaire! Une licence épouvantable!*
>
> *On m'a donné à lire leurs copies, je veux dire leurs mémoires, dépêches, relations comme ils disent. Je n'arrêtais pas de marquer des fautes!*
>
> *Les plus nobles mots de notre idiome employés à des usages autant nouveaux que grossiers!*
>
> *Ces vocables qu'on ne trouve dans aucun lexique, est-ce du toupi? de l'astèque? de l'argot de banquier ou de militaire?*
>
> *Et qui s'exhibent partout sans pudeur comme des Caraïbes emplumés au milieu de notre jury d'agrégation!*

[Dear grammar, beautiful grammar, delicious grammar, daughter, spouse, mother, mistress and livelihood of professors!

Everyday I find new charms in you! There is nothing of which I am not capable for you!

The will of all the religious school inspectors in Spain has brought me here! The scandal was too great! I have thrown myself at the feet of the King.

What's going on over there? what is happening to Castilian? All those rascally soldiers set loose completely naked in that hateful New World,

Are they going to make us a new language for their own use and convenience without the consent of those who have been given the right and privilege to furnish for all time the means of expression?

A language without professors is like justice without a judge, like a contract without a notary! A dreadful license!

I have been given their exercises to read, I mean their accounts, dispatches, reports as they say. I didn't stop for a minute checking off all the mistakes!

The most noble words of our language, put to uses as vulgar as they were new!

What are these vocables that cannot be found in any lexicon? Tupi? Aztec? banking or military slang?

And they show themselves off everywhere shamelessly, like feathered Caribbeans in the midst of our Ph.D. examining boards!] [19]

It would be difficult to find a more mordant satire of literary critics and of *"les sales professeurs"* ["nasty professors"] than this, especially when one considers what Claudel had to say elsewhere about the sanctity of grammar:

La grammaire ne devrait pas être autre chose qu'une recommandation prudente du meilleur usage et le musée des formes les plus délicates de l'idiome. Rien ne lui donne le droit de s'arroger l'autorité d'un code.

Le grammairien a des principes ridicules: celui-ci, entre autres, qu'une forme n'est légitime que lorsqu'elle est analysable rationnellement.

. . . Toutes les grammaires à partir de Vaugelas indiquent que la règle du bon parler français est l'usage, mais en réalité on ne tient aucun compte de cet usage ni des nécessités du français tel qu'il est fait pour notre poumon et notre boîte sonore.

[Grammar should be no more than a prudent recommendation of the best usage and the museum of the most delicate forms of the language. Nothing gives it the right to assume the authority of a code of laws.

The grammarian has ridiculous principles: among others, the one that says that a form is legitimate only when it is rationally analysable.

. . . All systems of grammar, from Vaugelas on, indicate that the rule for speaking correct French is usage, but in

19. *Le Soulier de Satin*, pp. 159-160.

reality usage is not taken into consideration, nor are the needs of French as it is made for our lungs and our sounding box.][20]

But aside from being satire, this passage from *Le Soulier de Satin* also points out various tenets of the symbolist poets. Much of the discussion in the scene from which this passage is taken is really a riposte to the critics of Claudel himself—not to mention its reflection of his superb sense of humor—as well as to those who found fault with the symbolists in general and, most assuredly, with Mallarmé in particular: "And that way of joining ideas! In order to bring them together, syntax has contrived many a noble detour to permit them bit by bit to approach each other and become acquainted."[21] And the following diatribe is quite probably directed at Lasserre's acid criticism of Rimbaud in which he says that Rimbaud used impardonable ellipses:[22] "But those wretches push straight on and when their passage is blocked, they simply jump!"[23] Even a caustic reference to the members of the *Académie Française* is here: "As concerns me—you know that I have composed a few modest works that I have taken the liberty to bring into your chamber *en masse*—, / When there is a place in the Academy, can I hope to fill a desk in the shadow of Your Munificence?"[24] Of all modern poets, it would seem that it is Claudel who best lends himself to treatment in the book publishers' series of *"les auteurs par eux-mêmes."* A biographer of an individual's intellectual and personal life would be at a loss to find an author whose published works furnish a richer mine than Claudel's, in which we can read even the most intimate details of his private life. But even more than expressing his humor, his pet peeves, and his private rages, each of Claudel's works is an attempt to express completely the essential thought behind his work as a whole; each is really a variation on a single theme or on a group of themes which he conceptualized at the outset, which he enlarged and broadened in his later works, but which remain basically identical.

20. Claudel quoted from an interview with Frédéric Lefèvre, *Les Sources de Paul Claudel* (Paris: Librairie Lemercier, 1928), pp. 153-54.
21. *Le Soulier de Satin*, p. 160.
22. See *Les Chapelles Littéraires*, pp. 11-16. Lasserre's book was published in 1920, a full four years before Claudel completed *Soulier*.
23. *Le Soulier de Satin*, p. 160.
24. *Le Soulier de Satin*, p. 168. Actually, Claudel himself aspired to becoming a member of the *Académie Française* but was bitter over not having been elected to it as of the early twenties. He eventually was elected, however, and occupied Racine's chair.

In *Rimbaud's Poetic Practice,* W. M. Frohock refers to the "osten-sible subject" and the "hidden motive" in Rimbaud's works. He points out that the "ostensible subject" of *Le Bateau Ivre,* for ex-ample, is the "adventure of the poet-boat through scenes that never were on land or sea," whereas the "hidden motive" is a "defeated effort to gain and retain a particular form of felicity."[25] This kind of internal motive complementing an external statement was basic to Claudel's thinking as well. In a letter to Jacques Rivière, he is quite explicit about the relationship between apparently superficial simplicity and inner depth: "I rather tend today to regard simplici-ty as an abnormal, artificial, violent, and otherwise illusory element. Nothing exists without a certain internal rapport."[26] What is implic-it in the statements by both Frohock and Claudel is that, inherent in the works of Claudel and Rimbaud, there is an aspect of symbol-ism that reveals the poet's inner self and involves him inextricably with the apparently simple, but actually complex, statements of his poetry. Thus, in *La Muse Qui Est la Grâce,* Claudel's bark leaves port in search of a reality—or a paradise—outside of human exis-tence; and just as the *bateau ivre* sees previously unimagined visions, the poet-bark catches a glimpse of God on His throne and of the marvels of existence outside of the human domain. As is true of the *bateau ivre,* the "ostensible subject" is the bark's adventurous trip; the "hidden motive," however, is "felicity attained" or "desire fulfilled," as is suggested by the bark's turning back towards the earth in order to find its form of happiness. Desire is one of the themes common to Claudel and Rimbaud; but for Rimbaud, it is in a state of suspension, whereas Claudel finally realizes or resolves de-sire. Extending this concept to other poetic works of Claudel as well as to his dramas, it becomes apparent that whether he is talk-ing about a beautiful spring night on the Rhône (as in *La Cantate à Trois Voix,* in which the three virgins—one is tempted to call them "vestal virgins"—await the return or arrival of Læta's fiancé), or, as in *L'Annonce faite à Marie,* about the sacrificial death of Violaine (which, for all its Christian trappings, is little more than paganistic human immolation, since Violaine must die in order that her loved ones be redeemed, and we see her stretched out on the table in the final scenes of the play, as on a sacrificial altar), the poet is stating symbolically the "hidden motive" of "felicity attained" or of "felicity on the verge of fulfillment."

25. *Rimbaud's Poetic Practice,* p. 11.
26. *Correspondance: Rivière et Claudel,* p. 139.

But, in the works of both these poets, there is an even more essential hidden motive, which strikingly reveals one of the fundamental reasons for the affinity that Claudel felt for Rimbaud, and which must have seemed to him to constitute a Rimbaud-Claudel unity. Even more than a "defeated effort to gain and retain a particular form of felicity," the hidden motive in Rimbaud is a compulsive questioning, a continual and constant search, an inevitable departure. The main point of *Le Bateau Ivre,* the "hidden motive," is summed up in the lines that make the transition from the freedom of unbridled wanderings to the restriction of the port and of the "prison ships' horrible eyes"; from the projected visions, the hypothetical situation in which felicity may possibly be attained, to the reality of defeat or disappointment: *"Est-ce en ces nuits sans fonds que tu dors et t'exiles, / Million d'oiseaux d'or, ô future Vigueur?"* The form of these two lines reflects the substance of the whole of Rimbaud's poetry: a question, a search, but never an answer; an expression of revolt and discontent, a series of problems poetically posed but never resolved. It is as the *Vierge Folle* says of her *Epoux Infernal* in *Une Saison en Enfer:* "he has perhaps secrets for *changing life?* No, he is only looking for them." Even some of Rimbaud's most assertive statements reveal themselves eventually as an effort to find an answer to some question and to posit possible essences, rather than to be an answer in themselves. Just as in the comparatively early *Le Bateau Ivre* the visions of the poet-boat are all put to doubt with a pivotal question at the moment when night becomes day,[27] much later, in the first of *Veillées* from *Illuminations,* Rimbaud transforms his affirmative theses into quasi-negations by asking a question:

> *C'est le repos éclairé, ni fièvre ni langueur,*
>   *sur le lit ou sur le pré.*
> *C'est l'ami ni ardent ni faible. L'ami.*
> *C'est l'aimée ni tourmentante ni tourmentée. L'aimée.*
> *L'air et le monde point cherchés. La vie.*
> *—Etait-ce donc ceci?*
> *—Et le rêve fraîchit.*

27. Curiously enough, this poem was written almost simultaneously with his so-called *Lettres du Voyant* in which Rimbaud states his poetic concepts quite categorically. Or should we assume that they, too, are basically "questions"?

[It is enlightened repose, neither fever nor languor,
　on the bed or on the meadow.
It is the friend neither impassioned nor weak. The
　friend.
It is the beloved neither tormenting nor tormented. The
　beloved.
The air and the world not sought after. Life.
—Was it this then?
—And the dream cools.]

Apparently positive discoveries—the friend, the loved one, pure and
innocent existence, each in a state of essential being—reveal themselves to be hopeful fantasies, unrealizable dreams (at least for Rimbaud), through the posing of a simple question that asks whether
"this was it," and thereby themselves become questions, "Is this
what a friend, a loved one, or life itself is or should be?" Even in
the prose poem *Départ* in which there are apparently only statements, *"Assez vu . . ." "Assez eu . . ." "Assez connu . . .":*

Assez vu. La vision s'est rencontrée à tous les airs.
Assez eu. Rumeurs des villes, le soir, et au
　soleil, et toujours.
Assez connu. Les arrêts de la vie.—O Rumeurs
　et Visions!
Départ dans l'affection et le bruit neufs!

[Enough seen. The vision occurred in all airs.
Enough had. Murmurs of cities, in the evening, and
　in the sun, and always.
Enough known. The hindrances of life.—O Murmurs and
　Visions!
Departure into new affection and sound!]

a question is implicit in the new search suggested by this *"départ*
dans l'affection et le bruit neufs," the "question" whether some
new reality will result from the departure. If, however, rather than
a search for some new reality, this departure is an answer to the
"Rumeurs et Visions," a riposte to them, a reaction against them,
an attempt to run from them, a refusal to accept visions as feasible
or realizable, a prefiguration of Rimbaud's renunciation of literature in *Une Saison en Enfer* (unless *Départ* was written after *Une*
Saison en Enfer, in which case it would be a restatement of the
renunciation), then it is only a provisional answer, hardly indicating
any final resolution, for escape is only transitional.

A specific example of this "inevitable departure" in the works of Claudel is to be found in *La Muse qui est la Grâce*. At the beginning of this ode, the bark is impatient to leave, impatient to embark on the high seas. However, as we have previously pointed out, the bark encounters in this departure not only visions and vain hopes (vain hopes being a form of question, in the same way that *Départ* is a question) but also—and what is even more important—the answer to the perplexing problem of the reason for its own existence, of its proper place in the universe:

> *J'ai un devoir qui n'est pas rempli! un devoir*
> *envers toute chose, pas aucune*
> *A quoi je ne sois obligé . . .*
> *. . . mon devoir n'est pas de m'en aller,*
> *ni d'être toujours ailleurs, ni de lâcher aucune*
> *chose que je tiens,*
> *Ni de vaincre, mais de résister, et de tenir à*
> *la place que j'occupe!*

> [I have a duty which is not fulfilled! a duty
> towards every thing, not one
> To which I am not obligated . . .
> . . . my duty is not to go away, nor to be
> always elsewhere, nor to let go of anything
> which I hold,
> Nor to conquer, but to resist, and to hold
> firm to the place I fill!] [28]

It returns with an answer to a question as well as with the certainty of having discovered new manifestations of the felicity that it had already attained—though it had previously been uncertain of having done so—and that has now been reaffirmed. The bark returns triumphant and reassured. To its original question—"What do all men matter to me now! It is not for them that I am made . . . What does any one of them matter to me?"—comes the answer: "When I hear your call, not a being, not a man, not a voice that is not required for my unanimity."

In *La Cantate à Trois Voix* there is also a problem to be resolved: the question of the reason for the women's long vigil, to which the answer is a promise of fulfillment with the coming of daybreak and the return of the conqueror-fiancé: "Tomorrow the *full* Summer

28. *La Muse qui Est la Grâce*, Vol. 1 of *Œuvres Completes* (1950), pp. 122-123.

begins!" And in Claudel's plays, especially in *Le Soulier de Satin,* the answer to each quest comes in the resolving of desire. Don Rodrigue, for example, finally finds rest, peace—fulfillment—in the certainty of Christianity (as emphasized by his deliverance into the hands of la Religieuse) and in an awareness of the reflection of God in nature.

Whereas Rimbaud's poetry points essentially to the visions that were to remain only visions, unrealizable—for Rimbaud—except as exquisitely expressed essences, and posits the hidden motive of a defeated quest for felicity, a philosophical and metaphysical question mark, Claudel's theme lies in the resolution of that questioning. In this sense Claudel's works are a continuation of Rimbaud's poetry and form a basic unity with it; the paradox of Claudel's affinity for the blasphemous child-poet is at least partially resolved for those to whom it seems unlikely that one should accept Rimbaud as either consciously or even inherently Christian. To be sure, Claudel sees Rimbaud as the converted Catholic, and his works as manifestations of dormant Catholicism; yet, actually, Catholicism is only incidental and peripheral to Rimbaud's influence on the vast panorama of Claudelian poetry. What is more important is that both Rimbaud and Claudel are "inspired" poets, and the basis for their inspiration really goes much deeper than particular religious beliefs.

4.
Claudelian Protagonists in a Rimbaldian Setting

Rimbaldian aspects of the Claudelian hero

Without question, of all Claudel's works, the one that is closest to Rimbaud in theme, in time—even partially in style—is *Tête d'Or*. The first version of this play was written in 1889, three years after Claudel's first encounter with Rimbaud's poetry, and published anonymously by the *Librairie de l'Art Indépendant* in 1890. The title alone identifies it with Rimbaud: "gold" was his symbol for the ideal, as it was Claudel's. The lyricism in this play, the elliptic speech, the density of imagery, the patterns of color and sound, without being pastiches, are nevertheless much more characteristic of Rimbaud's prose poems than of Claudel's later *verset* in which the use of "liturgical" repetitions makes the Rimbaldian influence less apparent, at least in stylistic terms. The kind of image that Claudel uses here is comparable to Rimbaud's images, as in this description of the dawn,

> *Et le matin par qui la mer s'embrase et dont les*
> *feux immenses*
> > *Colorent les toits et les pylônes, renaît!*
> > *Je sens la fraîcheur du vent.*

> [And the morning through which the sea blazes
> up and whose huge fires
> > Color the roofs and the towers, is being reborn,
> is dawning!
> > I feel the coolness of the wind.] [1]

in which the coloring of the *"toits et les pylônes"* and the movement of the *"fraîcheur du vent,"* as well as certain vowel tones such as ô in *"pylônes,"* recall Rimbaud's *Aube:*

---

1. *Tête d'Or*, Vol. 6 of *Œuvres Complètes* (1953), p. 138.

A la grand'ville, elle fuyait parmi les clochers et les dômes,
et, courant comme un mendiant sur les quais de marbre, je la
chassais.

[In the heart of the city, she fled among the steeples and domes,
and running like a beggar on the marble quays, I chased her.]

But it is principally the characterization of the title role that reflects the spirit of Rimbaud, that evokes Rimbaud's *"fils du soleil,"*
his "sun's son" (*Vagabonds*), for in Tête d'Or himself Claudel has
created a dramatic character who, through his projected goals and
final acts, owes more than just a similarity of tone to Rimbaud.

Tête d'Or—who is referred to as Simon Agnel in act one and as
Le Roi in act three, and whose various names indicate successive
stages of development—is the sort of full-blooded and high-spirited
individual, the adventurer and conqueror epitomized in other Claudelian heroes such as Amalric in *Partage de Midi* or Rodrigue in *Le
Soulier de Satin;* all three are reminiscent of Rimbaud in their
single-minded strength and purpose. Tête d'Or, however, is much
more the independent individual than either of the other two, much
more subject to an indomitable pride, and, consequently, much more
alone. He is the epitome of the lone wolf. Like Rimbaud, Tête d'Or
attempts to build his world through the power of his own strength
and ability, unaided; he wishes to be supreme, powerful above everyone, and he has his own secrets for success in attaining his goals unassisted, his own "secrets for *changing life,"* as the *Vierge Folle* had
said of her *Epoux Infernal* in *Une Saison en Enfer.* But he is
doomed to an eventual fall by the very fact of his prowess and in-
flexible, proud determination. Having buried his wife in the darkness of night and seen his friend Cébès die after a long agony, Tête
d'Or pursues a course of action which seems to be a reaction against
those who, through their deaths, have failed him and who thereby
have imposed on him the need for an assertion of human will as opposed to divine will; he reacts to Cébès's death—pushing the corpse
away from himself and shouting *"Horreur!"*—in a way that suggests
that he is violently asserting the reality of his own existence and of
mortal life as a protest against the frailty of humanity, that he is
forcefully expressing a horror of weakness, and above all, perhaps,
a horror of weakness within himself. In particular, his reaction to
the death of this man, to whom he had sworn a profound friendship
but had expressed only a hesitant committal during his night of
agony (Cébès dies just as dawn is about to break), permits of a parallel with the first lines of *Vagabonds:*

*Pitoyable frère! Que d'atroces veillées je lui dus! "Je ne me
saisissais pas fervemment de cette entreprise. Je m'étais joué
de son infirmité. Par ma faute nous retournerions en exil, en
esclavage."*

[Pitiable brother! What ghastly sleepless nights I owed him!
"I didn't really take this business very seriously. I had played
on his weakness. Through my fault we would go back into
exile, into slavery."]

Tête d'Or puts all his ferocious strength into asserting his freedom
from "exile" and "slavery" by assuming power over the kingdom,
usurping it through killing the emperor and banishing the emperor's
daughter. This banishment is symbolic of a supreme assertion of
his own will over divine will, for the Princess represents Christ: having wandered to a "far country"[2] where she is in "exile" and "slavery," she is "crucified" on a pine tree to which her hands have been
nailed as to a cross; moreover, she has been "betrayed" by a weak
deserter from the army.

Tête d'Or, in his defiance of authority, in his refusal to submit to
a higher authority than himself, in his role of *"l'homme révolté,"*
becomes a Nietzschean superman for whom God, the emperor, is
dead. He makes a positive statement of his denial of God, saying
that he does not believe "there exists in this room of the World /
Any other God than ignorant man."[3] But his actions also admit of
a parallel with Rimbaud. His battles, an attempt to "possess every
landscape" (as in *Alchimie du Verbe*), are fought in the blazing heat
of southern climes, like Rimbaud's struggles in Africa; his victories
take place in the sunlight, in broad daylight, and it is in this way
that he is *"le fils du soleil."* He too looks to the "god of fire" *(Alchimie du Verbe),* for the image of the sun is the poetic leitmotif that
symbolizes his actions throughout the play from the time he assumes power, and many of his soldiers "wear the image of the sun."
In his final battle, he is deserted by his army but remains to fight
the enemy alone, since "When we are very strong,—who retreats?"
(Phrases).

Like Rimbaud, Tête d'Or never gives a direct answer to a question. When, for instance, he arrives at the crucial moment of his

2. For this reference to a "far country," see the New Testament, Luke 15: 13.
It is in this chapter of Luke that we find the three "lost" parables: "the lost
sheep," "the lost coin" and "the lost son," the last being frequently referred
to by Claudel.
3. *Tête d'Or*, p. 371.

life, at the point when he is about to die, the moment for defining
and determining his beliefs, and is asked, "What are you saying?"
he answers, "Nothing. It doesn't matter." Yet he had just denied
God's existence before being asked that question. His denial is
comparable to Rimbaud's blasphemy, and his answer reflects a distrust not at all unlike Rimbaud's distrust of others' capacity for understanding and ability to understand him. Tête d'Or's death was
necessary, for he could no more succeed alone than could Rimbaud.
His one final attempt to assert his Nietzschean-Rimbaldian solitude
comes in his wish to be left alone to die on the hilltop. But even
this is impossible, since he now becomes aware of the presence of
the Princess on the same hilltop. These final scenes with the Princess, in whose arms Tête d'Or dies, point to a comparison between
Tête d'Or's death and Rimbaud's death "in the arms of the Church."
Furthermore, it is true of Tête d'Or as it was for Rimbaud that
"women nurse those fierce invalids, home from hot countries"
(*Mauvais Sang*). Not being able to succeed alone, it is only in a final
recognition of the Princess—Christ, and therefore the Church—that
Tête d'Or can find peace.

Through all of this, Tête d'Or is heard exhorting nature as his witness. His words are often cryptic. Like Rimbaud, who "invented
the colors of the vowels" (*Alchimie du Verbe*), Tête d'Or "invents
words beginning with O,"[4] including Omega, the All-inclusive: he
will make a god of himself. In his closeness to nature, in his attempt
to attain the ultimate through his own "invention," in his refusal to
recognize any power outside of himself until the very end when he
invests the Princess with his own robes, in his visions, in his witness
of light, in his "rebirth" out of darkness into light as well as his
death towards the end of the day (rather like "the twilight of the
gods"), Tête d'Or is none other than the Rimbaud of *Les Illuminations* and *Une Saison en Enfer*.

In another of Claudel's principal plays, *Partage de Midi,* we find
not just one but three characters who each represent some aspect
of Rimbaud and also of Claudel. Amalric, De Ciz, and Mesa are
really three different aspects of a single personality. Just as Violaine and Mara in *L'Annonce Faite à Marie* symbolize opposing elements of Claudel's psyche, the essential characteristics of these
three male roles, when juxtaposed, form a Rimbaud-Claudel unity.
Amalric is the full-blooded flesh and high spirit that characterize
so much of Rimbaud; he is the adventurer, the strong, vigorous,

4. *Tête d'Or (deuxième version)*, p. 300.

physically oriented male. De Ciz is the businessman-speculator who was sensitive to Rimbaud and who is described as having had a "certain Arthur Rimbaud" as a business partner in Harrar and as having boarded the ship at Aden. Harrar and Aden, of course, were both centers of Rimbaud's operations in East Africa. Another bit of Rimbaud's biography is added when Amalric suggests that maybe this Rimbaud smuggled arms. These references to Rimbaud were included in the second version of the play, written in 1948, but not in the first, written in 1905 and published the following year. In all probability, Claudel did not know much about Rimbaud's life at the time he first wrote the play, or, perhaps, as he grew older and wanted to give even greater emphasis to the role of Rimbaud in his own life, he felt that he must include him in what was obviously a very personal story. (Possibly it was simply that in his old age, Claudel had lapses of artistic good taste.)[5] In any case, these specific mentions of Rimbaud suggest that the play must not be considered without tak-

5. Actually, despite our attempts to justify these mentions of Rimbaud, Claudel's introduction of him into *Partage de Midi* strikes us as being a bit of unfortunate writing. Apparently, Claudel's adoration of Rimbaud had a tendency to obscure the better part of his artistic good judgment, for, in this case, the addition adds nothing to the play dramatically nor to an understanding of the characters as *dramatis personae*. In fact, the effect of this addition borders on the comic. What compounds the misfortune of this lapse of artistic taste is the fact that, although Claudel had a fine and subtle sense of humor, the comic effect was certainly unintended here. To create such an effect would have been completely out of character, for Claudel was never facetious in his mentions of Rimbaud (with one exception: in a sarcastically humorous critical barb, he writes, in *Quelques Réflexions sur la Peinture Cubiste*, Vol. 17 of *Œuvres Complètes*, p. 214, "*M. Jean Paulhan vient de publier dans la Nouvelle N. R. F. sur la peinture cubiste deux articles remarquables et qui m'ont vivement intéressé. Il insiste sur le caractère, dit-il, 'sacré' de cette tentative. Et ce n'est pas ma faute si ce mot a aussitôt réveillé en moi un souvenir de Rimbaud: 'Je finis par trouver sacré le désordre de mon esprit.'*" [the Rimbaud quotation is taken from *Une Saison en Enfer*]); Rimbaud's name alone, the very thought of him, was enough to involve Claudel in a traumatic experience, as he says in his prayer *Pour les miens: "Mais qu'aurait-il pu me dire alors qui vaille cette traction soudaine sur le cœur que si souvent je ressens en plein courant de la conversation et cette interruption de je ne sais quelle continuité qui me réveille en pleine nuit."* But from Claudel's point of view and even that of literary criticism, De Ciz' Rimbaud does have a function, for he points to the deeply personal character of the play—as we pointed out earlier, *Partage de Midi* is, by Claudel's own admission, an autobiographical play. With this inclusion of Rimbaud, it is brought to our attention even more vividly than before, that, as in most of Claudel's principal male characters, there is in Amalric, De Ciz and Mesa, a positive element of the imaginative, sensitive yet physically vigorous adventurer-wanderer which links them with Rimbaud.

ing Rimbaud's thought into account, and that furthermore, he is to
be compared with Mesa; for the mention of Rimbaud's name coin-
cides with Mesa's admission to Amalric that he does not know
"very much about women." Rimbaud is here in order to give us a
better and fuller understanding of Mesa, just as in many ways he
complements Claudel's works. Mesa is a poet. His very name, Mesa,
which means "an isolated volcanic plateau," indicates the potential-
ly explosive yet subdued violence, the introversion and aloofness
that are part of his personality. His small experience of women and
his aversion to them and, in particular, to Ysé at first, brings to
mind Rimbaud's phrase, "I do not like women" (*Délires*). And,
just as this Rimbaud of *Partage de Midi* seemed to Ysé "untamed"
and averse to her companionship (she says, "he used to look at me
like an idiot"–"*de son œil d'abruti*"–"the sun first and me after"),[6]
Mesa seems to her to be unattainable. But if Mesa resembles Rimbaud, he also has much in common with Claudel. His position as a
diplomat in China, his admission that he has been refused for the
priesthood and is therefore a spoiled priest, all of these biographical
details associate him with Claudel; there can be no question but that
Mesa represents the "Claudel" aspect of the composite personality
mentioned above. In these three men, Amalric, De Ciz, and Mesa,
we discover Rimbaud-Claudel-the adventurer, Rimbaud-Claudel-the
diplomat-businessman-speculator, Rimbaud-Claudel-the introverted,
mysogynous poet.

As in *Tête d'Or*, the sun plays an important role in *Partage de Midi*,
for the blinding sun of midday destroys the vision of night, or at
least hides it from immediate view. Of the four principal characters,
Amalric in particular is associated with "the full force of the sun"
which he calls "the full force of my life!"[7] Mesa too points to the
sun and refers to it as a source of dominating power:

> MESA, montrant le soleil.—*Le foyer? Le voilà,*
> *notre foyer, troupe errante!*
> *Ne le trouvez-vous pas allumé comme il faut?*
> *On s'arrange ensemble tout de même!*
> *Regardez-le, le patron là-haut, avec un milliard*
> *de rayons tout occupé après la terre,*
> *Comme une vieille femme après les mailles de son*
> *crochet!*

6. *Partage de Midi*, p. 111.
7. *Partage de Midi*, p. 206.

[MESA (*showing the sun*): Home? There it is, our home, wandering troop!
Don't you find it lighted up like it should be?
We manage just the same!
Look at him, the boss up there, with a billion rays
all taken up with the earth,
Like an old woman with her crochet stitches!][8]

He says that it is the direct midday sun that isolates these fragments of humanity and leaves them free of the earth, free of any binding obligations, and presumably free to act according to their own will; they are free "in the middle of the complete horizon," between the sea and the sun, Rimbaud's eternity:

Elle est retrouvée!
—Quoi?—l'Eternité.
C'est la mer mêlée
Au soleil.

[It is found again!
—What?—Eternity.
It is the sea mingled
With the sun.]

When we consider the ensemble of Claudel's dramatic works, it becomes all the more apparent that the theme of the dynamic individual isolated in the sun was not just incidental. In *Le Soulier de Satin*—perhaps Claudel's greatest play, certainly the most comprehensive, and the one of which he said, "This drama sums up the work of my whole life"[9]—the theme of the willful adventurer-conqueror is once again prominent, in the role of Rodrigue. Rodrigue too is a Rimbaud-Claudel composite, since, although his mission is partially involved with Africa and therefore with Rimbaud, he is, like Claudel, who spent many years as French ambassador in Rio de Janeiro (1914-18) and in Washington (1928-33), "the man of America." His wanderings also take him to Japan where he plays a kind of counterpart to Claudel who, as a diplomat, spent considerable time in Tokyo. He is to be further compared to Claudel in that his general mission was to proselytize, "to bring Catholicism to the world." Moreover, the parallels go beyond his travels, for, like Claudel and Rimbaud, Rodrigue is separated from women; even though

8. *Partage de Midi*, p. 206.
9. Claudel quoted in *Les Sources de Claudel*, p. 137.

he does attempt to become united with Dona Prouhèze, he is never successful. Typical of most of Claudel's heroes, he lacks female companionship and understanding; more precisely, he is misunderstood, or not understood at all, by women, and conjugal love remains beyond his reach. In his solitude, his actions are governed by his own will; he refuses to submit to any terrestrial authority other than his own.

However, the similarities between Rodrigue and Rimbaud are not limited to temperament; there is even a physical and biographical resemblance between them. After having lost favor with the king and having lost his prodigious influence at the Spanish court as well, Rodrigue is described as "the one-legged man,"[10] for he has had a leg amputated—like Rimbaud. But despite this diminution of his person, Rodrigue's role still is "to enlarge the earth,"[11] just as Rimbaud's was to invent a new poetry and attempt to find a new universe. In the loneliness of his retreat and imprisonment, he draws incomprehensible pictures, comparable to Rimbaud's hermetic images in poetry. When he returns to Europe after his wanderings, Rodrigue is comforted by his "spiritual daughter," Sept-Epées, just as Rimbaud was comforted by his sister Isabelle at Roche and at the Hôpital de la Conception at Marseille during the late summer and fall months of 1891: "Women nurse these fierce invalids, home from hot countries" (*Mauvais Sang*). And Rodrigue too might well have said, "I will be mixed up with political affairs" (*Mauvais Sang*); it is precisely for political reasons that he loses his power as viceroy of India. When speaking with Sept-Epées, he allows his imagination to wander in what seem to be fantastic visions, like Rimbaud who, on his deathbed, was "in a kind of uninterrupted dream," saying to his sister Isabelle "bizarre things very softly, in a voice that would have charmed me if it had not been stabbing my heart. What he says are dreams,—however, it is not at all the same thing as when he was feverish. One would say, and I believe it is so, that he does it on purpose."[12] And Rodrigue is looking for the terrestrial paradise, just as Claudel said that Rimbaud "had spent his life trying to bring" his left foot back to "the terrestrial Paradise."[13] And in precisely the same terms as Rimbaud, who had said that the

10. *Le Soulier de Satin*, p. 263.
11. *Le Soulier de Satin*, p. 307.
12. Letter from Isabelle Rimbaud to her mother, 28 octobre 1891, in Arthur Rimbaud, *Œuvres Complètes* (Paris: Bibliotèque de la Pléiade, Gallimard, 1954), p. 585.
13. *L'Epée et le Miroir*, p. 91.

poet "arrives at the unknown," Rodrigue wishes to discover and comprehend "the unknown."[14] Finally, at the end of the play, he delivers himself, "body and soul," to the care of a nun, or, rather, he is sold to her as a bargain: "For sale, what the Jews have not sold!"[15] Cared for by a nun at the end of his life, he is like Rimbaud "converted" to Catholicism on his deathbed and visited by a priest.

The similarities between Rodrigue and Rimbaud, even down to a two-syllable name beginning with R, are too striking to be purely coincidental. Moreover, the theme of the adventurer-*fils du soleil* is too obvious in the works of Rimbaud for Claudel not to have found in them, as well as in Rimbaud's life, a great deal of thematic inspiration for the role of Rodrigue. Even on his deathbed, speaking with Isabelle, Rimbaud was preoccupied with the sun: "I will go under the earth . . . and you will walk in the sun." In the type of individual whom he represents, even in isolated actions and physical characteristics, Rodrigue is very much the Rimbaud-Claudel adventurer, the converted, proselytizing Catholic who cannot attain his goal through a purely terrestrial search, for the earth is "the apple of Paradise"—temptation; he must submit to a Godly and religious life in order to find peace and fulfillment. In *Tête d'Or,* the individual never relents, right up until the moment of his death, a fact that points to an ever closer resemblance between Tête d'Or and Rimbaud than between Rodrigue and Rimbaud. But with Rodrigue there is a slight difference—perhaps even a capital one: he makes a conscious final avowal of his capitulation by giving up to God not only his soul, as he had previously done in dedicating himself to spreading God's message, but his body as well; in this sense, he represents Rimbaud "the illumined" Catholic that Claudel claimed he was even during his poetic career. Rodrigue too might

14. *Le Soulier de Satin,* p. 307.
15. The comparison of this quote from *Solde* in *Les Illuminations* with Claudel's dramatic intentions is particularly appropriate since Claudel was not very *large d'esprit,* not very broad-minded, in certain respects, and was more than just slightly anti-Semitic. See *Prière pour les miens,* page 421—both in the text and in the footnote—and also his letters to André Gide. One may object that Claudel had Jews among his best friends. However, it is quite possible to have a Jewish friend—whom one disassociates from ethnic peculiarities—and yet be anti-Semitic. In any case, Claudel almost invariably refers to Jews in derogatory terms in his writings. Was this a reflection of the Church's long condemnation of the Jews as the crucifiers of Christ, only recently redeemed by the Church?

well have said, "I will be free to possess truth in one soul and one body" (*Adieu*).

Throughout Claudel's dramas, the adventurous individual isolated in the sun is inevitably and ineluctably confronted with defeat, an *échec*. In order to be fulfilled as individuals, in order to find their completeness, these *"fils du soleil,"* Tête d'Or, Rodrigue, Amalric-De Ciz-Mesa, must all return to the Black Virgin of night. Mesa and Ysé, drawn together in the sun, are separated in the *partage de minuit;* Tête d'Or dies at nightfall; it is night when Rodrigue is sold to the nun. The way in which Claudel resolves these men's fate is undeniably his own, but their characteristic traits and the principal image with which they are associated, the sun, are eminently drawn from the Rimbaud context of male "weakness or strength: there you are, it is strength" (*Mauvais Sang*) and "Here is the punishment. —Forward, march!" (*Mauvais Sang*)

The Claudelian hero as a poet: aesthetic parallels between Rimbaud and Claudel

There is another type of male in Claudel's dramas, a male who is more specifically Rimbaud-the-poet, or Rimbaud-the-apologist-for-poetry, whose ideas reflect an image of Rimbaud without associating him with the theme of the adventurer. In *La Ville,* the poet Cœuvre, whose name is a symbolist *calembour* for *"cœur"* and *"œuvre,"*[16] is, like Rimbaud in Charleville and later in Paris, "an object of astonishment and derision"[17] in the city where he resides; because he is a poet, he must "undertake [his] venture all alone."[18] His loneliness is stressed all the more by the fact that he has certain aspirations for poetry that do not seem realizable. Like Rimbaud, who said he had flattered himself in thinking that he had invented a form of "poetic language accessible some day to all the senses" while reserving for himself "all rights of translation" (*Alchimie du Verbe*) and who had been certain of being able to find a "universal

16. Lasserre says that the name *Cœuvre* is a symbolist *calembour* for *"qui œuvre"* (cf. *Les Chapelles Littéraires*, p. 63). But in the Claudelian context of *"âme et corps"* that refers directly to the last lines of Rimbaud's *Une Saison en Enfer, "cœur et œuvre"* seems to be a more likely interpretation; certainly an alternative one.
17. *La Ville*, p. 161.
18. *La Ville*, p. 168.

language," Cœuvre wanted "to propose to the world a soluble and delectable word."[19] Like Rimbaud, who "invented the color of the vowels" and who stated that "each word" is "an idea," Cœuvre has had his poetic inventions and his "intelligible word":

> CŒUVRE.—Lorsque j'étais un poëte entre les hommes,
> J'inventai ce vers qui n'avait ni rime ni mètre.
> Et je le définissais dans le secret de mon cœur
> cette fonction double et réciproque
> Par laquelle l'homme absorbe la vie et restitue,
> dans l'acte suprême de l'expiration,
> Une parole intelligible.

> [CŒUVRE: When I was a poet among men,
> I invented that verse-line that had neither
> rhyme nor meter.
> And I defined it in the secret of my heart as that double
> and reciprocal function
> By which man absorbs life and restores, in the supreme
> act of exhalation,
> An intelligible word.] [20]

Throughout *Une Saison en Enfer,* one of Rimbaud's recurrent themes is that the unknown and the truths revealed by poetry cannot be reached through science, for "science does not go fast enough for us!" (*L'Impossible*); "and science is too slow" (*L'Eclair*). He says that "divine love alone grants the keys of science" (*Mauvais Sang*), that understanding requires more than just knowledge. Similarly, Cœuvre tells Bésme that in order to understand what the poet says and does, he will need "some other knowledge" than that of "the wiseman," a knowledge that can be found by "opening your eyes to what is."[21] It becomes all the more obvious that Cœuvre's words are a Claudelian rendition of the Rimbaud text when one considers the sentence immediately following "the keys of science": "I see that nature is but the display of goodness." In its revelation of the essential role of nature, this was, for Claudel, one of Rimbaud's key phrases. However, the similarity between Cœuvre and Rimbaud is not limited to their solitude in nature.

19. *La Ville,* p. 162.
20. *La Ville,* p. 228.
21. *La Ville,* p. 153.

Cœuvre's "duty" had been to discover "the unknown" through poetry; but by becoming a bishop he has put aside that duty and done so with pride: Rimbaud says, "I have my duty, I shall be proud of it after the fashion of several others, by setting it aside" (*L'Eclair*). And just as Rimbaud tells "the story of one of my follies" (*Alchimie du Verbe*), Cœuvre, having joined the Church, makes a "confession" of his poetic efforts. Rimbaud's *"plus de mots"* ["no more words"] (*Mauvais Sang*) is rendered by Cœuvre's *"la vie sociale n'est que le verset double de* l'action *de grâces ou hymne, / Par lequel l'humanité absorbe son principe et en restitue l'image"* ["life in society is simply the counterpart versicle of the *action* of graces or hymn, / By which humanity absorbs its principle and restores its image"].[22] For both Rimbaud and Cœuvre, "grace," that is to say, "poetry"—since for Claudel poetry is a form of grace—becomes action; they no longer write, they live in society. However, Cœuvre is not just the Rimbaud who met with a literary *échec* and who was reduced to silence, even though he is growing old waiting for this "word which is nourishment" and even if "silence is nothing, compared to the oblivion in which I now am."[23] Like Claudel's temporary renouncement of poetry and also like Rimbaud's total literary silence as interpreted by Claudel, Cœuvre's "oblivion" is the result of having made a "sacrifice" to God by giving up poetry. The similarities between Cœuvre and Rimbaud are not just of a negative nature, however. Cœuvre makes several pronouncements about poetry that are virtually verbatim quotes from Rimbaud's works.

One of the ideas basic to Rimbaud's aesthetic doctrine was that the poet "must be a seer"; he must be capable of unveiling the unknown, he must "inspect the invisible" (*Lettre du Voyant*). Claudel too says that the domain of poetry "is the universe of invisible things," and its goal is to "plunge to the depths of the definite in order to find the inexhaustible"[24] (*Positions et Propositions I*). For both Claudel and Rimbaud, poetry is more than a form; it is a means of gaining a vision and an awareness of the unknown; it is a state of the soul, a way of seeing things. It is in their capacity for being aware of the unknown that both are seers. However, the poet is not a seer simply by being; he must work at it. "One must *make* oneself a seer," says Rimbaud in the *Lettre du Voyant*. One must

22. *La Ville*, p. 228.
23. *La Ville*, pp. 161-162.
24. *Positions et Propositions I*, p. 95.

will oneself to it. Similarly, for Claudel, "the Orator, like the poet, is one who knows how to put himself into a state of transport voluntarily."[25] In order to arrive at this willed poetic state, the poet relies first on his intelligence, through which, according to Rimbaud, he makes a thorough examination of his inner being: "The man who wishes to be a poet must first make a thorough study of himself; he searches his soul, he inspects it, he tempts it, he learns to know it." But beyond this, his poetry is dependent on his emotions, on his faith, on the degree to which he has developed his sensitivity to "ineffable torture for which he needs complete faith and superhuman strength, through which he becomes the sickest, the most criminal, the most damned of them all,—and the supreme Savant!" For Claudel too, "poetry cannot exist without emotion."[26] However, this emotion must be tempered by intelligence, good taste, understanding. All of the poet's faculties must be as vigilant and attentive as possible, "each ready to furnish what it can and what is needed, memory, experience, fantasy, patience, undaunted and sometimes heroic courage, taste capable of judging immediately what is contrary or not to our as yet obscure purpose";[27] but above all, "intelligence that looks, evaluates, questions, advises, represses, stimulates, separates, condemns, reassembles, distributes and spreads out order, light and proportion everywhere."[28] Yet, in the final analysis, the poetic *élan* is not a matter even of intellect, for "it is not intelligence that makes poetry, intelligence watches us making poetry."[29] The intellect is merely a "control"—a concept expressed by Rimbaud in his oft-quoted, and too often misquoted and misunderstood phrase, *"JE est un autre"* ["I is another"]. For Claudel, the actual poetic experience depends on "a certain 'poetic faculty' which has more direct rapport with imagination and sensitivity than with the power of reasoning" (*Positions et Propositions I*);[30] and insofar as the individual is in "a harmonious state of intelligence"—insofar as he has made, in Rimbaud's terms, the preparatory effort of "cultivating his soul" (*Lettre du Voyant*)—he will be a poet. Through an intelligent, though not necessarily conscious control of his emotions—in fact, he should not be conscious of the control, he should not be self-conscious, his "cultivation of the soul" should be completely

25. *Positions et Propositions I*, p. 59.
26. Ibid.
27. Ibid.
28. Ibid.
29. Ibid.
30. *Positions et Propositions I*, pp. 57-58.

assimilated as an integral part of his experience and of his life—he will have made himself a seer:

Le poëte qui a le magistère de tous les mots, et dont l'art
est de les employer, est habile, par une savante disposition
des objets qu'ils représentent, à provoquer en nous un état
d'intelligence harmonieux et intense, juste et fort. Mais, alors,
nous serons les poëtes, les faiseurs de nous-mêmes.

[The poet who has magisterial control over all words, and whose art is to use them, is able, through a well-informed disposition of the objects that they represent, to provoke in us a state of intelligence, both harmonious and intense, accurate and strong. But, then, we will be poets, makers of ourselves.]

(*Art Poétique*)[31]

Having made this intelligent effort, having plunged to the depths of the definite, having become the supreme savant, he will have become the inspired poet. The poet, the individual who fills up the "whiteness" of the paper (in Claudel's terms), is, for Rimbaud, only an instrument; he does not create so much as he records: "I am present at the unfolding of my thought: I look at it, I listen to it."[32] Thus, the poet does not create form; whatever form a poem may have is created *through* him, through this unconscious, intelligent control (unconscious because the poet does not think about it or reflect upon it, as in automatic writing; intelligent because he has already acquired poetic sophistication in the manner of expressing a spontaneous idea or a vision): "If what he brings back from [the descent into the unconscious] has form, he gives form; if it is formless, he gives no form" (*Lettre du Voyant*). This, of course, is precisely why Claudel wrote sarcastically and contemptuously in his journal, "Why don't I write in lines of twelve feet?" Yet, though the poet does not choose form, he must be endowed with a desire to express himself, an instinct for poetry, as it were. This desire, "this thrust of the soul which is expressed in man by words, is expressed in animals by cries or song" (*Positions et Propositions I*).[33] Rimbaud expressed the idea much more simply and much more succinctly in a letter to his former schoolmaster Izambard: "One must be born a poet, and I have recognized that I am a poet."

31. *Art Poétique*, Vol. 5 of *Œuvres Complètes* (1953), p. 111.
32. *Lettre du Voyant*, p. 270.
33. *Positions et Propositions I*, p. 60.

In *La Ville*, in answer to Besme's question, "But you, Cœuvre, who are you and what use are you?" Cœuvre explains just what it is to be a poet, his role, his functions. For Cœuvre, the poet is inspired. He does not participate intellectually in the poetic creation; he conceives in his sleep, in what Rimbaud calls "the plenitude of the great dream" (*Lettre du Voyant*):

> *O Besme, je ne parle pas selon ce que je veux,*
> *mais je conçois dans le sommeil.*
> *Et je ne saurais expliquer d'où je retire ce*
> *souffle, c'est le souffle qui m'est retiré.*

> [Oh Besme, I do not speak according as I want,
> but I conceive in my sleep.
> And I could not explain where I draw this breath
> from, the breath is drawn from me.][34]

He does not force the creation; rather, he is its instrument:

> *Dilatant ce vide que j'ai en moi, j'ouvre la*
> *bouche,*
> *Et, ayant aspiré l'air, dans ce legs de lui-même*
> *par lequel l'homme à chaque seconde expire*
> *l'image de sa mort,*
> *Je restitue une parole intelligible.*

> [Expanding this emptiness which I have in me,
> I open my mouth,
> And, having breathed in the air, in that legacy
> from himself by which man *exhales* every second
> the image of his death,
> I restore an intelligible word.][35]

In terms almost exactly parallel to Rimbaud's explanation of the poet's role (Rimbaud wrote, *"j'assiste à l'éclosion de ma pensée"* ["I am present at the blossoming forth of my thought"]), Cœuvre describes the poetic process at which he is present but in which he does not consciously participate:

34. *La Ville*, p. 154.
35. *La Ville*, pp. 154-55.

*Je constate, j'assiste; mais, pas plus que je ne
vais ouvrir un bourgeon avec mes doigts,
    Ou fouiller au ventre de la mère pour lui arracher
son fruit, si tu demandes
    Que je mette moi-même la main à l'œuvre,
que je dirige ces forces dont je contemple le branle
éternel et que je propose mon idée,
    La pensée me manque et mon cœur interdit se
refuse à comprendre.*

[I ascertain, I am present; but, no more than I
will open a bud with my fingers,
    Or grope in the belly of the mother in order to
draw her fruit out of her, if you ask
    That I myself put my hand to the work, that I
direct those forces of which I contemplate the
eternal impetus and that I offer my ideas,
    Thought fails me and my confounded heart
refuses to understand.][36]

Insofar as the poet uses what is present, what has become a real part
of his universal vision—for Cœuvre, "all things are present"—he is
what Rimbaud calls "an author, a creator, a poet":

*LÂLA, à Cœuvre.—Mais maintenant c'est vous
qui expliquez
    Ce livre que vous avez en vous, le monde,
    Votre école, est devenu votre écolier.*

[LÂLA (*to Cœuvre*): But now it is you who
explain
    That book that you have in you, the world,
    Your school, has become your pupil.][37]

It is in this way, in the way he transcribes his visions, his world, his
"school," that he creates a poetic reality. As Claudel says in his
discussion of *L'Otage*, "reality is only a rough sketch and it is the
artist's right to complete it. In the place of few and incomplete
directions, he has substituted a meaning."[38] The poet's reality is
his inspired vision. However, Lâla is wrong in one sense: the poet
does not explain, he ascertains. When Besme says to Cœuvre, "You

36. *La Ville*, p. 198.
37. *La Ville*, p. 160.
38. *L'Otage*, p. 313.

explain nothing, but all things become explainable through you," he is expressing essentially Rimbaud's idea that poetic reality is the vision itself and not the intelligent awareness or explanation of that vision, which, indeed, he may well forget: "he would end by losing the understanding of his visions, he has seen them!" (*Lettre du Voyant*). Cœuvre himself says virtually the same thing: "I am like a man who has crossed a river, and vomiting water he arrives on the other side. / And no one understands what he is saying, and he himself as he speaks forgets."[39] And inasmuch as it is the poetic vision which counts, irrespective of its "meaning" or of its peripheral implications, the logical conclusion is that poetry is an expression of essences. Rimbaud states that the poet "exhausts the poisons within him in order to keep only the quintessences." Claudel is even more explicit: "poetry . . . brings out the pure essence of things" (*Positions et Propositions I*).[40] And Besme, summing up what Cœuvre has told him about the poet's role, says, "By means of this song without music and this word without a voice, we harmonize with the melody of this world."[41]

This "word without a voice," this "song without music," these visions, these poetic essences, will be expressed in words, of course, since words are the poet's medium. But words are not important for their semantic value alone; in their sonorous and visual qualities they must have some direct relationship with what they represent, with what they symbolize. For Rimbaud, the language of the poet will be "of the soul, for the soul, summarizing everything, perfumes, sounds, colors. . . ." Claudel takes this even further and interprets words according to the shape of the letters that make them up: "Notice the three T's of temptation, like three successive extensions of the index finger."[42] Words are not just designators, they are signs, what Rimbaud defines as "every word being an idea." For the Claudelian poet, words are "sonorous phantoms" of what they symbolize, and they constitute a picture both intelligible and delectable:

39. *La Ville*, p. 167.
40. *Positions et Propositions I*, p. 61.
41. *La Ville*, p. 154.
42. *La Rose et le Rosaire*, p. 218. In *L'Œil Ecoute* (page 84), Claudel quotes another author on the subject, as a point of interest: *"Un ami fantaisiste prétend qu'idéographiquement soi et soie, c'est le même mot, s représente le fil, o le cocon, i le ver et le point sur l'i l'œil ou trou (dans soie, l'e représente le brin maintenant prêt à s'entortiller)."*

*. . . nous employons dans la vie ordinaire les mots non pas
proprement en tant qu'ils* signifient *les objets, mais en tant
qu'ils les* désignent *et en tant que pratiquement ils nous per-
mettent de les prendre et de nous en servir. Ils nous en don-
nent une espèce de réduction portative et grossière, une valeur,
banale comme de la monnaie. Mais le poète ne se sert pas
des mots de la même manière. Il s'en sert non pas pour l'uti-
lité, mais pour constituer de tous ces fantômes sonores que
le mot met à sa disposition, un tableau à la fois intelligible et
délectable.*

[. . . in everyday life we use words not, properly speaking,
insofar as they *signify* objects, but insofar as they *designate*
them and insofar as practically they allow us to take them
and use them. They give us a kind of portable, rough reduc-
tion of objects, a certain value, banal like change. But the
poet does not use words in the same way. He uses them not
for their practical usefulness, but to create a picture both
intelligible and delightful.]

(*Positions et Propositions I*)[43]

As Cœuvre says, the poet "restores an intelligible word" from the
images he sees; "every verse line . . . / Puts rhythm into or rhymes
with, allows or includes / An element exterior to itself."[44] And inasmuch as each word has qualities that evoke the essence of the
image it symbolizes, it becomes an integral part of the poet's soul.
Claudel might well have said that this mystical poetic transformation is like the bread and wine of the Eucharist, which, during the
Mass, become transubstantially the body and the blood, the soul
and the divinity of Christ.[45] Rimbaud called it "alchemy of the
word." Through "the word," the poet will make his poetic, or
mystical image visible. He will create a new universe, and, in Rimbaud's terms, he will "change life"; as Claudel writes in *La Muse
Qui Est la Grâce,* "all things are necessary to me. . . . They are not
made for me, their order is not with me, but with the word which

43. *Positions et Propositions I*, p. 60.
44. *La Ville*, p. 155.
45. Claudel himself sees an image of the Eucharist in many things, and sometimes in the least expected situations. One curious example is the carniverous
lion in *Positions et Propositions II*, p. 205: *"La perfection des lions étant de
manger des moutons et celle des moutons d'être mangés par eux, les uns ne
manquaient pas aux autres. Et qui sait si cette loi qui fait que tous les êtres
ne peuvent vivre qu'en se dévorant entre eux n'est pas une image obscure du
sacrifice et de la communion?"*

has created them"[46]—the same "word" that figures in the first paragraph of one of the gospels that Claudel was particularly fond of quoting, the Gospel according to Saint John: "In the beginning was the Word, and the Word was with God, and the Word was God." Words then, like God, create. But this "changing of life" cannot be effected by words individually. Words do not exist as isolated entities; they must also be considered in the aggregate—that is to say, one must consider the images or visions evoked by the juxtaposition of words, the interrelationship of words, as well as their individual symbolic values. The proximity of one word to another may very well evoke an idea that is new and independent of the meanings of either of the words taken separately; *"l'heure bleue,"* for example, evokes not only time and color (and, for some, perfume), but also mood, though neither *heure* [hour] nor *bleue* [blue] separately suggests a state of mind. It is in this way that Rimbaud's "universal language" will involve "thought catching hold of thought and pulling" [*"la pensée accrochant la pensée et tirant"*]. Rhythm and movement (progress) give vibrant, pulsating life to the poet's visions; the ideas suggested by this juxtaposition of words, as well as by the words themselves, form the poem and create a new reality that is not static: "The poet would define the quantity of the unknown awakening in its time in the universal soul: he would give more—[more] than the formula of his thought, [more] than the annotation *of his march towards Progress!* Enormity becoming the norm and absorbed by everyone, he would truly be *a multiplier of progress.'*[47] It is through poetry, not science, that the world will be renewed and will progress towards perfection and fulfillment. As Claudel says, the poet will create a universe and put it in motion; "with a poem," he will do "what other people have done around me with the canon which opens old Empires, with the [explorer's] collapsible boat" (*La Muse qui est la Grâce*).[48] And inasmuch as a poem is the expression of his truth and therefore a communication of that vision to other men, the poet has a great responsibility; he is, as Rimbaud says, "burdened with humanity." This is precisely why Cœuvre, the poet, becomes a bishop; as a bishop, he is entrusted with the soul of humanity.

46. *La Muse qui est la Grâce* from *Cinq Grandes Odes*, Vol. 1 of *Œuvres Complètes*, p. 127.
47. Rimbaud, *Lettre du Voyant* in *Œuvres Complètes* (Pléiade), pp. 271-272.
48. *La Muse qui est la Grâce*, p. 119.

Poetry, then, for both Rimbaud and Claudel, is not an end in itself. It has no relationship whatever with the Parnassian concept of art for art's sake. It is the distillation of a mystical experience, the means of bringing a revelation to mankind; and in this sense it has a real social significance. Rimbaud refers to this revelation, the ultimate goal of poetry, as "the unknown"; he never actually defines it. But Claudel is much more specific: "poetry is one with prayer, because it brings out the pure essence of things which are God's creatures and witnesses of God."[49] The revelation is of God's existence and presence. In Claudel's terms, Christianity and mysticism are synonomous. Given this context, there can be little doubt that Claudel identified Rimbaud with Christianity mainly because of the mystical aspects of his poetry, which explains why he uses the words "Christian" and "mystic" interchangeably when referring to Rimbaud.

When one considers that Claudel believed that "suffering resembles grace,"[50] is a form of grace, and that Rimbaud had stated that the poet-seer must endure "all forms of love, of suffering, of madness" before attaining poetic "grace," it can hardly be surprising that Claudel should make so forcefully a point of Rimbaud's "Catholicism" and of his deathbed "conversion," for Rimbaud underwent excruciating suffering at various periods of his life, but especially during his last, fatal illness. Yet, although mysticism goes a long way towards giving us an insight into Claudel's hagiographic adoration of Rimbaud, its implications in Claudel's Christian beliefs are really secondary to understanding the nature and depth of the influence of Rimbaud on Claudel. What is particularly significant for our present study is the similarity between the Rimbaldian and Claudelian aesthetic doctrines, and the exact parallels between them and the poetic mysticism expressed in the role of Cœuvre. With these similarities in mind, it becomes clear that Cœuvre, like Rodrigue and Mesa, is really a Claudel-Rimbaud composite. Yet even though Cœuvre is a mystical poet and symbolic of much of the religious element in Claudel, he is none the less human; he has much in common with the other male roles we have mentioned.

Just as Tête d'Or represents Rimbaud-the-adventurer, Cœuvre represents Rimbaud-the-poet; one symbolizes the "body" and the other the "soul" of Rimbaud, two aspects of the same individual. Both plays, Tête d'Or and La Ville, were written at approximately

49. *Positions et Propositions I*, p. 61.
50. *Positions et Propositions I*, p. 60.

the same time, 1889 and 1890 respectively; the similarity in concept of these two principal male roles is therefore understandable.
Furthermore, Claudel himself points to a similarity of tone when
he says that these two plays were written while he was undergoing
the four years of spiritual struggle during his conversion. The
second versions of both plays were published at the same time, in
1901, in a single volume. Changes made by Claudel in Tête d'Or's
lines, as well as in Cœuvre's, underline the similarity of temperament that is one of the bonds linking them. In the second edition,
the role of Cœuvre in particular was given greater stress than in the
first version and his position as a central character in the play was
amplified. It is in this second version of La Ville that we become
acutely aware of one of Claudel's principal themes, and of one of
the traits of his male characters, which suggests that Tête d'Or and
Cœuvre are really opposite sides of the same coin and which all of
Claudel's principal male roles have in common: an aversion to
women, an insouciance of them, or at least something that separates them from women. Cœuvre confides pointedly to Lâla, "And
the book which I studied was in the hand of no master, and, filled
with joy, I was not concerned about women."[51] Although Cœuvre
does marry Lâla, he is eventually separated from her. He too, like
Tête d'Or and Rodrigue, must find his spiritual fulfillment, not
through poetry, nor through women, but through God. And his
abandonment of women and of poetry in an effort to arrive at a
complete realization of his religious *élan* is in keeping with Claudel's
explanation of Rimbaud's literary silence. These are *positive* rather
than *negative* elements, in the same way that other Claudelian
heroes are positive in their involvement with the attainment of a
mystical goal.

The fallen angel: woman as a deterrent to man's perfection

One of the motivating forces in the lives of these men and at the
same time an obstacle to their fulfillment, actually their great weakness, is *la femme*. From Claudel's point of view, woman is the exact opposite of man, not only sexually but also psychologically.
Claudel's male characters are positive and determined in their search
for some specific goal and in their assertion of themselves as individ-

51. *La Ville*, p. 162.

uals; his female characters are negative in that they are constantly trying to lure men away from that goal. In effect, women are, for Claudel, little short of perfidious; he sees them as jealous and calculating creatures. In terms similar to those used by Rimbaud in his sarcastic reference to "boredom, the hour of 'dear body' and 'dear heart'!" (*Enfance*), Claudel defines men's physical passion for women: "Woman is there," he says, "with her body and her jealous heart to keep men from being angels and to maintain the rights of original sin."[52] (The fact that Rimbaud's terms undoubtedly refer to Verlaine—especially when seen in the light of *L'Epoux Infernal* from *Une Saison en Enfer*—is beside the point since Claudel does not accept the notion of Rimbaud's homosexuality.) For Claudel, woman's role is to destroy whatever harmony might be established on earth and to keep men from attaining perfection: "Women will always be the danger of any paradise."[53] Woman's love is ridiculous and hardly worth dying for, hardly worth all the "philosophizing" that some men, such as Suarès, indulge in: "Everyone knows that it is not fitting to die for the love of a woman. It is more than ridiculous. It is positively indecent."[54] And it is principally on account of its theme of terrestrial love between man and woman that Shakespeare's *Romeo and Juliet* is condemned by Claudel: "Can you imagine anything more slapdash and more botched than *Romeo and Juliet*, or written in a more abominable jargon? If Shakespeare had done only things of this kind, and he did quite a few of them, you could understand Voltaire's judgment!"[55] (One wonders whether Claudel's admiration of other plays by Shakespeare was based less on his dramatic power than on the fact that Voltaire, whom Claudel abominated, did not like him. His wholesale condemnation or approval of an author or of any individual is often based on his emotional reaction to a single thing which that person expressed or did. His dogmatism and his attempts to convert some of his contemporaries were more a matter of *"taper dessus"* in an emotional way than of persuasion through rational arguments. Claudel's works certainly demand an emotional acceptance, *un sentiment,* rather than a rational understanding of his themes, and they often defy any logical interpretation. He asks his audience, or his reader, not so much to understand as to accept in

52. *Conversations dans le Loir-et-Cher,* Vol. 16 of *Œuvres Complètes* (1959), p. 69.
53. *Conversations dans le Loir-et-Cher,* p. 130.
54. *Contacts et Circonstances,* Vol. 16 of *Œuvres Complètes,* p. 307.
55. *Contacts et Circonstances,* p. 318.

good faith the assertions for which he gives no more explanation than he does for his insistence on the importance of Rimbaud in his life.)

Apart from generalities about women, Claudel makes specific references to them in terms that are almost invariably derogatory, often gratuitous, and sometimes questionable, when they are not downright erroneous. For example, he imparts, for no apparent reason, the dubious information that "the proximity of a woman in her menstrual period is enough to disturb the culture of mushrooms and the hidden fermenting of wine in the cask."[56] And although he admired Richard Wagner, or at least certain of his works such as *Tannhäuser* and *Parsifal,* despite his opinion that Wagner was "inspired generally by spirits from below, though sometimes a ray strayed on him from above," his admiration did not extend to the German composer's wife whom he referred to as "the sinister Cosima."[57] Great ballerinas were no less vulnerable and fared no better; he calls the greatest of them all "the sinister Pavlova," perhaps because he had "little taste for the conventional art of the ballet as it is practiced on many subsidized stages, sometimes with a stupid perfection."[58] What is even more curious is that throughout his works he refers to many women whom he knew personally or in public as basically unvirtuous, and not once in the twenty-six volumes of his *Œuvres Complètes* does he even slightly redeem women by a mention of his own faithful wife. The only possible virtue of women in Claudel's eyes seems to be that they bear children and make good housekeepers—when they are not off on some perfidious seduction. It would seem that Claudel regarded his own marriage as a kind of Christian duty; that since he was not permitted to become a priest after his sterile attempt at life in a monastery, he felt he had to fulfill his duty by having a wife and children. Or perhaps it was, for him, a form of penance; certainly his marriage followed fairly closely on the adulterous Ysé episode recounted in *Partage de Midi,* and the idea of terrestrial love is never expressed as a real possibility or as any kind of fulfillment. (Possibly, having arrived at his mid-thirties and finally discovered the corporeal pleasures of passion, he chose to follow Saint Paul's advice to the Corinthians: "It is better to marry than to burn.") In any case, Claudel was not very generous in his opinions about anyone; but when it came to women, he was positively venomous.

56. *Figures et Paraboles,* p. 175.
57. *Contacts et Circonstances,* p. 330.
58. *Positions et Propositions I,* p. 126.

Claudel's antifeminist attitude, which pervades his secular works and finds a place even in his Biblical exegeses—in *Les Aventures de Sophie,* for example, the story of Sarah is compared to Rimbaud's "parable of the *Epoux Infernal*";[59] for Claudel, Sarah is yet another unillumined female—is still more prevalent in his plays. In *Le Soulier de Satin,* Dona Prouhèze is essentially the temptress for Rodrigue. She is dominating and domineering, particularly in her relationship with Don Camille, who says of woman, "she brings death and the desert with her."[60] Don Rodrigue is never united with Dona Prouhèze, except by proxy through her daughter Sept-Epées (though even Sept-Epées, Rodrigue's "spiritual daughter," manages to misunderstand his flights of imagination and imagery). Her loveless *"mariage de convenance"* with Don Camille is clearly an extension of Rimbaud's *"amours mensongères"* ["lying loves"] (*Adieu*). This theme of the "love lie" is elaborated even more explicitly in *Partage de Midi* by Mesa who says, "But every love is only a comedy / Between man and woman; questions are not asked"[61]—the essentials are not discussed. There can be no real dialogue between man and woman, no meaningful exchange. Mesa's statement is Claudel's version of "love must be reinvented" (*Délires I*). Just as "the comradeship of women" was "forbidden" to Rimbaud, Ysé is truly "forbidden" to Mesa who says, "Let me look at you, for you are forbidden."[62] Her eventual seduction of him does not alter the fact that there can be no *rapprochement* between the two of them, even at the end of the play. Though *Partage de Midi* is the dramatization of a personal experience in Claudel's life, the broad implications of Ysé's role are obvious: Ysé is not just a single individual; she is a sort of everywoman. She embodies the gross elements of woman's basic incompatibility with man: the coquettish superficiality (as in Rimbaud's *Les Reparties de Nina*), the incapacity for understanding (as in *Vierge Folle*), the inability to be a true companion (as in *Mauvais Sang:* "But debauch and the comradeship of women were forbidden me. Not even a companion."). Considering the opening scenes of the play and Ysé's role from this point of view, it becomes obvious why Claudel brought the mention of Rimbaud into the play, for elsewhere he has said that Rimbaud did not need women, that for Rimbaud, "woman was not strong enough to serve as a wine

---

59. *Les Aventures de Sophie,* Vol. 19 of *Œuvres Complètes* (1962), p. 49.
60. *Le Soulier de Satin,* p. 24.
61. *Partage de Midi,* p. 31.
62. *Partage de Midi,* p. 135.

press for this powerful vintage,"[63] and his contempt for them is at least part of the reason for Claudel's general exclusion of women from the terrestrial paradise. In all probability his attitude should also be attributed to the adulterous experience that is the "ostensible subject" of *Partage de Midi;* he himself said that it was an experience that colored his life for many years afterward. However, that is not the whole of it, for the antifeminist attitude is apparent even in earlier works written before this incident took place. In *Tête d'Or* and *La Ville,* Claudel is equally trenchant on this subject, and the proximity of the writing of these plays to the Rimbaud experience leaves little doubt as to the origin of his attitude, or at least as to the confirmation of an attitude that was already evolving in the young Claudel at the time he first read Rimbaud. Our *rapprochement* of the Rimbaud text with Mesa's comment about his rapport with Ysé seems completely in context and could hardly be more explicitly Claudel's intention than if he had pointed out the Rimbaud quotation himself. And although the muteness of the Rimbaud of *Partage de Midi,* when he is confronted with Ysé's commentaries about the sunset, may be an indication of Arthur Rimbaud's real life refusal to become involved with poetry at the time of his life in Harrar, the juxtaposition of it with Ysé's presence at twilight (a prefiguration of the *partage de minuit* at the end of the play) emphasizes the depth of his antipathy for women.

However, the theme of adultery in *Partage de Midi* goes much deeper than either Claudel's personal experience or his reading of Rimbaud; it has its roots in Biblical history as well, in the story of David and Bathsheba. There are, for example, similarities between the plot of Claudel's play and the Biblical narrative: Mesa, hoping that De Ciz will die so that Ysé will be free to marry him, arranges for De Ciz to take a protracted business trip to the interior of China where he is murdered, just as David sent Uria the Hittite away to be killed in battle; David's illegitimate son by Bathsheba and Mesa's by Ysé both die. Even the language waxes Biblical on occasion: "the gnashing of teeth," used by Mesa to describe his anguish over his affair with Ysé, is an expression often used in the Bible (it is also, incidentally, one that is incorporated into *Adieu* from *Une Saison en Enfer:* "For I can say that victory is won: the gnashing of teeth, the hissings of fire, the pestilential sighs are abating"); and when Mesa comes back to Ysé in the third act, he ecstatically describes the event, *"Parce que je t'avais perdue et voici que je t'ai retrouvée"*

---

63. *L'Epée et le Miroir,* p. 148.

["Because I had lost you and here I have found you"],[64] in terms similar to those used by the father in the parable of the prodigal son, *"Car mon fils que voici était mort, et il est revenu à la vie; il était perdu, et il est retrouvé"* ["For this my son was dead, and is alive again; he was lost, and is found"]. And the comparison that Mesa makes between himself and the prodigal son is too striking to be neglected: *"Me voici au milieu de ces peuples païens et il m'y a retrouvé, / Et je suis comme un débiteur que l'on presse et qui ne sait point même ce qu'il doit"* ["Here I am amongst these pagan peoples and he has found me, / And I am like a debtor who is being pressed for payment and who doesn't even know how much he owes"].[65] Like the prodigal son to whom Claudel compared Rimbaud, Mesa returns from a pagan "far country." ("Pagan" was one of Rimbaud's words that Claudel was fond of repeating.) With the intermingling of Rimbaldian and Biblical themes, vocabulary, and style, the two capital influences on Claudel's life and works become unmistakably evident in *Partage de Midi*.

In *La Ville* one finds a similar use of Biblical references complementing and counterbalancing the Rimbaldian theme of "the hell of women back there" (*Adieu*). Lâla, through her infidelity, her incapacity to fulfill her promise of love and marriage to Lambert, her continual vacillation, is again the woman of Rimbaud's *"amours mensongères"*—the ephemeral loves which can never have any real significance because they have no basis in spiritual reality and because they involve "perfidious women." Lâla is the promise that cannot be kept, for hers is the unrealizable promise of terrestrial love and understanding: "I am the promise which cannot be kept, and my grace consists of that: / I am the sweetness of what is, with the regrets of what is not"[66]—she is "the sweetness of what is" because Cœuvre finds her physically desirable, and "the regret of what is not" because he cannot be united with her if he wishes to discover love. She cannot be associated with Rimbaud's "let us go to the Spirit," for she appeals to the senses. This is the initial reason for Ivors' denying her a place among the men of the "new city":

> LÂLA.—*Car Cœuvre n'est pas comme un oiseau,*
> *mais comme un lion qui va vers le gué et comme un*
> *grand cheval attelé au char de Jupiter.*

---

64. *Partage de Midi*, p. 83.
65. *Partage de Midi* (Version pour la scène), p. 133.
66. *La Ville*, p. 229.

Mais moi, comme un oiseau que l'on entend sans le voir,
Chacun se plaît à attacher son sens à la mélodie.
IVORS.—Femme, ta place n'est point avec nous.

LÂLA: For Cœuvre is not like a bird, but like a lion
that goes toward the ford and like a large horse harnessed
to Jupiter's chariot.
But I, like a bird that is heard without being seen,
Everyone takes pleasure in attaching his own meaning
to the melody.
IVORS: Woman, your place is *not* with us.][67]

It is also the reason for her having been separated from Cœuvre,
for in order to find God's grace or the reality of His Creation, His
munificence, His love, which is what Cœuvre was attempting to
find through poetry, he must rise above temptations and banal joys
or revelries of the flesh. His leaving Lâla is his way of saying, "I
can laugh at the old love lies, and strike those deceitful couples
with shame" (*Adieu*). But Lâla's actions do not reflect only Rimbaud's statements about women or love. Her role also suggests a
parallel with the allegory of the bondwoman in Galatians; being
concerned with the flesh and therefore with the law, with "what
is," she is rejected in favor of faith and God's grace, as manifested
by Cœuvre's actions. (This parallel is further indicated by Lâla's
reference to herself as "the promise which cannot be kept," since
the bondwoman is opposed to the freewoman who is associated
with the "promise" that has been kept by Christ's appearance on
earth.[68] With Lâla disposed of, Ivors and Cœuvre are free to estab-

67. Ibid.
68. The Bible, Galatians 3: 17. "And this I say, that the convenant, that was
confirmed before of God in Christ, the law, which was four hundred and seven-
ty years after, cannot disannul, that it should make the promise of non effect."
Galatians 3: 22-25. "But the scripture hath concluded all under sin, that the
promise by faith of Jesus Christ might be given to them that believe. But before faith came, we were kept under the law, shut up unto the faith which
should afterwards be revealed. Wherefore the law was our schoolmaster *to
bring us* unto Christ, that we might be justified by faith. But after that faith
is come, we are no longer under a schoolmaster." Galatians 4: 22-26. "For it
is written, that Abraham had two sons, the one by a bondmaid, the other by a
freewoman. But he *who was* of the bondwoman was born after the flesh; but
he of the freewoman *was* by promise. Which things are an allegory: for these
are the two covenants; the one from the mount Sinai, which gendereth to bondage, which is Agär. For this Agär is mount Sinai in Arabia, and answereth to Jerusalem which now is, and is in bondage with her children. But Jerusalem which is above
is free, the mother of us all." Galatians 4: 30-31. "Nevertheless what saith the

lish a natural order and law through faith: "As for us, establishing ourselves in the middle of the City, we will constitute the laws."[69] The "City" is really the "Jerusalem above," the New Jerusalem. There seems at first to be a certain inconsistency in this symbolism in that Ivors is the son of the bondwoman-Lâla and by all rights should not be included in matters of faith, since, according to Galatians, "the son of the bondwoman shall not be heir." However, in his repudiation of Lâla, Ivors is apparently sufficiently cleansed to be admitted into the congregation of those who are blessed with awareness of an existence full of grace. And in any case, his legitimate place in the New Jerusalem is confirmed by a passage from Romans, in which it is stated that "the promise" will be "sure to all the seed; not to that only which is of the law, but to that also which is of the faith of Abraham; who is father of us all."[70]

Woman, then, represents for Claudel the human soul, human nature—as does Sarah—but not the illumined individual. She is the woman of Rimbaud's *Lettre du Voyant,* who does not yet have the capacity for being an illumined poet. Rimbaud, however, says,

> *Quand sera brisé l'infini servage de la femme, quand elle vivra pour elle et par elle, l'homme,—jusqu'ici abominable,—lui ayant donné son renvoi, elle sera poète, elle aussi! La femme trouvera de l'inconnu! Ses mondes d'idées différeront-ils des nôtres?—Elle trouvera des choses étranges, insondables, repoussantes, délicieuses; nous les prendrons, nous les comprendrons.*

> [When the infinite bondage of woman is broken, when she lives for herself and by herself, man,—abominable until now,—having given her her discharge, she too will be a poet! Woman will find the unknown! Will her worlds of ideas be different from ours?—She will find strange, unfathomable, repulsive, delicious things; we will take them, we will understand them.]

This is an aspect of the Rimbaldian woman that Claudel seems to have neglected. For Claudel, woman is aware of the attraction of the earth, of the flesh, of corporeal existence, but she can never know the possibility of being counted among the angels, for, as we

---

scripture? Cast out the bondwoman and her son: for the son of the bondwoman shall not be heir with the son of the freewoman. So then, brethren, we are not children of the bondwoman, but of the free."
69. *La Ville,* p. 230.
70. See *The Bible,* Romans 4: 14-16.

have seen, part of Claudel's interpretation of the role of women is that they are on earth "to keep men from becoming angels." In a sense, Claudel, in his role as a man, is saying, "I who said that I was a magus or an angel, exempt from all morality, I am returned to the soil, with a duty to seek, and rough reality to embrace." Rimbaud made this last statement in *Adieu* from *Une Saison en Enfer,* after saying that he has given up his search for a terrestrial paradise, "It is of Eden I was thinking" (*L'Impossible*), and after his return from "the hell of women back there." His fall from grace, as it were, his loss of the opportunity of becoming equal with God and even with the angels, was simultaneous with his "season in Hell" and with a sterile relationship with women—at least from Claudel's point of view, since he refused to believe that there was any homosexuality in the Rimbaud-Verlaine relationship, even though the truth could hardly be clearer than Rimbaud makes it in *Une Saison en Enfer.* [71] The importance of Claudel's interpretation of Rimbaud's "confession" cannot be too strongly emphasized, for, as André Gide wrote, Claudel claimed to be defending or upholding the Rimbaud of *Une Saison en Enfer,* who certainly gives the impression of having repudiated women or at least of having placed them in the kind of context in which we find them in Claudel's works.

Violaine in *L'Annonce faite à Marie* presents a striking exception to this general pattern of Claudelian women. She embodies human compassion, a deep sense of personal sacrifice, and a genuine simplicity and openness of feeling and emotion, and completely lacks the vain selfishness and thoughtlessness epitomized in women like Ysé or Lâla. But she is an exception in the same way that the Vir-

---

71. As Enid Starkie points out in her book *Arthur Rimbaud,* p. 184: "There is also *Le Bon Disciple,* a poem found in Rimbaud's pocket-book after the arrest of Verlaine in Brussels, and this leaves little doubt as to the nature of their relationship. The last verse runs:

> *Toi le jaloux qui m'as fait signe,*
> *Ah! me voici, voici tout moi!*
> *Vers toi je rampe, encore indigne!*
> *—Monte sur mes reins et trépigne.*

. . . And finally it seems only puerile innocence and futile quibbling to interpret otherwise than obscenely the poem *Ces Passions* (Parallèlement)." Miss Starkie might also have pointed out that *Le Bon Disciple* is a sonnet in reverse —in "perverse," as it were—since it begins with two tercets and ends with two quatrains rather than the other way around as is usual in French sonnet form; moreover, the sonnet is traditionally a "love lyric," and the expression *"faire l'amour"* has only *one* possible interpretation in French. Verlaine was not above making such obscene pleasantries.

gin Mary is an exception, and, like the Virgin Mary, she intercedes with God. On the other hand, her sister Mara—dark Mara—is symbolic of all the destructive and forboding elements in other Claudelian women. In *Tête d'Or,* the Princess too seems to be an exception in certain respects, particularly in her symbolism of Christ through her crucifixion on the pine tree. But she actually plays a double role, for she is banished from the kingdom after Tête d'Or kills her father, just as women are not to be allowed in paradise, just as "women will always be the danger of any paradise." Apparently, despite her association with Christ, the Princess cannot escape the curse of her sex.

Even if it is possible for man to surrender his body to woman in a physical act, as Mesa does, this is nevertheless not a surrender of what is important to him, his soul. Ysé reproaches Mesa for not having given himself to her entirely, to which he answers that there is no way to do that, "there is no way to give you my soul, Ysé."[72] The giving of the soul united with the body in one comprehensive gift would be the discovery of truth, for, as Rimbaud says, "I will be free to *possess truth in one soul and one body.*" But since Mesa does not give his soul to Ysé, it is obvious that, in Claudel's terms, woman is not symbolic of truth, just as she is not symbolic of love. She is essentially obstructionist, and the resolution of Rimbaud's longing search must be found elsewhere.

A Rimbaldian setting: "body and soul," nature, time

The final paragraphs of *Une Saison en Enfer* express certain ideas that form the basis for the broad structural outline of most of Claudel's plays and for the setting of the obscurity of night as a preparation for victorious entrance into the all-revealing, brilliant, dazzling daylight:

> *Point de cantiques: tenir le pas gagné. Dure nuit! le sang séché fume sur ma face, et je n'ai rien derrière moi, que cet horrible arbrisseau!... Le combat spirituel est aussi brutal que la bataille d'hommes; mais la vision de la justice est le plaisir de Dieu seul.*

72. *Partage de Midi,* p. 131.

Cependant c'est la veille. Recevons tous les influx de vi-
gueur et de tendresse réelle. Et à l'aurore, armés d'une ardente
patience, nous entrerons aux splendides villes.

Que parlais-je de main amie! Un bel avantage, c'est que je
puis rire des vieilles amours mensongères, et frapper de honte
ces couples menteurs,—j'ai vu l'enfer des femmes là-bas;—et
il me sera loisible de posséder la vérité dans une âme et un
corps.

[No hymns! Hold the ground gained. Arduous night! The
dried blood smokes on my face, and I have nothing behind
me but that horrible bush! . . . Spiritual combat is as brutal
as the battle of men: but the vision of justice is the pleasure
of God alone.

This, however, is the vigil. Let us welcome all the influx of
vigor and real tenderness. And, at dawn, armed with an
ardent patience, we shall enter magnificent cities.

Why did I talk about a friendly hand! (How silly to talk
about a friendly hand!) It's all to my advantage that I can
laugh at old lying loves and put to shame those deceitful
couples,—I saw the hell of women back there;—and I shall be
free to *possess truth in one soul and one body.*]

In each of the Claudel plays we have referred to in the previous
chapters, *Tête d'Or, L'Annonce faite à Marie, Le Soulier de Satin,*
with the exception of *Partage de Midi,* the opening scenes take
place at night. The waiting, the agony and anxiety of uncertainty,
the "spiritual combat," are all enveloped by the night: "this is the
vigil" of the "arduous night!" Simon Agnel buries his wife at night,
just as it is the *partage de minuit* that separates Mesa from Ysé. Tête
d'Or's first decisive battle, like "the battle of men," is fought at
night, after which the deliverance of the kingdom is announced at
dawn; "this atrocious night"[73] is over for the emperor. In *La Ville,*
much the same things happen: the horrors of the battle, the fire
that consumes the city, Cœuvre's decision to marry Lâla, and his
spiritual struggle to abandon poetry, all take place at night, and it
is with the coming of dawn and daylight that everything will be resolved. Tête d'Or says, "Today has come," after the nightlong vigil
and battle, "when I must show who I am";[74] and at the end of *La
Ville,* it is midday when Ivors announces, "we will constitute the

73. *Tête d'Or,* p. 92.
74. *Tête d'Or,* p. 141.

laws," just as Rimbaud had said, "at dawn, we shall enter magnificent cities." Yet, although both Claudel's and Rimbaud's night is "atrocious" (in *Le Bateau Ivre,* Rimbaud wrote, *"Toute lune est atroce"* ["Every moon is atrocious"]), it is not "the night without hope" that Claudel says one finds in the works of Baudelaire, Poe, and Mallarmé.[75] On the contrary, night is a preparation for the dawn, its principal light, the moon, a reflection of the day: "Oh you who at night give evidence of the sun that you see!" (*La Ville*).[76] It holds the promise of rebirth in daylight: "Oath taken at night. Only promises and not an act nor an oath."[77] (Although this last quotation, from *L'Otage,* is a negative statement, the point is that night is equated with the idea of "a promise.") Rimbaud's drunken boat wanders for ten nights and asks whether it is in "those endless nights that you are sleeping and exiled, / Millions of golden birds, Oh future Strength?" just as at the end of *Une Saison en Enfer* the poet says that we must receive "all the influx of strength" during the night in order to apply that strength to our tasks in the "magnificent cities" at dawn. In *La Muse qui est la Grâce,* Claudel's bark departs at night, and it is the night that welcomes it upon its return to take up its preordained place on earth; the "strength" of the bark has been acquired at night. In *La Cantate à trois voix,* the three sisters, Fausta, Beata, and Læta, behold a beautiful spring night, a *"nuit sans aucune nuit"* ["a night without night"] (flooded with light), like the *"nuit entre les nuits"* ["the night of nights"] in *La Ville* (the night is incomparably beautiful; the stars and the moon form an ocean of "white light"); and with the dawn will come completion, the reuniting of the three sisters with "the fiancé." It is, for the sisters, a beautiful night of sparkling stars and a brilliant full moon that holds the promise of an even more beautiful day when "he whom Fausta loves comes back perhaps," when "the *full* Summer . . . begins" (it is midsummer night, the summer solstice); a night which will bring back "him whom I will marry" tomorrow at dawn. It holds the promise of joy and hope, just as the night enfolds and joins everything together in complete harmony for the bark. For both Rimbaud and Claudel, night is identified with the acquisition of strength and vigor, with the dreams, hopes, and visions that will or should be realized in broad daylight, with the reality of the unknown or the inexhaust-

75. *Positions et Propositions I,* pp. 112-113.
76. *La Ville,* p. 164.
77. *L'Otage,* p. 65.

ible, or at least with the realization that reality may (for Rimbaud) or can (for Claudel) be attained, as in *La Cantate à trois voix* and *La Muse qui est la Grâce*. Night has an even more all-pervasive significance for Claudel in that it separates man from woman (as in *Tête d'Or, Le Soulier de Satin, Partage de Midi*) and prepares him for the discovery of truth "in one body and one soul" from which woman has been excluded (though only temporarily, for Rimbaud). It illumines rather than obscures, for it is the promise that with the dawn will come truth: it unites "the soul and the body."

The importance of these two aspects of man, suggested by the development of them in the plays and in certain poetic works of Claudel, is specifically stated in *Contacts et Circonstances:*

> *Il suffit en effet d'ouvrir les yeux, de visiter les musées, de se promener dans un de vos quartiers populaires, pour comprendre que, en Belgique, le corps et l'âme sont des réalités fortement unies, fortement étreintes, fortement comprises, fortement traduites, que Breughel y répond à Memling et Jordaens à Van Dyke, que la rude Wallonie a produit des musiciens sublimes comme Lassus, comme Grétry et comme César Franck, et qu'à cette table plantureuse qu'est votre beau pays, tout couvert des productions les plus magnifiques de la nature et de l'industrie, ne cesse pas de présider l'Esprit de la Pentecôte.*

> [You have only . . . to open your eyes, to visit museums, walk in one of your popular quarters, in order to understand that, in Belgium, the body and the soul are realities strongly united, strongly embraced, strongly understood, strongly expressed, that here Breughel corresponds to Memling and Jordaens to Van Dyke, that rough Wallonie has produced sublime musicians like Lassus, like Grétry and like César Franck, and that at this abundant table, your beautiful country all covered with the most magnificent produce of nature and of industry, the Spirit of the Pentecost does not stop presiding.] [78]

One is not independent of the other; and there seems to be much the same relationship between the soul and the body as there is between the night (or the vigil) and the day (or the dawn). Just as the night is the reflection of the day and proof of its existence, virtually the embodiment of the day, the body is the reflection of the soul and is formed by it: "It is the soul which makes the body" (*Le*

78. *Contacts et Circonstances*, p. 246.

Soulier de Satin).[79] The very properties of the body are governed by the soul: "The human soul is that by which the human body is what it is, its action, its continually operative seed, and, as the School says, its form."[80] And both are presided over by "the Spirit of the Pentecost,"[81] that is, "the Holy Spirit." A passage from *Conversations dans le Loir-et-Cher* makes it even more apparent that Claudel equates truth with God and considers the unity of body and soul a prerequisite to be realization of this truth:

> *Oui, nous sommes plus heureux que les Apôtres et la Sainte Vierge elle-même qui ne pouvaient que voir et toucher le Fils de Dieu, tandis que nous le possédons tout entier, corps et âme, être à être, et non seulement Lui-même mais cela qui au-dedans substantiellement ne cesse de Le faire Lui-même.*

> [Yes, we are more blessed than the Apostles and the Holy Virgin herself, who could only see and touch the Son of God, whereas we possess Him completely, body and soul, being to being, and not only Himself but that which inside substantially does not cease making Him Himself.][82]

This theme of the inseparability of the body and soul, of their necessity for interdependence, is repeated over and over again throughout Claudel's works to indicate completeness, as in, "the only movement that remains possible for the body and the soul is smoking, is exhaling like a samovar or like the vapor which escapes from your mouth in cold weather."[83] It has great importance in Claudel's very concepts of poetry, for poetry is in effect a manifestation of the relationship of the body with the soul. Poetry is the metaphor of existence, just as Claudel says, "the body is the metaphor of the spirit"; poetry reflects visions in much the same way as the body reflects the soul. There is, for both Rimbaud and Claudel, an irrefutable mystical alliance between the two. But it is an alliance that cannot be expressed, or at least that is not expressed in their works, in any rational way. As with so much of what Claudel asserts, he takes the theme of "the body and the soul" and repeats it as a self-evident truth, without any particularly deep analysis. In fact, Claudel's poetry is no more a poetry of the intellect than is

79. *Le Soulier de Satin*, p. 192.
80. *Sur la Cervelle* in *Connaissance de l'Est*, p. 149.
81. *Contacts et Circonstances*, p. 246.
82. *Conversations dans le Loir-et-Cher*, p. 113.
83. *Conversations dans le Loir-et-Cher*, p. 144.

Rimbaud's, but rather an outpouring of the soul. It is in a realization of the importance of the relationship of the physical or the concrete, the plastic, the exterior aspects of their work, with the inner, soulful emotions expressed in their poetry that we understand the fundamental similarity of their poetic concepts expressed by "one soul and one body." The theme itself owes more to theology than to anything specifically peculiar to Rimbaud. However, the fact that this theme does not appear in *L'Endormie* (written before Claudel read Rimbaud), or in any of Claudel's poetic efforts before *Tête d'Or*—though it does appear in *Tête d'Or* and *La Ville*—suggests that the theme was awakened in Claudel by his reading of Rimbaud, in whose works it is eminently apparent as the essence of projected truth, the basis of communication between poetic reality and banal existence. It has its counterpart in the thesis-antithesis of much of Rimbaud's poetry (as in *"science et patience,"* a play on the words *"science"* and *"pas science"* from *L'Eternité*) and in his juxtapositions of the vulgar and the obscene with the sublime (as in *Premières Communions*); this is also one of Claudel's early devices in parts of *Connaissance de l'Est,* where he contrasts the exotic beauty of the Orient with the "dirt" of the West, and in which he bemoans the encroachment of civilization on the simplicity and pristine beauty of nature. Actually, the final phrase from *Une Saison en Enfer* is one of Rimbaud's "questions" that Claudel answers to the effect that truth, joy, happiness (these are all aspects of the same fundamental awareness, according to Claudel)[84] are to be found in a communication between God and man through Christianity.

The setting for this discovery of truth is nature. Nature unifies body and soul, says Claudel, since it appeals not only to the senses, but also to the intellect: "Nature has found the way to make herself heard not only by our ears, but also by our intelligence. She speaks."[85] It is all-inclusive. The themes of the adventurer, the poet, castigated woman, all are bound together in Claudel's works by a profound awareness of nature. Ysé's love of sunsets is one small example of the appeal of nature to Claudel's characters. Cœuvre's adulation of the moon, Tête d'Or's feeling of unanimity

84. *Positions et Propositions II*, p. 254: *La joie et la vérité, c'est la même chose, et du côté où il y a le plus de joie, c'est là où il y a le plus de vérité. Cette joie, je ne vous dirai pas ce que c'est . . . Mais je vous parlerai simplement des conditions nécessaires pour y communiquer. Ces conditions sont l'ordre et le sacrifice."*
85. *J'Aime la Bible*, p. 355.

with the earth, the three sisters' evocation of the Rhône, the stars, the moon, the fragrances of flowers in *La Cantate à trois Voix*, point to an attitude that recalls Rimbaud's phrase, "I lived, gold spark of *pure* light *in nature.*"[86] Claudel makes specific references to this phrase when speaking of the ecstasy of communication through art, and in so doing points out the poet's mystical role in bringing the universe into focus and demonstrates in what way the artist has "the right to complete reality":

> *Ou supposons que rien de tout cela ne soit sérieux et qu'il n'y ait plus que cette ivresse, cette extase! "J'ai vécu, étincelle d'or de la lumière nature! J'ai tendu une corde de clocher à clocher et je danse!" (A. R.) Mais la nature elle-même, elle n'est pas faite pour m'engloutir! C'est moi le maître! c'est moi qui la fais lever de cette fausse immobilité que moi, qui en sais plus long que vous, j'appelle simplement "une tenue." C'est moi qui lui explique qui elle est! elle est mon audience! elle est cette matière à mes ordres! je passe la revue! c'est moi qui au sein de ce chaos profère le nom de Dieu!*

> [Or suppose that none of all that is serious and that there is nothing more than this drunkenness, this ecstasy! "I lived, gold spark of *pure* light *in nature!* I have stretched a cord from steeple to steeple and I dance!" (A. R.) Why, nature itself is not made to engulf me! *I* am the master! it is I who raise her up from this false immobility which I, who know more about it than you, call simply "an attitude." It is I who explain to her what she is! She is my audience! she is matter under my orders! I'm the one who passes inspection! I'm the one who in the midst of chaos utters the name of God!]
>
> > *(L'Œil Ecoute)*[87]

He himself makes the comparison between Rimbaud's closeness to nature and his own discovery of inspiration through a communication with the sensual allure of natural phenomena:

> *On n'entend pas la protestation de cette vaste forêt qui va de Brocéliande à l'Ardenne et qui a toujours été un des territoires favorisés du rêve et de l'invention poétique et musicale. C'est de là que sont sorties les Chansons de geste, les*

---

86. *Alchimie du Verbe* in *Une Saison en Enfer*, p. 236.
87. *L'Œil Ecoute*, p. 152.

*paysages enchantés de la tapisserie, les romans d'Alexandre
Dumas, les poèmes de Verlaine et de Rimbaud qui ont ouvert
des avenues immenses à travers les dures constructions parnas-
siennes, et, pour ne parler que de la région liégeoise, la musique
de César Franck, de Grétry, de Lekeu et de Vieuxtemps . . .
Cette Meuse . . . guida jadis la course de Rimbaud à travers ce
"grand mouvement de sapinaies," dont moi-même à ce moment je recevais le souffle, sévère et aromatique pardessus les
clôtures du lycée de Bar-le-Duc, ce sont les eaux sacrées sur
lesquelles s'est penchée la bergère de Domremy et où se sont
reflétées les figures inspiratrices de Saint Michel et de Sainte
Marguerite.*

[One does not hear the protest of that great forest which
goes from Brocéliande to the Ardennes and which has always been one of the favorite territories for dreams and poetic and musical invention. It has been the source of the
Chansons de geste, the enchanted landscapes of tapestry,
Alexander Dumas's novels, the poems of Verlaine and of
Rimbaud which opened immense avenues through the
harsh Parnassian constructions, and, speaking only of the
Liège region, the music of César Franck, Grétry, Lekeu and
Vieuxtemps . . . This river Meuse . . . once guided Rimbaud's
journey through this "great movement of the pine forests,"
from which I myself received at that time the harsh, aromatic
breath above the enclosure of the *lycée* Bar-le-duc, they are
the holy waters over which bent the shepherdess from Domremy and in which were reflected the inspiring faces of Saint
Michael and Saint Marguerite.]

(*Contacts et Circonstances*)[88]

(Notice in this text the *rapprochement* of Rimbaud with Jeanne
d'Arc, just as Rimbaud compares himself with "the shepherdess"
in *Une Saison en Enfer:* "I saw myself in front of an infuriated
crowd, facing the firing squad, crying because of the unhappiness
that they have not been able to understand, and forgiving!—like
Joan of Arc!" He might also have added, as surely Claudel would
have done, "Like Christ!") Claudel's only specific references to
nature in another poet's works are drawn from Rimbaud, as in the
two texts just quoted above and as in other passages throughout
his works, such as,

---

88. *Contacts et Circonstances,* pp. 257-258.

. . . Un cœur pur pénètre le ciel et l'enfer" (Immit., X, 1.2, ch. 4). Et j'ajouterai: la terre aussi. "Je vis," dit un autre grand converti, Arthur Rimbaud, "que la nature est un spectacle de bonté." La cabane coiffée de roses, où l'on loge les outils du jardinage, voisinera désormais avec l'église habillée de feuilles.

[". . . A pure heart penetrates heaven and hell" (*Immit.*, X, 1.2, ch. 4). And I will add: earth also. "I saw," said another great convert, Arthur Rimbaud, "that nature is a display of goodness." The rose-covered shed where the gardener's tools are kept, will henceforth be side to side with the leaf-dressed church.]

(*Accompagnements*)[89]

This is not to say that he does not associate other poets with an awareness and love of nature; he mentions Francis Jammes as being "this man of nature who prefers the book of the Creation to all others, and to whom the Creation tells about the Creator," and he says that Verlaine is a "poet of nature" and that "it is always in one of the never forgotten salubrious corners of his home country that he tries to find cures and salvation."[90] But it is Rimbaud who remains Claudel's authority on nature, as it were—Rimbaud whom Claudel associated with nature as much for his direct communication with it through his predilection for long walks as for its dominant role in his poetry. Nature is especially prominent in connection with color and musical imagery in the poetry of both Rimbaud and Claudel. And just as Rimbaud refers to himself as a "gold spark of *pure* light *in nature*," Claudel expresses a fervent belief in "the communion of man with nature through roadways."[91] Claudel, along with Rimbaud and Verlaine, was another "fancier of the high road."

The theme of nature is apparent from the very first of Claudel's works. The setting of *L'Endormie*, for example, is a forest inhabited by wood nymphs. As Wallace Fowlie rightly points out, Claudel "has written of Nature as he studied her from the highest branch of an old tree he used to climb as a boy. This was the site of his first dialogue with Nature and of his first impressions from which he drew throughout his life."[92] Yet, however the early works reflect these first impressions, this theme of nature becomes even

89. *Accompagnements*, p. 150.
90. *Accompagnements*, p. 112.
91. *Conversations dans le Loir-et-Cher*, p. 177.
92. *Paul Claudel*, p. 9.

more intensified in Claudel's post-Rimbaud period, in which nature is not just a setting but the very element out of which the poetry grows. It is in the works beginning with *Tête d'Or* that we find a larger, all-inclusive view of nature and its cosmic implications, a nature that, while terrestrial in its evocations of the seas, the rivers, the floral ecstacies, is also celestial. The *Bateau Ivre*'s cataclysmic transformation into a *presque île,* which in turn becomes a sort of macrocosm "thrown by the hurricane into the birdless ether," which "pokes holes in the sky," among the stars, and which is "spotted with electric lunula," is rendered by the soliloquy of the moon in *Le Soulier de Satin,* by the bark's voyage through the heavens in *La Muse qui est la Grâce,* and expresses the basic idea of nature's profound impact on man. Tête d'Or's sensitivity to the elements of nature and his solitude in a natural setting further demonstrate that Claudel's finding a source of strength and inspiration in nature is comparable to Rimbaud's.

A setting, however, is not only a matter of place, of the things surrounding one—with which one has some form of intimate communication; it also involves time. Rimbaud wished to identify himself ideally with "the ancient feast." It is the primitiveness of ancient Gaul, the brutality of untamed peoples not yet subject to the encroachment of modern social norms, mores, and scientific progress, the innocent, unsullied spontaneity of men not yet constrained and contaminated by lawful society that particularly appeals to him; in *Une Saison en Enfer,* he invokes "the purity of ancient races." He rejects modern science and says, almost nostalgically, that he longs for *"l'Europe aux anciens parapets,"* that is, not only Europe *with* its old parapets, but also the Europe *of* the old parapets, Europe as it was centuries ago, "ancient Gaul." Similarly, Claudel does not accept the rationalism and the *scientisme* of the modern materialistic world that Renan represented for him. In *La Ville,* Besme gives Cœuvre a sapphire, "this drop of abstract night, pupil of the primordial blindness"[93] ("blindness" in that it has not yet seen the corruption of contemporary society and therefore is innocent for having been formed at a time remote from the present, "primordial"), the essence of primitive beauty. The desirability of antiquity is further evoked in *Le Soulier de Satin* when Don Gusman says, "I want to appease the old masters with the True Cross. I want this old world, our conquest, to become our heritage."[94] Claudel's plays do not, for the most part, take place

93. *La Ville,* p. 204.
94. *Le Soulier de Satin,* p. 140.

in contemporary times. More often than not, no specific time is mentioned at all, though the atmosphere is usually evocative of something medieval. Claudel gives the impression of thinking back nostalgically to *"le temps ancien"* ["time past"] and in particular to the Middle Ages which he conceives of as being much closer to perfection than the modern world; he says, "evil is old; it goes back to the end of the Middle Ages."[95]

Both Rimbaud and Claudel have this theme of nostalgia for the past in common with the Romantics. In fact, much of what they say in terms of theme and often even subject matter is directly related to the early nineteenth-century poets whom they referred to as "real poets," although Claudel qualified this by saying, "many French poets of the nineteenth century had talent and even genius, but they did not have faith . . . they lacked religion" (which explains why he wrote to Gide of his "hatred . . . for the Romantics").[96] Rimbaud even called them *voyants,* seers. Yet there is a very real difference between Rimbaud and Claudel and the Romantics as concerns their attitude towards the past. The romantic idea in wishing for *le temps ancien* is founded principally on a desire for escape; actually, distance in space works for them as well as distance in time, as is true for Chateaubriand's René, for example. Moreover, the Romantics, Victor Hugo, Musset, Lamartine, even Vigny, are satisfied mainly with the superficial aspects of past eras—the chivalric attitude, the heroic bravura of legendary figures, the local

95. *Contacts et Circonstances*, p. 227.
96. *Positions et Propositions II,* p. 143. *"La poésie française pendant les XVIIe et XVIIIe siècles a été simplement un moyen concis, spirituel et harmonieux d'exprimer des pensées. C'était une façon de parler en proverbes et sentences frappantes, un peu à la manière des gens de la campagne. Au XIXe siècle c'était bien de la vraie poésie, mais c'était la poésie sans Dieu. Beaucoup de poètes français du XIXe siècle avaient du talent et même du génie, mais ils n'avaient pas la foi. Et si leur œuvre fait à certains l'effet d'un amas de décombres, je voudrais vous montrer que la cause de ce rapide déclin n'est pas qu'ils manquaient de talent, mais qu'ils manquaient de religion, c'est-à-dire qu'à leur talent et à leurs œuvres manquait un ingrédient essentiel."* Rimbaud, letter to Paul Demeny, pp. 272-273, *"Les premiers romantiques ont été voyants sans trop bien s'en rendre compte . . . les seconds romantiques sont très voyants: Théophile Gautier, Leconte de Lisle, Théodore de Banville."* It should be noted that the text in *Positions et Propositions II* was written and delivered as a lecture in Baltimore on 14 November 1927, after Claudel had read Rimbaud's letter to Demeny. His correspondence to Gide before reading Rimbaud's text suggests complete disdain for the Romantics: *Correspondance: Claudel et Gide*, p. 169. *". . . auteur* [Boileau] *que j'aime surtout en raison de la haine que j'ai pour les romantiques."*

color of past epochs—as a vehicle for contemporary *malaise* and *mal du siècle,* and concern themselves with little more than posturing. For Rimbaud and Claudel, however, a moralistic consideration is of paramount importance; the consciousness motivating acts and the spontaneity of action rather than the acts themselves is what interests them. And it is mainly Claudel's preference for the psychology of primitiveness, the directness and the seeming simplicity of men of the distant past, that suggests that he owes a great deal of his attitude to Rimbaud as much if not more than to the orthodoxy of medieval church pageantry or even to the Romantics' penchant for the Middle Ages.

5.
Elemental Rapports in
Rimbaud & Claudel:
Sound & Light as "Correspondences"

From Versailles to the pyramids of Egypt, modern engineers have highlighted historically important architectural achievements by subtle use of sound systems and illumination. In such *"son et lumière"* projects, the interaction of light and sound is arranged in such a way that the play of lights on various monuments complements the sound effects and the sound in turn gives greater intensity to the lighting. In a sense, Rimbaud and Claudel have vividly evoked their poetic themes with a similar technique; in order to accentuate the "architectural" lines of their poetry and to convey the essential meanings of their visions and sensations, both poets rely extensively on images related to light and sound. Moreover, these fundamental elements seem to be eminently interdependent; neither one takes precedence over the other. Claudel himself was certainly aware of the importance of this relationship in the creation of a poem, for he says that "the essential element in any form of art is rapport," and that "the rapport in poetry is between ideas, images, feelings, and especially sound."[1]

Certainly in Rimbaud's poetry—with its innumerable references to vividly colored visual images such as *"blessures écarlates et noires"* ["scarlet and black wounds"] (*Being Beauteous*), *"pigeons écarlates"* ["scarlet pigeons"] (*Vies*), *"grandes juments bleues et noires"* ["great blue and black mares"] (*Ornières*), *"ces poissons d'or"* ["those golden fish"] (*Le Bateau Ivre*)—the emphasis he places on color and its importance to his visual concepts are obvious and have led at least one critic, Marguerite-Yerta Méléra, to state in her article *"Les Voyages d'Arthur Rimbaud,"* that visual sensations are above all important to Rimbaud, that "his senses are moreover very unequally developed; he exists especially through the sight of his flesh and of his mind. His sense of hearing can also stimulate sensations, but often they are visual sensations, the sound be-

1. *Accompagnements*, p. 20.

ing transposed into images."[2] However, in *The Art of Arthur Rimbaud,* A. R. Chisholm expresses an opposite point of view and writes that "the usual form of [Rimbaud's] sensations is auditory."[3] This statement seems to be given authority by lines such as,

> *Reprenons l'étude au bruit de l'œuvre dévorante qui se rassemble et remonte dans les masses.*

> [Let's return to our study with the sound of the consuming work that reassembles and revives in the masses.]

> *(Jeunesse)*

> *. . . les poissons d'or, les poissons chantants . . .*

> [. . . the golden fish, the singing fish . . .]

> *(Le Bateau Ivre)*

(although the fish are "golden," the further qualification of them is that they are "singing"; the final impression is one of sound)

> *. . . il est l'affection et le présent puisqu'il a fait la maison ouverte à l'hiver écumeux et à la rumeur de l'été.*

> [. . . he is affection and the present since he has made the house open to the frothy winter and to the summer's uproar.]

> *(Génie)*

A short passage from *Sonnet,* also in *Les Illuminations,* seems further to corroborate Chisholm's assertions: *"la force et le droit réfléchissent la danse et la voix à présent seulement appréciés"* ["force and right reflect the dance and the voice only now valued"]. As final proof of his theory, Chisholm cites, among others, the following phrase: *"Le monde sera réduit . . . en une maison musicale"* ["The world will be reduced . . . to a musical house"]. Unfortunately, he has neglected to quote the whole passage: *"Quand le monde sera réduit en un seul bois noir pour nos quatre yeux étonnés,—en une plage pour deux enfants fidèles,—en une maison musicale pour notre claire sympathie,—je vous trouverai"* ["When the world is reduced to a single black wood for our four astonished eyes,—to a beach for two faithful children,—to a musical house for our luminous understanding,—I shall find you"] (*Phrases*). Rimbaud says, "I shall find you" not only when the world is reduced to "a mu-

2. Marguerite-Yerta Méléra, *"Les Voyages d'Arthur Rimbaud"* in *La Revue Universelle,* Vol. 35, No. 18, 15 décembre 1928, p. 661.
3. A. R. Chisholm, *The Art of Arthur Rimbaud* (Melbourne University Press, 1930), p. 19.

sical house," but also, and equally, when the world is reduced to a
"single black wood for our four astonished eyes." Both qualifications—visual as well as musical—are necessary to complete Rimbaud's "phrase." Nor is this purely coincidental. In qualifying the
essence of the poet-seer in his letter to Demeny, Rimbaud wrote
that the poet must "inspect the invisible [visual] and hear the unheard [sonorous]." His images were not intended to be primarily
auditory or primarily visual. If we are to accept as valid the evidence of his theory as he presented it to Demeny, we must conclude that these two elements were meant to be interdependent.
Moreover, this essential interdependence is apparent not only in
Rimbaud's pronouncements about poetic theory or in the juxtaposition of references to light and sound, but also in his poetic practice, in the way tones of vowels and consonants complement images. Consider the following image from *Aube: "A la grand'*
ville, elle fuyait parmi les clochers et les dômes, et courant comme
un mendiant sur les quais de marbre, je la chassais" ["In the heart
of the city, she fled among the steeples and domes, and running like
a beggar on the marble quays, I chased her"]. The image of marble
quays on which rays of early morning sun are playing is suggested
by the warm tones of the vowels and consonants, and the constant
play of light spreading from the tops of steeples to the lower
domes and finally to the ground level of the quays is accompanied
by the continuous vibrant quality of the "musical" tones. It would
be difficult to find a better example of sound that is complementary to the visual image—complementary and unifying.

Just as critics have done a disservice to Rimbaud's poetry in neglecting the effect of its stylistic elements in all of their ramifications,
they have been prone to misjudge certain aspects of Claudel's poetic
practice or to indicate a preference for one of them over another.
For example, in words reminiscent of A. R. Chisholm's evaluation
of Rimbaud's imagery, J. Samson, in his book *Paul Claudel Poète
Musicien* on the musical aspects of Claudel's works, suggests that
"the voice is everything."[4] It would be misrepresenting Samson to
say that he does not recognize the importance of visual concepts in
Claudel's works, for he qualifies his earlier statement by saying that
"Claudel does not explain what he sees, he feels things and translates them into images and rhythmic concepts."[5] However, he tends

4. J. Samson, *Paul Claudel Poète Musicien* (Paris: Editions du Milieu du
Monde, 1957), p. 105. Samson is quoting Charles du Bos, but his comment
is, *"C'est très juste,* That is quite right."
5. *Paul Claudel Poète Musicien,* pp. 249-250.

to negate this statement by further qualifying it in the following terms: "When we finish reading it, what remains in our mind? A residue of images? Yes, but of images in movement; and when the images have left our memory? a rhythmic feeling."[6] The question one must ask oneself at this point is simple enough: suppose one is oriented towards visual concepts (as would be the case for a painter) rather than musical ones (as is the case for Samson who happens to be particularly interested in music in general)? One's perspective is then completely different. Arguments like Samson's tend to neglect certain basic facts, such as, in the case of Claudel, the author's own rhetorical questions, which leave little doubt as to his opinion concerning the importance of certain poetic elements, at least in theory. For example, in his preface to Samson's own book, Claudel asks whether words do not have "color, just as they have timbre?"[7] When mentioning sound, he often includes a reference to color or uses a verb that suggests color:

> ... il se sent tellement adapté à l'oreille qui l'écoute, qui refuse certaines idees et qui en exige certaines autres, qui colore, amplifie ou amortit tout ce qu'elle reçoit.

> [... he feels so attuned to the ear which listens to him, which refuses certain ideas and insists on certain others, which colors, amplifies or muffles everything it receives.]
> (*Conversations dans le Loir-et-Cher*)[8]

> Regardez tout ce qu'un seul rayon de Schubert vient faire fourmiller tout à coup au fond de l'âme d'un commissaire-priseur.

> [Look at all that a single ray of Schubert comes and stirs up in the depths of the soul of an appraiser.]
> (*Conversations dans le Loir-et-Cher*)[9]

(note that *"rayon"* usually refers to light, whereas Schubert is a composer of music, sound)

> Ne prétendez pas décomposer la lumière: quand c'est elle qui décompose l'obscurité, produisant, selon l'intensité de son travail, sept notes.

6. *Paul Claudel Poète Musicien*, pp. 249-250.
7. *Paul Claudel Poète Musicien*, pp. 250-251.
8. *Conversations dans le Loir-et-Cher*, p. 93.
9. *Conversations dans le Loir-et-Cher*, p. 25.

[Don't claim to decompose light: when it is light that decomposes darkness, producing, according to the intensity of
its work, seven notes.]
                (*Proposition sur la lumière* in *Connaissance de l'Est*)[10]

*Et l'intensité des tons varie, suivant une gamme dont le jaune
forme la tonique, selon la mesure plus ou moins complète où
la matière répond aux sollicitations de la lumière.*

[And the intensity of the tones varies, following a scale of
which yellow forms the tonic, according to the more or less
complete measure in which matter responds to the solicita-
tions of light.]
                (*Proposition sur la lumière* in *Connaissance de l'Est*)[11]

Color is used to describe the quality of a particular sound:

. . . cette note jaune

[. . . this yellow note]
                (*Conversations dans le Loir-et-Cher*)[12]

. . . ces cris percants de vert

[. . . these piercing shouts of green]
                (*Conversations dans le Loir-et-Cher*)[13]

. . . le cri du rouge contre le vert

[. . . the shout of the red against the green]
                (*Contacts et Circonstances*)[14]

. . . j'entends encore ce cri rouillé

[. . . I still hear that rusty shout]
                (*Conversations dans le Loir-et-Cher*)[15]

. . . admettez comme la note fondamentale ce rouge sombre.

[. . . allow as the fundamental note this somber red.]
                (*Conversations dans le Loir-et-Cher*)[16]

10. *Connaissance de l'Est*, p. 140.
11. *Connaissance de l'Est*, p. 141.
12. *Conversations dans le Loir-et-Cher*, p. 101.
13. *Conversations dans le Loir-et-Cher*, p. 106.
14. *Contacts et Circonstances*, p. 299.
15. *Conversations dans le Loir-et-Cher*, p. 201.
16. *Conversations dans le Loir-et-Cher*, p. 47.

Instruments or objects that produce or that are associated with sound are described as having a particular color or properties of light and illumination (Claudel equates light with color: *"Qui dit lumière dit couleur"* ["He who says light says color"][17]):

> . . . *tels que des grelots rouges*

> [. . . like red bells]
> > (*La Maison Suspendue* in *Connaissance de l'Est*)[18]

> . . . *nos sombres cloches qui sonnent les vêpres*

> [. . . our somber bells that ring vespers]
> > (*Conversations dans le Loir-et-Cher*)[19]

(*"sombres"*—indicating a lack of light or the presence of only a little light—describes the quality of *"cloches"* which produce sound)

> . . . *les clochetons dorés*

> [. . . the little gilded bells]
> > (*Conversations dans le Loir-et-Cher*)[20]

Shades of color are compared to the tones of a full orchestra: *"Comme une simple note rouge fait chanter l'orchestre jusque-là inanimé des verts"* ["How the hitherto lifeless orchestra of greens is made to sing by a simple red note"] (*Conversations dans le Loir-et-Cher*)[21] The colors of the spectrum are referred to as "the painter's orchestra" (*Positions et Propositions I*).[22] The tone of the human voice, which Claudel compares to "vermilion blood," is described as being "the very essence of purple":

> *Que le sens sacré de la parole et le son de la voix humaine*
> *Tombe dans la pensée mot par mot et s'y dissolve,*
> *comme les gouttes de sang vermeil et l'essence même de la pourpre*
> *Une par une en un cristal limpide!*

> [May the sacred meaning of the word and the sound of the human voice

---

17. *Conversations dans le Loir-et-Cher*, p. 62.
18. *Connaissance de l'Est*, p. 133.
19. *Conversations dans le Loir-et-Cher*, p. 48.
20. *Conversations dans le Loir-et-Cher*, p. 55.
21. *Conversations dans le Loir-et-Cher*, p. 157.
22. *Positions et Propositions I*, p. 121.

Fall into thought word by word and dissolve, like drops
of vermilion blood and the very essence of the purple
One by one into a limpid crystal!][23]

In this passage from the *Cantique des Parfums* in *La Cantate à
Trois Voix,* the intense colors, both strong and somber (*vermeil* is a
strong shade of red—a rich, intense color—and *pourpre,* a deep, somber shade, is the sign of Roman and Byzantine royalty and of the
dignity of a cardinal) are intensified by the repetition of the "intense and somber" nasal tones of the vowels, interspersed with and
highlighted by the sibilant consonant S which slows down the movement of the *verset.* The effect here is induced by the colors mentioned and by the sounds that accompany them; the comparison itself is, in terms of the vocabulary, one of color and sound. (Very often such insistent use of a particular dominant sound in a single
passage is tantamount to alliteration in Claudel's works.)

Space does not permit listing here all the hundreds of allusions to
complementary colors and sounds in Claudel's works. One or two
further references, however, should clarify the matter completely.
Consideration should be given, for instance, to the title of one of
Claudel's works about art, *L'Œil Ecoute* [*The Eye Listens*], in
which he again juxtaposes words that suggest color and sound. And
to dispel any doubt about the conclusions based on our earlier observations, it should be noted that in *Conversations dans le Loir-et-
Cher,* two of the essential points of discussion are sound and color,
and a third is architecture. Thus, two of the principal subjects in
this book are involved with visual concepts, and all three can be included under the heading *son et lumière.*

It may seem at first that this concept of visual and sonorous rapports is comparable to Baudelaire's theory of correspondences. In
fact, there seems to be such a correlation between light and sound
in the works of Rimbaud and Claudel that they might be defined
in Baudelairian terms—*"Les parfums, les couleurs et les sons se ré-
pondent"* ["Perfumes, colors, and sounds respond to each other"]
(*Correspondances*)—but for the fact that the olfactory impressions
are negligible in Rimbaud, and, in Claudel's works, do not have the
same functions as color and sound. Marguerite-Yerta Méléra could
well have written of Claudel, as she did of Rimbaud, that "his sense
of smell is not very active."[24]

23. *Cantique des Parfums* in *La Cantate à trois voix,* p. 215.
24. *"Les Voyages d'Arthur Rimbaud,"* p. 661.

In Rimbaud's poems, occasional references to specific aromas and to the sense of smell in general are to be found, as in the following examples:

Les tilleuls sentent bon dans les bons soirs de juin!
L'air est parfois si doux, qu'on ferme la paupière;
Le vent chargé de bruits,—la ville n'est pas loin,—
A des parfums de vigne et des parfums de bière . . .

[The linden trees smell good in the good June evenings!
The air is sometimes so sweet, that you close your eyelids;
The wind laden with sound,—the town isn't far,—
Has the scent of grape-vines and the smell of beer . . .]

(Roman)

Quand, sous les poutres enfumées,
Chantent les croûtes parfumées . . .

[When, under the smoke-blackened beams,
The perfumed crusts sing . . .]

(Les Effarés)

. . . il était entêté
A se renfermer dans la fraîcheur des latrines:
Il pensait là, tranquille et livrant ses narines.

[. . . he was determined
To shut himself up in the cool of the latrines:
There he meditated, quiet and surrendering his nostrils.]

(Les Poëtes de Sept Ans)

. . . cela finit par une débandade de parfums.

[. . . it ended in a riot of perfumes.]

(Matinée d'Ivresse)

. . . une odeur de bois suant dans l'âtre

[. . . a resinous odor of wood on the hearth]

(Phrases)

. . . et les parfums pourpres du soleil des pôles

[. . . and the purple perfumes of the sun at the poles]

(Métropolitain)

Loin des vieilles retraites et des vieilles flammes, qu'on entend,
qu'on sent

[Far from the old retreats and the old flames that you hear, that you smell]

(Barbare)

. . . des anses d'amours morts et de parfums affaissés.

[. . . coves of dead loves and sunken perfumes.]

(Fairy)

It should be pointed out that the first of these allusions to perfumes come from Rimbaud's early poems, written when he was newly acquainted with Baudelaire's works. The last five of these olfactory references, from *Les Illuminations,* constitute the bulk of such references in his prose poems. Moreover, with the exception of *"latrines"* and possibly *"les tilleuls sentent bon,"* these are not the strong pervasive perfumes that Baudelaire mentions in poems like *Le Chat,*

> *De sa fourrure blonde et brune*
> *Sort un parfum si doux, qu'un soir*
> *J'en fus embaumé, pour l'avoir*
> *Caressée une fois, rien qu'une.*

> [From her blond and brown fur
> Comes a scent so sweet, that one evening
> I was embalmed by it, for having
> Caressed her once, just once.]

or *Le Flacon:*

> *Il est de forts parfums pour qui toute matière*
> *Est poreuse. On dirait qu'ils pénètrent le verre.*

> [There are strong perfumes for which all matter
> Is porous. One would say that they penetrate glass.]

In fact, Rimbaud's "perfumes" are not generally even essential to the images and ideas he is portraying. While *"les tilleuls sentent bon," "des parfums de vigne,"* and *des parfums de bière"* from *Roman* do convey the image of a soft night in late spring or early summer, *"débandade de parfums"* from the later *Matinée d'Ivresse* does not intensify the poem's central image, except insofar as it suggests confusion; it certainly does not point to any particular aroma to which one might attach some symbolic significance. Curious too is the fact that the last of the above references to perfumes taken from *Les Illuminations* qualifies them as *"affaissés"*—

depressed, bent over with age, or sunken and nonfunctional. In at least one instance even flowers have sounds rather than scents for Rimbaud. In *Aube*, the flowers speak to the poet, but no fragrance emanates from them: *"La première entreprise fut, dans le sentier déjà empli de frais et blêmes éclats, une fleur qui me dit son nom"* ["The first adventure was, in the path already filled with fresh and pale shimmerings, a flower who told me her name"]. Though it would be inexact to state that olfactory references do not exist in Rimbaud's poetry, nevertheless, they are secondary. And of particular importance for our present study is the fact that in *Les Illuminations* and *Une Saison en Enfer*—the works that Claudel mentions as having particularly influenced him—the five quotations mentioned above are the only important references to perfumes.

Certainly one does find olfactory sensations implied in Claudel's works as well. He mentions *"le parfum sacerdotal"* ["the sacerdotal perfume"] (Claudel was not entirely unaffected by the purifying incense of the Church, just as Rimbaud was not indifferent to the incense burned during Mass: *"Sur mon lit d'hôpital, l'odeur de l'encens m'est revenue si puissante; gardien des aromates sacrés, confesseur, martyr"* ["On my hospital bed, the odor of incense came back to me so strong: guardian of the sacred aromatics, confessor, martyr"], as he writes in *L'Eclair*). Elsewhere Claudel refers to *"la trompette nasillarde des fromages"* ["the nasal trumpet of cheeses"][25] (but Claudel is joking here) and *"le pet noir"* ["the black fart"][26] (one wonders whether *vert*, green, might not be more appropriate, since *vert* is the color Claudel uses most often when referring to nature). Other examples of odors proliferate in his works, such as,

> *Ce que l'odeur de la saumure et du goudron est pour un fils de marin, celle de la paperasse l'a été pour moi et cette occulte fermentation qui se dégage des écritures superposées*

[What the odor of brine and tar is for a sailor's son, that of official papers was for me and the occult fermentation that emanates from superimposed writings]

(Contacts et Circonstances)[27]

and,

> *Ce beau soleil, ce n'est pas pour rien que Dieu l'a mis là! Il n'y a qu'à y aller, montons-y! Mais non pas, ce n'est pas le*

25. *Conversations dans le Loire-et-Cher*, p. 103.
26. *Conversations dans le Loire-et-Cher*, p. 104.
27. *Contacts et Circonstances*, p. 241.

soleil! c'est cette odeur délicieuse qui m'attire! Oh! si je
pouvais tout le temps la respirer! le temps de mourir et de
nouveau elle est là! Ce n'est pas le soleil visible que je veux,
c'est cette espèce d'esprit exhilirant, cette odeur délicieuse
qui fait mon cœur défaillir!

[That beautiful sun, God did not put it there for nothing!
You can just go there, let's go! But no, it is not the sun
that attracts me! It is that delicious aroma! Oh! If only I
could breathe it all the time! time enough to die and it is
there again! It is not the visible sun that I want, it's this
kind of exhilarating spirit, this delicious odor that makes my
heart sink!]

(*Le Soulier de Satin*)[28]

Such odors usually exert a limited power of recall in a Proustian or
Bergsonian manner, or of attraction in order to emphasize a particular object, but they do not have the properties of color and sound
in that they do not emphasize or are not associated with some particular sentiment or idea. They are restrictive rather than broadly
inclusive. That is to say that, whereas visual imagery is often qualified in sonorous terms in Claudel (and vice versa)—the sound complementing or expanding the image—the olfactory references generally only qualify without amplifying the objects or sensations
they are applied to; in any case, they are seldom associated with
color or sound, nor are they evocative of any particular theme.
Here, too, the heavily aromatic air that pervades Baudelaire's poems
is virtually nonexistent. One section of *La Cantate à trois voix* does
deal with the fragrance of flowers—of the rose, in particular—and is
entitled *Cantique des Parfums* [Song of Perfumes] (as in Solomon's
Song of Songs), but this is what might well be called the exception
that proves the rule. Actually, rose is usually a color for Claudel,
and even violets—so often referred to by other poets for their scent—
suggest color; in any case, these flowers are really evocations of a
mood suggested by their appearance rather than by their smell.

Certain images or words that are especially reminiscent of Baudelaire actually have completely different applications in Rimbaud and
Claudel. For example, *ambre*, amber, is primarily an aroma, a perfume in Baudelaire's works:

28. *Le Soulier de Satin*, p. 261.

Il est des parfums frais comme des chairs d'enfants,
Doux comme les hautbois, verts comme les prairies,
—Et d'autres, corrompus, riches et triomphants,

Ayant l'expansion des choses infinies,
Comme l'ambre, le musc, le benjoin et l'encens,
Qui chantent les transports de l'esprit et des sens.

[Some perfumes are fresh as children's flesh,
Soft as oboes, green as prairies,
—And others, corrupt, rich and triumphant,

Having the expansion of things infinite,
Like amber, musk, benzoin and incense,
Sing the raptures of the mind and of the senses.]

(*Correspondances*)

Les plus rares fleurs
Mêlant leurs odeurs
Aux vagues senteurs de l'ambre . . .

[The rarest flowers
Mingling their fragrance
With the faint scent of amber . . .]

(*L'Invitation au Voyage*)

But for Rimbaud, it is a color (mentioned only once):

Ce soir, à Circeto des hautes glaces, grasse comme le poisson,
et enluminée comme les dix mois de la nuit rouge—(son
cœur ambre et spunk),—pour ma seule prière muette comme
ces régions de nuit et précédant des bravoures plus violentes
que ce chaos polaire.

[This evening, to Circeto of the icy heights, fat as fish, and
flushed, illuminated like the ten months of the red night—
(her heart amber and spunk)—for my one prayer silent as
those regions of night and preceding daring exploits more
violent than this polar chaos.]

(*Dévotion*)

Ambre is also a color for Claudel: "*Entre ces gras replis violets,*
voici l'eau peinte comme du reflet des cierges, voici l'ambre, voici
le vert le plus doux, voici la couleur de l'or" ["Between these fat
violet folds, here is water painted like the reflection of tapers, here
is amber, here is the softest green, here is the color of gold"] (*La*

Dérivation in *Connaissance de l'Est*).[29] And when perfume is represented as having color for Rimbaud, it is not amber at all; it is purple, as in *"les parfums pourpres du soleil des pôles,"* ["the purple
perfumes of the sun at the poles"] (*Métropolitain*). But here again,
even though in this example there is a certain correspondence between color and perfume, it is exceptional, and such a treatment of
perfumes—comparable to Baudelaire's synesthesia—is extremely rare
in both Rimbaud and Claudel. There is, of course, no doubt that
both of them owe a certain debt to Baudelaire—as Rimbaud tacitly
states in his letter to Paul Demeny on May 15, 1871 (the second of
the so-called *Lettres du Voyant,* the first having been written to
Georges Izambard a few days earlier), "Baudelaire is the first seer,
king of the poets, a real *God*"—and as Claudel makes clear in *Ma
Conversion:* "I read the *Posthumous Writings* of Baudelaire, and I
saw that a poet whom I preferred to all Frenchmen had found faith
in his last years."[30] Their debt, however, seems virtually to have excluded Baudelaire's first "correspondence." And it can be safely as-
sumed that, although Rimbaud for one was indeed impressed with
and even partially influenced at the outset by Baudelaire's theory—
the letter to Demeny also states that "this language will be of the
soul for the soul, summarizing everything, perfumes, sounds, colors"
(Rimbaud not only refers to the same sensory perceptions as Baudelaire, he places them in the same order)—he did not by any means
assimilate it whole. In fact, despite Rimbaud's having further stated
that Baudelaire's poetry was an example of "inspecting the invisible
and hearing the unheard," that it was a poetry that did more than
express "the spirit of things dead"—statements which both apply
very well in a definition of the aesthetic doctrines of Rimbaud and
Claudel—Rimbaud and Claudel are actually very far from Baudelaire's concept of correspondences.

Among the divergences from Baudelaire's poetic approach to be
found in Rimbaud's works are the kinds of images he uses, the contrasts between these images, and his treatment of them. As A. R.
Chisholm writes in *The Art of Arthur Rimbaud,* Baudelaire "remains largely plastic in his poetic practice."[31] To illustrate his
point, Chisholm chooses as examples, *"balcons du ciel,"* ["sky

29. *La Dérivation* in *Connaissance de l'Est*, p. 72.
30. *Contacts et Circonstances*, p. 195.
31. *The Art of Arthur Rimbaud*, p. 5.

balconies"],[32] *"robes surannées"* ["old-fashioned dresses"],[33]
"fond des eaux" ["depth of the waters"].[34] These images are reflections of what Baudelaire sees and touches concretely in the
world that surrounds him; they do not go much beyond what is at-
tainable in the visual and tactile—or olfactory—world as it is; they
are fixed. Yet in Rimbaud's works we find a new creation. To begin with, the tactile sensations are virtually nonexistent. Moreover,
Rimbaud's images are not attached to the ground, as it were, are
not stationary or immalleable; they are free and float in a cosmos
that Rimbaud himself has created; they go beyond the real: they
express the *sur*-real in an attempt to discover the ultimate, the ideal,
or to re-create it, through transcendence of reality. For Baudelaire,
the ideal was a priori unattainable; Rimbaud begins with the assump-
tion that the attainment of the ideal is only a matter of the proper
procedure.[35] And whereas Baudelaire often appears to be retaining
a certain element of poetic posturing, Rimbaud achieves a unique
youthful spontaneity. Furthermore, though the correspondences
are suggested—as in *Voyelles*—and are obviously a part of Rimbaud's
early poetic concepts, they are, at least in the later poems, correspondences that he himself has invented; they are deeply personal associations, undeniably hermetic, and they are fluctuating and fluid. In
Baudelaire we are confronted with a kind of realist painter attempting to express the ideal in terms of concrete reality, whereas Rimbaud is more of an expressionist, in the etymological sense of the
word. It is not the object itself that produces color or sound in
Rimbaud's poetry; rather, these sounds and colors are produced
from the associations of the poet himself. To be sure, as we shall
see in *Voyelles,* the colors and the things to which they refer seem
to be taken from the world surrounding Rimbaud and are in this
sense an example of what Claudel calls "plunging . . . to the depths
of the definite in order to find the inexhaustible."[36] Yet a further
study of them clearly indicates that the colors Rimbaud associated
with certain sounds have with each other as well as with those
sounds a correlation quite disassociated from the realist paintings

32. Charles Baudelaire, *Recueillement* in *Les Fleurs du Mal* (Paris: Editions
Garnier Frères, 1961), p. 189.
33. Ibid.
34. Ibid.
35. Claudel says that Rimbaud was the first to have used "language and poetry,
not only as the expression of things known but in an attempt at discovery."
See *Journal*, Tome I, Cahier 4, March 1920, p. 470.
36. *Positions et Propositions I*, p. 95.

of Baudelaire, in which each element of an image has an inherent importance as well as an outer association with the other elements of the image and with the poetic world. If we say, for example, that the colors black and red have a correlation both with each other and with the sound I, then black relates to red, both colors relate to I (in that the strident tone of I evokes the violence of red which is outlined in its contours by black) and, in conjunction with each other, they all reflect the same abstract aspects or aspect of the poetic vision. It is in this manner that Rimbaud's free-floating colors and sounds—this flux—express the poet's deeply personal feelings, his ardent and exalted desires, and they are much more than an attempt to translate into poetry—or into what has been traditionally accepted as poetic form—what has already been expressed (by God, for Claudel) in the concrete world; they are, in a sense, a re-creation of the world, or the creation of a new world: in any case, a refocusing, a bringing of the world into a new perspective.

Briefly, we can say that in Baudelaire, the interrelationship of perfumes, colors, and sounds is objective, is based primarily on observation; in Rimbaud—at least in *Les Illuminations* and *Une Saison en Enfer*—the relationships are subjective and are an exteriorization of the poet's inner self, hermetic and difficult to understand as they may sometimes seem to be. Red, for example, is not just a representation of blood, of fire, of flames, of a sunset, or of all of these at once; it is a state of mind, a way of seeing things through the poet's own mind. Another dimension is involved, the dimension of the poet's soul. This is not just the "poetic soul" or a "poetic posture," but, rather, the very life and substance of the poet as an individual: "The first study of the man who wishes to be a poet is knowledge of himself, complete; he searches his soul, he inspects it, he tempts it, learns about it," says Rimbaud in his letter to Demeny. It is this dimension, along with the fluid and cosmic nature of its expression, that distinguishes Rimbaldian and Claudelian visions from Baudelairian correspondences, as Claudel has also clearly implied:

> *Ce n'est pas assez dire que nous regardons le monde exister, nous l'existons par la vue, nous nous associons par un assentiment intime à ce rythme, à cette expression et à ce dessein par quoi il existe...*

> [It is not enough to say that we watch the world exist, we make it exist through vision, we associate ourselves, through

an intimate acquiescence, with that rhythm, with that expression, with that design by which it exists . . .]

(Présence et Prophétie)[37]

Nous devenons ce que nous nommons, nous devenons (momentanément) ce que nous faisons par l'imagination.

[We become what we name, we become (momentarily) what we do through our imagination.]

(Du Sens Figuré de l'Ecriture)[38]

Rimbaud not only sees the heavens, for instance, he becomes part of them; he finds in them not so much an objective quality analogous to something he wishes to express, as a subjective element with which he infuses his own soul: *"Moi qui trouais le ciel"* ["I who poked holes in the sky"] (*Le Bateau Ivre*). All of this is not to say that we must or can place Baudelaire among the Parnassian poets with their *l'art pour l'art*. Rimbaud himself certainly does not, even if, in his enthusiasm and in the exalted inspiration of his letter to Demeny, he has somewhat exaggerated Baudelaire's role as a seer, in the sense that the poet becomes one with his poetry and is completely inseparable from it. Claudel does not place Baudelaire in the same category as the Parnassians, either, for he abominates the "hodgepodge" of the Parnassians. We wish, rather, to emphasize that Rimbaud's *"son et lumière"* (like Claudel's) was essentially different from Baudelaire's, in that it was primarily a subjective element of his poetry, and was in no real sense a mere duplication of what Baudelaire had done fifteen or twenty years earlier than Rimbaud, and long before Claudel.

The concept of color and sound as correspondences was not peculiar to the latter part of the nineteenth century and the beginning of the twentieth. As Enid Starkie points out in *Arthur Rimbaud*, "There was nothing startling or new in the conception of the connection between colors and sound, since Ballanche, Hoffman, Gautier, Baudelaire—and even Balzac—had all described the sensation of color being identical with that of sound, and of the possibility of stimulating one particular sense by appealing to another."[39] Nor was it confined to literature, for it had its counterpart in the art of musical composition. The Russian composer Scriabin, for one, carried out experiments that included projecting

37. *Présence et Prophétie*, p. 279.
38. *Du Sens Figuré de l'Ecriture*, p. 53.
39. Enid Starkie, *Arthur Rimbaud* (A New Directions Book, 1961), p. 164.

color on a screen while accompanying it with orchestrations supposedly having a correspondence with the changing tones and shades of color. The concept of *"l'audition colorée"* was part of the *Weltanschauung* of this period. Had Rimbaud and Claudel been Verlaine, they might well have written an *Art Poétique* beginning, *"de la musique et de la couleur avant toute chose"* ["music and color before everything"]. (Verlaine's poem begins: *"De la musique avant toute chose"* ["Music before everything"].) Claudel actually did write a book entitled *Art Poétique,* but it was little more than yet another occasion to express his religious convictions.[40] And it certainly lacked Verlaine's conciseness. However, this is not to say that neither Rimbaud nor Claudel has left us a key to his poetic concepts. Two works in particular stand out as comparable to Baudelaire's *Correspondances* and Verlaine's *Art Poétique:* the poem *Voyelles* by Rimbaud and Claudel's *Conversations dans le Loir-et-Cher*—a rambling work (on architecture, cuisine, America, as well as sound and color), to be sure, but one that nevertheless gives valuable insights into his poetic practice. In each of these works, we find principles concerning light and sound that apply to the poets' works as a whole and that also constitute a key to the symbolism of these two elements in the poetry and in the prose poems of Rimbaud and Claudel.

40. In one of the copies of *L'Art Poétique* in the Sterling Memorial Library at Yale University—on the flyleaf—one individual has noted that it is an admixture of "astrology, paraphysics, Catholicism, mysticism, superstition, scholasticism, intelligence, stupidity, witchcraft and intellectual inefficacy." Not everyone agrees with this point of view, however, since someone else's comment on the same flyleaf is, in rebuttal to the first comments, *"Mais c'est Polichinelle qui parle!"*

6.
Voyelles:
An Aesthetic Key to
Rimbaud's Poetry

Of all of Rimbaud's *Poésies,* the one poem—aside from *Le Bateau Ivre*—that has caused the greatest amount of literary controversy is the sonnet *Voyelles.* In the latter part of the nineteenth century, it was considered by certain poets as having all the elements of a symbolist manifesto, though a mystifying one—if not entirely incomprehensible. It was supposedly the key to a new aesthetic. Later, it was the rallying point for surrealist factions. And apart from the schools of poetry, literary critics have found in it a source of considerable discussion. Some have suggested that the colors Rimbaud assigned to the five vowels were taken from an ABC book he used as a child, or at least were fixed in his subconscious by his ABC book if they were not consciously borrowed from it. Others have worked out a whole system of mysticism based on the colors associated by Rimbaud with the vowels and have attempted to prove thereby that he was well acquainted with the works of Eliphas Lévi on occultism. Still other critics have gone to great lengths to explain Rimbaud's mysticism—including the origin of *Voyelles*—in terms of the Cabala and alchemical systems, as seems to be suggested by Rimbaud himself in the title of one of the sections of *Une Saison en Enfer, Alchimie du Verbe,* in his use of the word *"alchimie"* in *Voyelles,* in his allusions to mysticism in his letter to Demeny, and in his many references to alchemy and mysticism such as, *"Mais la noire alchimie et les saintes études/Répugnent au blessé, sombre savant d'orgueil"* ["But black alchemy and sacred studies / Are repulsive to the wounded man, somber savant of pride"] (*Les Sœurs de Charité*). One critic has found pornographic and erotic allusions in *Voyelles,* an interpretation that is in keeping with the obvious pornographic implications in poems like *Les Premières Communions* and *Le Cœur Volé.* Certain others have pointed out a close correlation between *Voyelles* and *Correspondances,* though certainly it cannot be said that the visual concepts and their relation to auditory and olfactory sensations as well as their associations with ideas as seen in *Voyelles* constitute a mere transposition of Baudelairian concepts, a simple and clever adaptation or restating of Baudelaire. However, more than a study of source materials—of which one can never be certain—an understanding of *Voyelles* requires analysis of the poem in terms of Rimbaud's poetic practice as it appears in the ensemble of his works, without recourse to exterior material.

In a discussion of the symbolic aspects of vowels and consonants, Claudel has given us an important clue to the understanding of this sonnet:

> *Vous savez tous par cœur le fameux sonnet par lequel un poète de votre terroir ardennais, Arthur Rimbaud, a donné une couleur aux voyelles:*
> *A noir, E blanc, I rouge, etc.*
> *L'interpretation visuelle que cet amateur a donnée aux voyelles, pourquoi ne l'étendrait-on pas aux consonnes? évidemment on ne peut pas donner la couleur à une consonne. Mais n'est-il pas évident que chacune d'elles, que chaque lettre en général a un dynamisme différent, qu'elle ne* travaille *pas de la même manière, qu'on peut la comparer à un engin qui sous une forme unique sert à toute espèce d'usages différents? Le T qui suggère à la fois l'idée d'une croix, d'un levier, d'une balance, d'un carrefour, ou l'O qui nous fait penser à la fois à une roue, à l'horizon, à l'ouverture d'un vase ou d'une bouche, à une poulie, à un volant d'automobile, etc.*

[You all know by heart the famous sonnet by which a poet from your Ardennes soil, Arthur Rimbaud, gave color to vowels:
A black, E white, I red, etc.
Why not extend to the consonants the visual interpretation which this lover of poetry has given to the vowels? obviously color cannot be given to a consonant. But is it not obvious that each one of them, that each letter in general has a different dynamism, that none *works* in the same way, that each can be compared to an engine that under a single form serves all kinds of different uses? T suggests at once the idea of a cross, of a lever, of scales, of an intersection; O makes us think at once of a wheel, of the horizon, of the opening of a vase or of a mouth, of a pulley, of the steering wheel of an automobile, etc.]

(*Accompagnements*)[1]

1. *Accompagnements*, p. 290.

As well as with color, vowels and consonants are to be associated, through their shapes, with certain sensations and ideas, as he makes even clearer in *Seigneur, Apprenez-nous à prier:*

Il y a un mot français dont le dispositif graphique traduit en quelques traits toute l'idée du tableau: c'est le mot: SOI. S, c'est l'escalier que je viens de décrire. I, c'est un flambeau allumé. Et O, c'est un miroir.

[There is a French word whose graphic disposition translates in a few strokes the whole idea of the picture: the word *SOI.* S is the staircase which I have just described. I is a lighted torch. And O is a mirror.][2]

Rimbaud himself has given us leave to read a certain symbolism into the shapes of letters and words, since he writes in *Alchimie du Verbe:* "I regulated the form and movement of each consonant" and in his letter to Demeny, "Moreover, every word being idea, the time of a universal language will come!"

The importance of visual concepts in *Voyelles* is apparent from the outset, since Rimbaud states in the first line of the poem that vowels have color: *"A noir, E blanc, I rouge, U vert, O bleu: voyelles"* ["A black, E white, I red, U green, O blue: vowels"]. Not only that, he has changed the order of them from the usual A, E, I, O, U. A makes a reasonable beginning for the sequence, since it is the first letter of the alphabet and the first of the vowels. O, however, is not the last of the vowels in the Roman alphabet; it is in the Greek—omega, but there are no other references in the poem to things Greek to support the view that this rearrangement of the vowels reflects Rimbaud's interest in classical studies. His childhood education also included a rigorous religious training and indoctrination; consequently he cannot have been unaware of Scriptural references, such as, "I am the Alpha and Omega, the beginning and the ending" and "I am the Alpha and Omega, the first and last" (Rev. 1: 8,11). In the first and second verses of the first chapter of Genesis, this beginning is further qualified: "In the beginning . . . darkness was on the face of the deep." Therefore, in this context of religious symbolism, A, the beginning, must be black. It seems unlikely that this is pure coincidence when one considers that in the second tercet of his sonnet, Rimbaud refers to a violet beam of light, *"rayon violet de Ses Yeux"* ["violet beam from His Eyes"]. The "blue O" has become a "violet omega," violet being a shade of purple. In the

2. *Seigneur, Apprenez-nous à prier,* Vol. 23 of *Œuvres Complètes* (1964), p. 23.

Gospel of John 19: 5, Jesus wears purple on the final day of his terrestrial life: "So Jesus went outside, wearing the crown of thorns
and the purple robe." Purple symbolized kingly or imperial status
for the Romans—as blue symbolizes French royalty—and, by being
forced to wear the purple robe, Jesus was mocked for his self-de-
scription as "King of the Jews." The color is all the more appropriate, for he is also the "King of Kings" (Rev. 19:16). In Rimbaud's
poem, the capitals S and Y of *"Ses Yeux,"* being associated with
alpha and omega and also with the purple robe, obviously refer to
God as well as to the King of Kings; for a good Catholic—like Claudel—Jesus and God are synonymous. If we consider the various
other associations Rimbaud makes with these colors and vowels,
their symbolism and the reasoning for them is not so mysterious
after all: between the beginning and the end there is life, existence;
and the colors that Rimbaud chooses for the other vowels may well
be described in terms of natural existence, existence in nature.

Apart from color, Rimbaud's vowels are associated with certain
scenes, or visions, and then in turn with sounds, odors, and, finally,
with feelings and emotions. It is in this order—color, visions, sounds,
and odors—that sensations have their proportional importance for
Rimbaud, and that the first four of them are mentioned in the
poem:

> *A, noir corset velu des mouches éclatantes*
> *Qui bombinent autour des puanteurs cruelles,*
> *Golfes d'ombre . . .*

> [A, black hairy corset of flashily bursting flies
> Which bombinate[3] around cruel stinks,
> Dark shadowy gulfs . . .]

In these first two lines, we find: *"noir"* (color), *"mouches éclatantes"* (visions, scenes of action or movement), *"qui bombinent"*
(sound), *"des puanteurs cruelles"* (odors). A fifth and final allusion in this first series is once again to the sense of sight, to light—
or to lack of light— *"golfes d'ombre."* Since there is an apparent
interrelationship between these allusions in that they are all involved with the senses, we can expect to find here what M. Sausy
refers to as an "association of sensations." He contends that "the
fly as a whole, if not the corset, has the shape of an *A.* For the

---

3. "bombinate": this is a neologism in Rimbaud's text as well. For further
explanation of Rimbaud's use of this word, see page 133 of this text.

poet, a fly is a flying *A.* "[4] Therefore, A, being synonymous with a
fly, is black, since flies appear to be black. And this color black is
especially intense when there is a whole mass of flies "bursting"
and "bombinating," *"mouches éclatantes qui bombinent."* The
word *"éclatantes"* itself intensifies the color, since it may mean
"bursting," "vivid," "flashing," or "brilliant" (as in *"l'éclat du soleil"*); but, since it may mean "loud," "ringing," as well as "bursting," it also anticipates the intensity of the noise made by these
buzzing flies, *"qui bombinent,"* and in this sense forms a transition
from the sensation of color to that of sound. Masses of flies are in
turn associated with decomposing wastes, and, in this case, most
probably with a stinking cadaver, *"des puanteurs cruelles,"* since
Rimbaud must have had occasion to see and smell more than one
of these "stinking cadavers" in the war-torn France of 1870-71. In
any case, the presence of masses of flies suggests something lifeless
or in a state of putrefaction.

Up to this point, a simple association of sensations works very
well and they appear to correspond to Baudelaire's three categories.
However, the transition from the color (in advanced stages of de-
composition, cadavers may turn black), "sound," and smell of a
decomposing cadaver to shadow-filled gulfs or bays, *"golfes
d'ombre,"* introduces another level of association: an association
of ideas. Death—suggested by the color of mourning, black, as well
as by the cadaver—is not a sensation; it is a state of being, or, rather,
of nonbeing, and also a concept. Moreover, in giving further consideration to the progression from A to a fly, to a mass of buzzing flies,
to a cadaver, it becomes apparent that each new association is dependent not on A (if a fly looks like an A when considered as a
whole, a cadaver certainly does not) but upon the immediately preceding image; and each represents an expansion, an opening-up, an
increase in size. This is not an expansion like that of Ionesco's
chairs; it is not a duplication or a simple enlargement of the original
image—not just an exploding A. Rimbaud had already used this
opening-up process in *Le Bateau Ivre:* the boat becomes a peninsula
and finally a constellation, a sort of macrocosm in the universe.
Later, in the first of *Veillées* from *Les Illuminations,* the concept of
tranquil repose is juxtaposed to the idea of the essential importance
of a "friend," which in turn is intensified by a deeper and more personally meaningful relationship, that of the loved one who becomes

4. Lucien Sausy, *"Le Texte Exact des VOYELLES"* in *Les Nouvelles Littéraires,* September 2, 1933, p. 4.

involved with the poet's life and upon whom depends his very existence:

> *C'est le repos éclairé, ni fièvre ni langueur, sur le lit ou*
> *sur le pré.*
> *C'est l'ami ni ardent ni faible. L'ami.*
> *C'est l'aimée ni tourmentante ni tourmentée. L'aimée.*
> *L'air et le monde point cherchés. La vie.*

> [It is enlightened repose, neither fever nor languor, on
> the bed or on the meadow.
> It is the friend neither impassioned nor weak. The friend.
> It is the beloved neither tormenting nor tormented. The
> beloved.
> The air and the world not sought after. Life.]

Each "concept" is enlarged, intensified, and has broader implications than the one immediately preceding it. Considered from this point of view, *"golfes d'ombre"* does not need to be explained in terms of A, even though Sausy says that "gulfs" are "kinds of reversed V's, therefore A again"; rather, it should be understood in terms of the preceding image or idea, which is "death." Rimbaud most likely associated "shadow-filled gulfs" with "the valley of the shadow of death" in the twenty-third Psalm. "Shadow" is a Biblical reference consistently associated with death or with impending death, and "gulfs" are accurately described by Sausy as being places "where those who pass on sink down with no possible way to escape." Finally, an extension of the image and a further association brings one to the expression or suggestion of an emotion: apprehension or fear of death, suggested by the "shadow" which hides or veils the unknown, or at least uncertainty, awareness of something indistinguishable in its detail. (As we shall see in a later chapter, the color black evokes precisely this sort of idea and sensation for Claudel.) A, then, is more than black, more than a simple vowel; it is the key to the opening-up of a whole series of ideas, emotions, and sensations, a "beginning." Moreover, black, this death of hopes, is among the principal colors used consistently by Rimbaud throughout his works, and it very often suggests precisely the kind of concepts associated with it in *Voyelles*, as in the following examples:

DEATH: *Sur l'onde calme et noire où dorment les étoiles*
　　　　La blanche Ophélia flotte comme un grand lys

[On the calm black water where the stars sleep
White Ophelia floats like a great lily]

(*Ophélie*)

Au gibet noir, manchot aimable,
Dansent, dansent les paladins,
Les maigres paladins du diable,
Les squelettes de Saladins.

[On the black gallows, nice one-armed fellow,
The paladins are dancing, dancing,
The devil's thin paladins,
The skeletons of Saladins.]

(*Bal des Pendus*)

DEAD
HOPES: *Si je désire une eau d'Europe, c'est la flache*
Noire et froide où vers le crépuscule embaumé
Un enfant accroupi plein de tristesses, lâche
Un bateau frêle comme un papillon de mai.

[If I desire a water from Europe, it is the
Cold black puddle where toward the sweet-scented twilight
A squatting child full of sadness, releases
A boat fragile like a May butterfly.]

(*Le Bateau Ivre*)

. . . *Elle, toute*
froide, et noire, court! après le départ de l'homme!

[. . . She, all
cold, and black, runs! after the man's departure!]

(*Mémoire*)

Jouet de cet œil d'eau morne, je n'y puis prendre,
ô canot immobile! oh! bras trop courts! ni l'une
ni l'autre fleur: ni la jaune qui m'importune,
là; ni la bleue, amie à l'eau couleur de cendre.

[Toy of this mournful eye of water, I cannot pluck,
o motionless boat! oh! arms too short! either this
or the other flower: neither the yellow one that troubles me,
there; nor the friendly blue one in the ash-colored water.]

(*Mémoire*)

THE
UNKNOWN: . . . *la plus sinistre fumée noire*

[. . . the most ominous black smoke]

(Métropolitain)

If we accept this sort of exegesis as valid, the rest of the vowels—
along with their particular color, sensation, and idea associations—
become obvious, and we find that this interpretation is in keeping
with what Claudel had to say about the association of ideas and
images:

> *Tant de romanciers à la mode nous invitent à faire une explo-*
> *ration à l'intérieur, dans ce château de Barbe-Bleue, qui se*
> *trouve être aussi celui de la Belle au bois dormant. Ils nous*
> *ont remis toutes les clefs, sauf une seule, la plus importante,*
> *celle de la petite cellule où est enfermée notre conscience.*
> *Et ce mot de cellule éveille justement dans mon esprit une*
> *autre image, car pourquoi ne passerais-je pas d'une idée à*
> *l'autre par le chemin de la juxtaposition aussi bien que par*
> *celui de la logique?*

> [So many popular novelists invite us to explore within, in
> this Bluebeard's castle, which also happens to belong to
> Sleeping Beauty. They have laid before us all the keys, ex-
> cept one, the most important, the one to the little cell where
> our conscience is locked up. And this word "cell" properly
> awakens in my mind another image, for why shouldn't I
> pass from one idea to another using the path of juxtaposition
> as well as of logic?]

(Seigneur, Apprenez-nous à Prier)[5]

We also realize not only that Rimbaud inspired a religious *élan* tantamount to fanaticism, as well as thematic material, but also that
there are definite Rimbaldian echoes in the technique of Claudel's
poetic attitudes.

> . . . *E, candeurs des vapeurs et des tentes,*
> *Lances des glaciers fiers, rois blancs, frissons d'ombelles;*

5. *Seigneur, Apprenez-nous à prier,* p. 12. Claudel underlines the importance
of this kind of association of ideas in reference to poetry in general and to
Rimbaud in particular. See *Journal,* Tome I, Cahier 3, November 1915, p. 344:
"C'est un procédé d'association d'idées tout à fait analogue à celui de la poésie.
Un Rimbaud en aurait fait un vers . . ."

> [. . . E, candors of vapors and tents,
> Lances of proud glaciers, white kings, shudders of umbellate
> blossoms;]

The E, with its three lateral prongs, suggests the blowpipes of proud, ancient glassmakers, *"lances des glaciers fiers"* (long before glass panes and mirrors were pressed they were blown, which accounts for the bull's-eye windowpanes in old homes). The prongs could also be the elongated shapes of immense, "arrogant" glaciers. Or, by extending and humanizing the image, these prongs become the phalanx of lances borne by the armor-clad troops of medieval "white kings" leading armies to the Crusades against dark-skinned Turks (in *Le Bateau Ivre*, written shortly before *Voyelles*, Rimbaud alludes to medieval Europe: *"Je regrette l'Europe aux anciens parapets"* ["I miss Europe of the [with its] old parapets"]). "White kings" also brings to mind the King of Kings, garbed as Rimbaud represents him in *Une Saison en Enfer:* "Jesus walked on the troubled waters, white with long brown hair." In turn, white suggests cold as well as white umbels or white umbellate blossoms, *"frissons d'ombelles."* But since *frissons* suggests not only "cold" and "white" but also "shudders," these "shuddering umbellate blossoms" must be blown by a breeze—the presence of an unseen wind, a certain mystery. In each case—the proud ancient glassblowers, the "fierce" (*fier* from the Latin *ferus*) white summit of glaciers, the greatness of armies and medieval kings, and the mystery of a breeze in white umbels—there is an aspect of the candor and simplicity of vaporous reveries and campers in the heart of nature, *"candeurs des vapeurs et des tentes."* "Candor" refers to "innocence," the unsullied purity of life in the open, under the stars— *"Mon auberge était à la Grande-Ourse"* ["My inn was at the Big Dipper"] (*Ma Bohème*)—the simplicity of tents pitched far from the complexity of modern civilization and its corrupting influence (as we find in *Le Bateau Ivre* and numerous poems of Rimbaud in which a longing for the simplicity of life in nature is expressed). Like innocence and virginity, *candeur* is symbolized by white (as in a white bridal gown, Ophelia's gown) and in fact the word derives from the Latin *candor,* brilliant whiteness; mists, vapors—mystery again—also have a quality of white about them. The progression here, then, is from the candid simplicity of existence in nature and of proud men's dreams amidst the immensity of glaciers in solitary nature—far from encroaching civilization—to phalanxes of power, to the authority of kings and of the King, and finally to the uncontrollable and mysterious all-enveloping wind, the essentially un-

knowable and unseen, comparable to *"golfes d'ombre."* And just
as there is a contrast between black and white in *Ophélie—"Voici
plus de mille ans que la triste Ophélie / Passe, fantôme blanc, sur le
long fleuve noir"* ["For more than a thousand years sad Ophelia /
Has been passing, a white phantom, down the long black river"]—
there is a contrast between the first and second series of images in
Voyelles: black and white, death and candid existence. Yet both
are involved with a suggestion of uncertainty, implied rather than
stated, the kind of perpetual question found throughout Rimbaud's
poetry, the unfathomable. Each of these vowels, in its own way,
suggests the vast unknown mystery of the ineffable, the ineluctable.

As in the case of the color black, certain of the ideas suggested by
white in *Voyelles* are associated with white in other poems by Rimbaud:

INNOCENCE,
SIMPLICITY,
PURITY,
CANDOR:

> *—Et le Poëte dit qu'aux rayons des étoiles*
> *Tu viens chercher, la nuit, les fleurs que tu cueillis,*
> *Et qu'il a vu sur l'eau, couchée en ses longs voiles,*
> *La blanche Ophélia flotter, comme un grand lys.*

[—And the Poet says that under the rays of the stars
You come at night to look for the flowers you picked,
And that he has seen on the water, lying in her long veils,
White Ophelia floating, like a great lily.]

(*Ophélie*)

> *Et quand, ayant rentré tous ses noeuds d'hystéries,*
> *Elle verra, sous les tristesses du bonheur,*
> *L'amant rêver au blanc million des Maries,*
> *Au matin de la nuit d'amour, avec douleur:*

[And when, having quieted all her knots of hysteria,
She sees, under the sadnesses of bliss,
The lover dreaming of a white million Marys,
The morning after the night of love, with pain:]

(*Les Premières Communions*)

> *Tant que la lame n'aura*
> *Pas coupé cette cervelle,*
> *Ce paquet blanc, vert et gras,*
> *A vapeur jamais nouvelle,*

[As long as the blade has
Not cut off that brain,
That white green fatty package,
With vapor never new,]

(*Honte*)

REVERIE: *Quelquefois je vois au ciel des plages sans fin
couvertes de blanches nations en joie.*

[Sometimes I see sky beaches all covered with
joyful white nations.]

(*Adieu*)

*Buvez! Quand la lumière arrive intense et folle,
Fouillant à vos côtés les luxes ruisselants,
Vous n'allez pas baver, sans geste, sans parole,
Dans vos verres, les yeux perdus aux lointains blancs?*

[Drink! When the night arrives intense and mad,
Elaborating at your side the streaming luxuries,
You are not going to drool, with no gesture, with no word,
Into your glasses, your eyes lost in the white distances?

(*L'Orgie Parisienne* ou *Paris se Repeuple*)

*O Douceurs, ô monde, ô musique! Et là, les formes, les sueurs,
les chevelures et les yeux, flottant. Et les larmes blanches,
bouillantes,—ô douceurs!—et la voix féminine arrivée au fond
des volcans et des grottes arctiques.*

[O sweetness, O world, O music! And here, forms, sweating,
hair and eyes, floating. And white tears, boiling,—O sweet-
nesses!—and a woman's voice in the depths of the volcanoes
and the arctic grottoes.]

(*Barbare*)

INELUCTABLE: *Un rayon blanc, tombant du haut du ciel,
anéantit cette comédie.*

[A white ray, falling from the top of the
sky, annihilates this comedy.]

(*Les Ponts*)

INFINITE: *L'infini roulé blanc de ta nuque à tes reins;*

[The infinite rolled white from the nape of your
neck to your loins;]

(*L'Etoile a pleuré . . .*)

If in *"E blanc"* there was a suggestion of candid existence, in *"I rouge"* we find an affirmation of all the violent passions to which man is subject:

> *I, pourpres, sang craché, rire des lèvres belles*
> *Dans la colère ou les ivresses pénitentes . . .*

[I, purples, spit blood, laughter of beautiful lips
In anger or penitent drunkenness . . .]

The shape of the vowel itself suggests an erect man, as in a stick drawing; or possibly, according to Sausy, a spurt of blood. But it is not the blue blood coursing through human veins as in *Les Reparties de Nina: "J'irais, pressant / Ton corps, comme une enfant qu'on couche, / Ivre du sang / Qui coule, bleu, sous ta peau blanche / Aux tons rosés"* ["I would move on, pressing / Your body, like a child one is putting to bed, / Drunk with the blood / That runs blue, under your white skin / With rosy tints"]; it is the spilled blood of violence, *"sang craché,"* and of men purple with anger, *"pourpres."* Red is also the color of lips, and I, turned on its side, evokes the menacing grimace of angrily clenched teeth: *"rire des lèvres belles / Dans la colère";* it also evokes the straight, unsmiling, sober gaze, the thoughtful and somber look of a guilt-ridden man who realizes in anguish the mistake of his excesses and of his heady drunkenness, who realizes too that an eventual atonement for his "revolt" can come only through righteous penitence, *"les ivresses pénitentes,"* through recognition of the inescapable presence of something beyond himself, of man's responsibility to a higher order than himself. Rimbaud cannot be placed among the existentialists, certainly not among the Sartrian existentialists, for, by placing man in this context of "shadow-filled gulfs," of the invisible wind in "shudders of umbels" that suggest mystery, and of the pious humility of "penitent intoxications," he recognizes not only that man is violent, menacingly choleric, expansively prone to willful and untempered excesses, but also that he is involved with an awareness of his own powerlessness when confronted with an inexplicable mystery requiring nothing short of humble penitence.

Red, then, is the passionate side of man, or of Rimbaud himself, and it is in this context that he uses this color in his poetry:

VIOLENCE,
ANGER: *Tandis que les crachats rouges de la mitraille*
              Sifflent tout le jour par l'infini du ciel bleu;

Qu'écarlates ou verts, près du Roi qui les raille,
Croulent les bataillons en masse dans le feu . . .

[While the red spit of grapeshot
Whistles all day through the infinite of the blue sky;
While scarlet or green, near the King jeering at them
Whole battalions collapse in the fire . . .]

(*Le Mal*)

Ils ont schako, sabre et tam-tam,
Non la vieille boîte à bougies;
Et des yoles qui n'ont jam. . . jam. . .
Fendent le lac aux eaux rougies!

[They have shako, saber, and tom-tom,
Not the old candle box;
And skiffs that have nev. . . nev. . .
Plough through the lake of reddened waters!]

(*Chant de Guerre Parisien*)

Et les Ruraux, qui se prélassent
Dans de longs accroupissements,
Entendront des rameaux qui cassent
Parmi les rouges froissements.

[And the Rustics who loll about
In long squattings,
Will hear branches breaking
Among the red rustlings.]

(*Chant de Guerre Parisien*)

PASSION: *. . . Il s'aidait*
De journaux illustrés où, rouge, il regardait
Des Espagnoles rire et des Italiennes.

[. . . He was helped
By illustrated newspapers where, red, he saw
Spanish and Italian girls laugh.]

(*Les Poëtes de Sept Ans*)

(lines like these point to the probability that *Les Poètes de Sept Ans* should really be entitled *Les Poëtes de Seize Ans*, Rimbaud's age at the time he wrote the poem)

Tu n'est jamais la Sœur de charité, jamais,
Ni regard noir, ni ventre où dort une ombre rousse . . .

[You are never the Sister of charity, never,
Neither black look, nor belly where sleeps a russet shadow . . .]
(*Les Sœurs de Charité*)

*Où, teignant tout à coup les bleuités, délires
Et rhythmes lents sous les rutilements du jour,
Plus fortes que l'alcool, plus vastes que nos lyres,
Fermentent les rousseurs amères de l'amour!*

[Where, suddenly dyeing the blueness, delirium
And slow rhythms under the glitter of the day,
Stronger than alcohol, vaster than our lyres,
Ferments the bitter redness of love!]
(*Le Bateau Ivre*)

REVOLT: *Ce soir, à Circeto des hautes glaces, grasse comme
le poisson, et enluminée comme les dix mois de
la nuit rouge. . .*

[This evening, to Circeto of the icy heights, fat as
fish, and flushed, illuminated like the ten months
of the red night . . .]
(*Dévotion*)

(this is apparently a reference to *"j'ai dansé sur les flots . . . dix
nuits"* ["I danced on the waves . . . ten nights"] from *Le Bateau
Ivre;* certainly, a similar mentality to that found in the earlier poem,
a continuity of thought, is indicated)

. . . je danse le sabbat dans une rouge clairière.

[. . . I am dancing the witches' sabbath in a red clearing.]
(*Mauvais Sang*)

In contrast with the intense emotions of humanity is the serene
calm of nature, the divine mystery which no form of alchemy can
really fathom or disturb; the inscrutability of its peace is reflected
in the "wrinkles" of "great studious brows" incapable of penetrat-
ing the depth of its secret and as hopelessly impotent as *Les Assis.*
Such are the implications of *"U vert"*:

*U, cycles, vibrements divins des mers virides,
Paix des pâtis semés d'animaux, paix des rides
Que l'alchimie imprime aux grands fronts studieux . . .*

[U, cycles, divine vibrations of viridian seas,
Peace of pastures scattered with animals, peace of the wrinkles
That alchemy prints on great studious brows . . .]

Its shape evokes a tuning fork with its cyclic beats, *"cycles,"* and also the image of a bay with calm ripples, or waves, in shallow green water, *"cycles, vibrements divins des mers virides"* (the sea takes on a deep blue color only in deeper waters; seen from land, enclosed as in a bay, water appears to be green, especially on Atlantic shores). This "divine" green calmness in turn evokes the pastoral setting of animals grazing peacefully in green pastures. Since these "divine vibrations" are associated with a pastoral scene, we are once again reminded of Rimbaud's description of Christ in *Nuit de l'Enfer* from *Une Saison en Enfer: "La lanterne nous le montra debout, blanc et des tresses brunes, au flanc d'une vague d'émeraude"* ["The lantern showed him to us standing, white, with long brown hair, on the flank of an emerald wave"], the "divine shepherd" bringing peace to the world and associated with nature. Moreover, it is an impenetrable nature, like the mystery of Christ's divinity, or at least one that does not bow to alchemy, *"paix des rides / Que l'alchimie imprime aux grands fronts studieux"*—since wrinkles on the forehead come especially from frowning or quizzical looks and therefore suggest incomprehension or fruitless study, and it is "alchemy" that has "imprinted" these "wrinkles." There is here at least some small suggestion of a paradoxical irony, since Rimbaud would become *"le fils du soleil,"* "the sun's son," through "Alchemy of the Word," if he could; yet he indicates that "alchemy" can lead only to defeat, long before saying so in *Une Saison en Enfer*. In effect, just as he was to mock science and materialism later on, he is mocking these "great studious brows" who would change nature, who would penetrate its secrets in other than a purely poetic way or through other than poetic associations. For Rimbaud, as for Claudel, only an acceptance of nature as it is, of its greenness, can erase the "wrinkles" and bring peace and, in a sense, salvation "to the great studious brows"; only that love of nature which he expresses elsewhere and which he likens to physical love of a woman as he imagines it must be: *"Et j'irai loin, bien loin, comme un bohémien, / Par la nature,—heureux comme avec une femme"* ["And I shall go far, very far, like a bohemian,/ Through nature,—happy as with a woman"] (*Sensation*). This theme of peace in and through nature, associated with green—and, at times, contrasted with red, is to be found in many poems written by Rimbaud both before and after *Voyelles:*

PEACE:

—Quand la femme, portée un instant, l'épouvante,
Amour, appel de vie et chanson d'action,

Viennent la Muse verte et la Justice ardente
Le déchirer de leur auguste obsession.

[—When woman, borne for a moment, appals him,
Love, call of life and song of action,
The green Muse and ardent Justice come
To tear him apart with their august obsession.]

(*Les Sœurs de Charité*)

Nos grands bois sentiraient la sève,
Et le soleil
Sablerait d'or fin leur grand rêve
Vert et vermeil.

[Our great woods would smell of sap,
And the sun
Would sprinkle with fine gold their great
Green and vermilion dream.]

(*Les Reparties de Nina*)

(contrast between red and green, between the passion and the peacefulness of love)

Un soldat jeune, bouche ouverte, tête nue,
Et la nuque baignant dans le frais cresson bleu,
Dort; il est étendu dans l'herbe, sous la nue,
Pâle dans son lit vert où la lumière pleut.

[A young soldier, his mouth open, his head bare,
And the nape of his neck bathing in the fresh blue watercress,
Sleeps; he is stretched out on the grass, under the clouds,
Pale on his green bed where light is raining.]

(*Le Dormeur du Val*)

(though the soldier is actually dead, the scene is one of peacefulness, of a soldier asleep in the peacefulness of nature; in this poem, too, green and red are contrasted, when the "red" of violence—two red bullet holes—is mentioned in the last line of the poem: *"il a deux trous rouges au côté droit"* ["he has two red holes on his right side"])

NATURE: *Le printemps est évident, car*
          Du cœur des Propriétés vertes,
          Le vol de Thiers et de Picard
          Tient ses splendeurs grandes ouvertes!

          [Spring is in evidence, for
          From the heart of the green Estates

The flight of Thiers and Picard
Holds its splendors wide open!
(Chant de Guerre Parisien)

. . . quoiqu'on n'ait fait jamais d'une cité
Ulcère plus puant à la Nature verte . . .

[. . . although man has never made of a city
A more stinking ulcer on green Nature . . .]
(L'Orgie Parisienne ou *Paris se Repeuple)*

(apparently even mid-nineteenth-century Paris had its pollution problems)

Les robes vertes et déteintes des fillettes
font les saules, d'où sautent les oiseaux sans brides.

[The little girls' green faded dresses
make willows, out of which hop unbridled birds.]
(Mémoire)

Up to this point of our study, we have been confronted with a series of contrasts between the mystery of death and the mystery of life, between violent, unbridled human passions and "the peace that passeth understanding," all symbolized and complemented by contrasts in associations of imagery and contrasts of color. However, in themselves they are incomplete; some unifying factor that also sums them all up is required to put them in their proper perspective. It is *"O bleu,"* an unending circle, that suggests this supreme element:

O, suprême Clairon plein des strideurs étranges,
Silences traversés des Mondes et des Anges:
—O l'Oméga, rayon violet de Ses Yeux!

[O, supreme Clarion full of strange stridors,
Silences crossed by Worlds and Angels:
—O the Omega, violet beam of His Eyes!]

The shape of O resembles the bell of a trumpet. It is the "supreme Clarion full of strange stridors," announcing on one hand the harmony of the spheres, *"Silences traversés des Mondes,"* and on the other, the day of final judgment, *"et des Anges."* It is the "Trumpet of trumpets" recalling the vastness of the heavens—which seem blue when seen from the earth—as well as the immensity of the kingdom of God; it is involved with the planets and the stars, *"Mondes,"* but also with the mystery of the Creator and of the afterlife, of an exis-

tence beyond this life or at least different from it, *"Anges."* All of
these are finally summarized in God Himself: *"O l'Oméga, rayon
violet de Ses Yeux!"* Given the capital letters of *"Clairon,"* *"Oméga,"* and *"Ses Yeux,"* the mention of *"Anges"* (also capitalized),
the imperial color of *"le rayon violet de Ses Yeux,"* and the use of
the adjective *"suprême"* (as in "the Supreme Being"), it would be
quibbling to deny that the last line of the sonnet is a distinct reference to God. It might be objected that this is yet another of Rimbaud's subtly ironic blasphemies, except that the tone of the rest
of the poem is in no way blasphemous; moreover, the idea of the
mystery of God and of His creation gives unity to all of the previous images. Certainly the mystery of the universe is elsewhere associated with the color blue in Rimbaud's works, as in *Soleil et
Chair: "Qu'elle bondisse libre, et l'Homme aura la Foi!/—Pour-
quoi l'azur muet et l'espace insondable?"* ["Let her bound free,
and Man will have Faith!/—Why the mute azure and the unfathomable space?"].

However, not only color but sound as well serves to qualify the
vowels and to give unity to the imagery. It is not so much that
each vowel has a particular sound as that each is associated with
the general concept of sound, rhythm, movement: A—*"bombinent"* (sound); E—*"frissons"* (movement); I—*"rire"* (sound); U—
"vibrements" (movement); O—*"Clairon"* (sound) and *"traversés"*
(movement). The alternation of sound and movement, the predominant musical characteristics of the first four vowels, is
summed up by a combination of them, each equally important,
in O. Within each of the series of images associated with these
vowels, there is a fundamental tone or rhythm: A—the rhythm
of the verse lines is uneven, but the syllables are mostly short, and
"bombinent"—a neologism that was probably suggested to Rimbaud by the Latin *bombus* [buzzing] and *bombinatio* and perhaps
too by the scientific name for a particular kind of fly, *Bombylius*—
is used for onomatopaeic effect; E—the vowel sounds are elongated,
stretched out, as in *"candeurs,"* *"vapeurs,"* *"tentes,"* *"lances,"*
and *"ombelles,"* slowing down the movement of the lines; I—a rap-
id succession of high close vowels effects a short, staccato rhythm;
U is characterized by the juxtaposition of nasalized mid and low
open vowels, as in *"vibrements divins"* and *"grands fronts"*; and
finally, O is identified with the slow, ponderous rhythm and full
tone evoked by low open vowels. Moreover, the frequency and intensity of contrasts between the vowel sounds within each series of
images as well as the frequency in the use of a particular vowel with-

in single lines of verse increase with each new series, again in a kind of opening-up process, just as the degree of emotional involvement is intensified in the first of *Veillées,* or of cosmic involvement in *Le Bateau Ivre.*

In the series *E blanc,* for example, we find only two instances of particularly striking contrasts: the "black" vowel A is used to express ideas associated with "white" E and is contrasted with E within a single word: *"can-deurs," "va-peurs."* In the I series, the passionate side of man is expressed not only by the images associated with I, but also by the staccato rhythm and insistently repeated shrill sounds of the high and mid close vowels, *i, a, é, è,* that, in contrast with the single low open vowel of *"pourpres,"* pile up and produce the effect of tension characteristic of the emotions described by Rimbaud (*"sang craché," "rire des lèvres belles," "la colère," "ivresses pénitentes"*) in much the same way as they suggest violence or intensity when associated with red in other of his poems: *"crachat rouge"* ["red spit"] (*Le Mal*), *"la nuit rouge"* ["the red night"] (*Dévotion*), *"Des Peaux-Rouges criards les avaient pris pour cibles"* ["Loud, shrieking Redskins had used them for targets"] (*Le Bateau Ivre*)—note that in this last example, the word *"criards"* means not only "shrieking" or "yelping" but also "loud" (as in "loud-colored" clothing) and thus intensifies both the sound and color—*"reflet vermeil"* ["vermilion reflection"] (*Les Etrennes des Orphelins*), and *"tas sombre de haillons saignant de bonnets rouges"* ["dark, somber pile of rags bleeding with red caps"] (*Le Forgeron*). In the series *U vert,* a change in the categories of contrasts introduces a new aspect of the opening-up process, for the importance of nature is emphasized not only by the contrasts between the "red" scenes of violence in the previous two verse lines and the "green" serenity of this first tercet, but also by the contrasts between the "red" vowels—*"cycles," "vibrements divins," "virides," "pâtis," "animaux," "rides," "alchimie," "Imprime,"* even *"studieux"*—and the "green" associations of imagery within the tercet itself. Rather than contradicting or attenuating the effect of colors and sounds associated with previous vowels, the juxtaposition of sounds and ideas to which Rimbaud assigns diametrically opposed values serves to heighten the contrast between images, colors, and sounds, thereby giving greater intensity to each of them, and, in this case, preparing the final resolution of those contrasts in the second tercet. The effect of the use of the "red" vowel I to express images associated with U, is to intensify the "greenness" of nature. Finally, in the second tercet, beginning with *"O, suprême Clairon,"* Rimbaud pulls out all the stops, as it were, and uses all of the vowels with varying degrees of contrasts in a baroque hyperbole of imagery and sound. Starting with the first associations of colors, sounds, and images suggested by *"A-noir,"* an expanding progression throughout the sonnet builds up to a final crescendo which is interrupted by an abrupt cadence: the high close vowels of *"Ses Yeux"* provide a sharp contrast with the low open vowels, *"O l'Oméga,"* that begin the final alexandrine. In all of these associations of ideas and sensations, there is only one allusion to olfactory experiences: *"puanteurs cruelles";* but these odors do not characterize the image of death, they simply recall something associated with death. This substantiates our earlier observation that olfactory sensations are secondary in Rimbaud's works.

The colors Rimbaud associates with the vowels in this poem are the predominant ones of his palette, those he uses most frequently in his poetry.[6] They belong to life—*"couleurs propres de la vie,"* as

6. The frequency of colors in Rimbaud's poetry is as follows: in the *Poésies*—exclusive of the *Album Zutique* and the Latin verses—twenty-nine different shades of color are mentioned, for a total of four hundred and six mentions of color (the number after each color designates the number of times that particular color is mentioned): *noir,* 75; *blanc,* 49; *vert,* 36; *rouge,* 32; *bleu,* 50; *argent,* 4; *lacté,* 1; *neigeux,* 2; *rougi,* 1; *rougeur,* 1; *carmin,* 1; *rubi,* 1; *écarlate,* 1; *ocreux,* 2; *vermeil,* 8; *roux,* 7; couleur de *sang,* 4; *rose,* 21; *orange,* 1; *bronze,* 1; *blond,* 10; *jaune,* 16; *azur,* 12; *ultramarin,* 1; *violet,* 8; *pourpre,* 1; *brun,* 14; *gris,* 10; *or,* 36. These shades divide up into six distinct color groups, in the following proportions: *ROUGE* (including *rose, sang, roux, vermeil, écarlate, carmin, rougeur, rubi, rougi, ocreux*), 79 or 19.4%; *BLEU* (including *azur, ultramarin*), 63 or 15.5%; *BLANC* (including *lacté, neigeux*), 52 or 12.8%; *VERT,* 36 or 9% and *OR* (including *jaune, blond*), 61 or 15% of all colors mentioned in the *Poésies.* 90% of the time, it is one of the colors from these six basic groups which is mentioned, whereas they represent only 80% of all the shades Rimbaud uses. If only the six basic colors which predominate are considered (*noir, blanc, rouge, vert, bleu* and *or*), the proportions are even more striking: 68.4% of *all* the mentions of color is accounted for by only 21.5% of all the shades Rimbaud uses, and with the exception of *or,* these are the colors found in *Voyelles.*

In *Les Illuminations,* twenty-six different shades of color are mentioned for a total of 90 mentions of color: *noir,* 13; *blanc,* 7; *rouge,* 9; *vert,* 5; *bleu,* 8; *or,* 11; *argenté,* 1; *opaline,* 1; *écarlate,* 2; *carminé,* 1; *roux,* 1; *rubi,* 1; *saignant,* 1; *rose,* 4; *ambre,* 1; *orange,* 2; *jaune,* 2; *blond,* 2; *azur,* 2; *indigo,* 1; *émeraude,* 1; *pourpre,* 1; *violet,* 4; *brun,* 2; *gris,* 6; *tricolor,* 1. Here again, there are six distinct color groups in the following proportions: *ROUGE* (*écarlate, rubi, carminé, roux, sang, rose*), 19 or 21.1%; *NOIR,* 13 or 14.4%; *BLEU* (*azur, indigo*), 11 or 12.2%; *OR* (*jaune, blond, ambre*), 16 or 17.6%; *BLANC* (*opaline, argenté*), 9 or 10%; *VERT,* 5 or 5%. Once again, we find almost the same distribution as in the *Poésies:* 90% of the time, it is one of the colors from

he says in *Being Beauteous*—are taken from nature, from the world around him. It may well be, as Verlaine said to Gide, that "he just saw them like that, that's all." It has been said that it was about the time he wrote *Voyelles* that he was studying occultism. Yet many of the examples we have chosen to illustrate his use of colors show that he was using them in the context and with the symbols of *Voyelles* long before he wrote this sonnet. This does not prove that he did not read Lévi, but it does suggest that what he read, if indeed he read anything at all on occultism, served in part to substantiate the kind of symbolism towards which he had already been previously evolving. One needs only to have been a sensitive child oneself and to have reread, as an adult, essays written when one was an adolescent, to discover that frequently ideas that have been published in books occur to a child long before he ever reads those books. There seem to be certain truths that are inescapable to an observant individual, even, and perhaps especially, to a precocious child; there can be no doubt that Rimbaud—whose themes of revolt and discontent and whose sensitivity to sound and color appear in *Le Soleil était encore chaud* as early as 1864, when he was barely ten years old—was just such a precocious child, and that consideration must be given to the poet's own genius, his own sensitivity, his own powers of observation and subjective exteriorization, his own inspiration. It may well be that the Jungian concept of the artist who has some innate subconscious association with alchemical processes, in an abstract sense, applies to Rimbaud, and that he had

---

these six basic groups that is mentioned, whereas they represent only 80% of the total number of different shades Rimbaud uses. And if only the six basic colors are considered, we find that 59% of the times color is mentioned, only 27% of the number of different shades is used. Thus the same observation applies here as in *Poésies:* with the exception of gold, these are the same colors as those used in *Voyelles.*

In *Une Saison en Enfer,* thirteen different shades of color are mentioned, for a total of twenty-nine mentions of color: *noir,* 4; *blanc,* 4; *rouge,* 3; *vert,* 2; *bleu,* 2; *or,* 7; *rubi,* 1; *brun,* 1; *émeraude,* 1; *jaune,* 1; *azur,* 1; *argent,* 1; *violet,* 1. Here, too, approximately 90% of all mentions of color are accounted for by 80% of the various shades in these six basic groups: *ROUGE (rubi),* 4 or 13.8%; *NOIR,* 4 or 13.8%; *BLEU (azur),* 3 or 10%; *BLANC,* 4 or 13.8%; *OR (jaune),* 8 or 31%; *VERT (émeraude),* 3 or 10%. If only the six basic colors are considered, we find that 76% of all mentions of color are represented by only 47% of all the shades mentioned, and that with the exception of "gold," they are found in *Voyelles.*

One final observation to be made about these colors is that of the six categories indicated, three are particularly noticeable and predominant in *Saison en Enfer* and *Illuminations: rouge, noir* and *or*—red, black and gold.

some psychic awareness of a sort of "alchemical" application of colors to his poetry. In this case, he need not have read Lévi to have become aware of these color associations, nor did he have to remember his ABC book. He need only to have had two eyes, two ears—but not a very good nose—and a certain power of observation and of imagination. For his poetry is above all a direct expression of his own existence, of his passions, of his emotions, of what he is observing and feeling as he writes. It is not essential or even really important that Rimbaud's vowels may or may not evoke the same sounds, colors, and associations of ideas that other people have experienced with particular colors and sounds; for what Rimbaud has transcribed is his own world; his own vision; his own fantasies of women who seem beyond his reach and outside the scope of his comprehension, as in *Les Reparties de Nina* or *La Maline;* his own "dreamed loves," as in *Ma Bohème.* It is in great part, perhaps more than anything else—more even than the virtuosity of his poetic technique—this immediacy of expression that gives to his poetry the impact it has upon the reader. Others have "looked back in anger," have written and recorded their lives in retrospect, whereas Rimbaud, having assimilated the techniques of poetry while still a child, expresses and records his life and visions, his "body and soul," as he lives and experiences them. If he says that he will only be able to explain to us the "latent births" of the vowels some day in the future, *"Je dirai quelque jour vos naissances latentes"* ["I will tell one day your latent births"], it is because he himself does not know them or has not analyzed them consciously; they are being born, as it were, simultaneously with the process of his poetic creation and inspiration. As Cœuvre says in *La Ville,* the poet does not explain, he utters. And in *Une Saison en Enfer,* which, in the words he used to answer his mother's question, means "what it says, literally and in every sense," Rimbaud writes, *"J'inventai la couleur des voyelles! . . . Je réglai la forme et le mouvement de chaque consonne, et, avec des rhythmes instinctifs, je me flattai d'inventer un verbe poétique accessible, un jour ou l'autre, à tous les sens"* ["I invented the color of vowels! . . . I governed the form and the movement of each consonant, and, with instinctive rhythms, I imagined that I was inventing a poetic language accessible some day to all the senses"]. For the artist, "invention" often means "recall," or a summoning up from the subconscious, or a refocusing and re-evaluation of lived experiences or inspiration simultaneous with the act of writing, painting, or composing. Thus, the fact that Rimbaud "invented" the color of the vowels suggests that at the time he wrote the poem, there was no more meaning to them than the acknowledgment of certain observations he had made, conscious or unconscious.

Only one of the colors that Rimbaud uses extensively in the rest of his poetry is absent in *Voyelles:* gold. Yet upon consideration of the symbolic value of gold for Rimbaud, it becomes apparent why it is not here. Gold represents unattainable perfection—at least, unattainable within the limits of his terrestrial struggle, except possibly through poetry (and this was eventually an *échec,* a defeat, for him)—the lost paradise, the ideal:

> *J'aurais voulu montrer aux enfants ces dorades*
> *Du flot bleu, ces poissons d'or, ces poissons chantants . . .*

[I would have wished to show children those sunfish
Of the blue wave, those golden fish, those singing fish . . .]

(Le Bateau Ivre)

> *—Est-ce en ces nuits sans fonds que tu dors et t'exiles,*
> *Million d'oiseaux d'or, ô future Vigueur?*

[—Is it in those endless nights that you are sleeping and exiled,
Million golden birds, O future Vigor?]

(Le Bateau Ivre)

> *Et quand il a fui—tel qu'un écureuil—*
> *Son rire tremble encore à chaque feuille,*
> *Et l'on voit épeuré par un bouvreuil*
> *Le Baiser d'or du Bois, qui se recueille.*

[And when he has fled—like a squirrel—
His laughter still trembles on each leaf,
And you see frightened by a bullfinch
The golden Kiss of the Wood, meditating.]

(Tête de Faune)

> *Pleurant, je voyais de l'or—et ne pus boire.*

[Crying, I saw gold—and could not drink.]

(L'Alchimie du Verbe)

As it is used in the above quotations, and especially in the last one from *Une Saison en Enfer,* it is clear that gold refers to the elusive *au-delà* that Rimbaud envisioned but never attained. *Voyelles,* on the other hand, represents all that was within the poet's reach or within his power to comprehend, all that comprised present existence, the realizable cosmos, as it were. Gold, therefore, being beyond the reach and vision of ordinary mortals and even of exceptional poets, logically has no place in *Voyelles*. Or if, as has been claimed, Rimbaud's gold is the alchemist's gold—unattained even though envisioned by Rimbaud—at least it does not reflect Lévi but, rather, something more deeply personal—Rimbaud's subconscious.

Verlaine has been accused of oversimplifying Rimbaud's poetic intentions. One wonders whether others, in their ardent enthusiasm for the striking beauty and hermeticism of his poems, and for analysis, are not equally guilty of overcomplicating these works. At least one individual, François Coppée, seems to have thought so:

> Rimbaud, fumiste réussi,
> Dans un sonnet que je déplore,
> Veut que les lettres O, E, I,
> Forment le drapeau tricolore.

> [Rimbaud, successful fraud,
> In a sonnet that I deplore,
> Wants the letters O, E, I,
> To form the Tricolor.][7]

Certainly, Rimbaud has given the world a poetry that has some meaning for everyone, even if no one is in agreement about it. But whatever his intentions actually were—and we can in all honesty only hypothesize and speculate about them—the fact remains that there is a unity in his poetry: a unity of concept, of performance, and of idea, to which we find an aesthetic key, if not a new aesthetic, in *Voyelles*. After the detailed analysis of the individual words and lines, of the rhyme and meter, of the most minute details of a poem, one must finally ask how the poem strikes one as a whole. What is its initial impact? What impression does it leave? What is its general tone? Whatever else *Voyelles* may imply, its tone is one of color and sound in association with certain ideas intensified by consistent symbolic values—a poetic concept of primary importance to Claudel.

7. François Coppée, *Ballade* (*Annales littéraires*, March 15, 1893), quoted in Rimbaud, *Œuvres Complètes*, p. 682.

7.
Correlations of Imagery

The implicit statement in *Voyelles* of the role of color and sound in Rimbaud's poetry and of their general importance in his poetic concepts becomes in *Conversations dans le Loir-et-Cher* a very explicit expression of the symbolic essence of these two elements, of their relationship to each other, and of their correlation with human emotions and feelings and with what Claudel refers to as the soul.

Imagery in color

Claudel begins his argument by making a comparison between the states of different souls and the variations or nuances of color:

> *Pour moi si pour mettre les âmes ensemble je voulais demander une image à l'art humain, ce ne serait pas les pierres que je choisirais qui durement se retiennent et s'empêchent l'une par l'autre de tomber, l'une à l'autre prêtant le secours de sa propre inertie. C'est les couleurs que je ferais apparaître.*

> If, in order to put souls together, I wished to ask of human art an image, I would not choose stones, which harshly restrain themselves and keep each other from falling, lending each other the help of their own inertia. I would make colors appear.
>
> (*Conversations dans le Loir-et-Cher*)[1]

These colors are not independent, any more than individuals are completely independent or can live isolated in the world; they have a relationship with some exterior, unifying force: *"chacune à elle-même insuffisante et reliée par le désir à l'iris"* ["each insufficient unto

---

1. *Conversations dans le Loir-et-Cher*, pp. 56–57.

itself and bound to the iris by desire"].[2] Yet each is distinct; each
has its own properties: *"chacune allumée par sa propre différence"*
["each lighted by its own difference"].[3] And, just as an object has
the property of a certain color but needs illumination for its particular color to be distinguishable, each soul needs light—which, for
Claudel, is God, the Giver-of-life, the Creator—for its individual qualities to become visible: *"travaillée dans sa substance même par la
lumière, elle révèle, où pas de pigments l'offusquent, sa propre
qualité"* ["worked in its very substance by light, it reveals, where
no pigments obscure it, its own quality"].[4] The correspondence between souls and colors in Claudel's thought is further established by
his definition of color as the soul illumined by light; *"le mélange de
l'âme avec la lumière"* ["the commingling of the soul with light"].[5]
And each color of the spectrum, especially each primary color, has
a specific value for Claudel. Furthermore, as is true of virtually everything he is involved with, these colors have a definite association with
his religious feelings. As he makes clear in *La Dérivation* from *Connaissance de l'Est,* colors evoke the very essence of his cosmic religious spirit:

> *A l'heure où la sacrée lumière provoque à toute sa réponse
> l'ombre qu'elle décompose, la surface de ces eaux à mon
> immobile navigation ouvre le jardin sans fleurs. Entre ces
> gras replis violets, voici l'eau peinte comme du reflet des
> cierges, voici l'ambre, voici le vert le plus doux, voici la
> couleur de l'or. Mais taisons-nous: cela que je sais est à moi,
> et alors que cette eau deviendra noire, je posséderai la nuit
> tout entière avec le nombre intégral des étoiles visibles et
> invisibles.*

[At the hour when sacred light produces as its whole response
the darkness that it decomposes, the surface of these waters
to my motionless navigation opens the flowerless garden. Between these fat violet folds, here is water painted like the reflection of tapers, here is amber, here is the softest green,
here is the color of gold. But let us be silent: what I know
is mine, and when this water becomes black, I will possess
the night, whole, with its full complement of visible and
invisible stars.][6]

2. Ibid.
3. Ibid.
4. Ibid.
5. Ibid.
6. *Connaissance de l'Est,* p. 72.

Claudel assumes for his basic colors five of those found in the stained glass windows of the cathedral at Chartres: blue, green, yellow-gold, black, and red. Chartres, with its dramatically vaulted ceiling, the lapidary ornateness of its sculptures and the elaborate detail of its windows, apparently appealed to his histrionic soul and to his interest in the theater, and was for him the quintessence of architectural perfection. The dominant color of its windows, blue, *bleu de Chartres*—the name given to a deep, rich shade of blue—is the first color discussed in *Conversations dans le Loir-et-Cher*. Associated with a religious monument, it appropriately designates God and His grace. All of the qualities mentioned by Claudel in connection with this color can be associated with the Divine Being. He says, to begin with, that blue is stable but not immobile: *"il n'y a pas de couleur immobile. Mais l'une est cependant plus que les autres stable . . . le bleu et le vert durent"* ["There is no motionless color. But one is nevertheless more stable than the others . . . blue and green endure"] .[7] Similar to Rimbaud's *"l'azur, qui est du noir"* ["azure, that is black"] ,[8] it is darkness become light, like a soul illuminated with God's grace: *"le bleu est l'obscurité devenue visible"* ["blue is darkness become visible"] .[9] It represents a certain equilibrium, a balance between night and day, not unlike Claudel's own religious faith to which he clung almost desperately as the balance between the temptation and moral chaos of mortal flesh and the intellectual effervescence of a pure spirit: *"L'azur entre le jour et la nuit indique un équilibre"* [The azure between the day and the night indicates an equilibrium"].[10] Blue symbolizes all that is fundamental, the basis of life, the genesis, the source from which life springs. It is also the color of water, which, in terms of evolution, is the element in which life first appeared before progressing to the land; and, more appropriate to our present context (Darwinism was anathema to Claudel), the color of the waters "in the Beginning" when "the earth was without form, and void; and darkness was upon the face of the deep. And the Spirit of God moved upon the face of the waters": *"Le bleu de toutes manières est quelque chose d'élémentaire et de général, de frais et de pur, d'antérieur au mot. Il convient à tout ce qui enveloppe et baigne"* ["In any case, blue is something elemental and general, fresh and pure, anterior to the word. It suits everything that envelops and bathes"].[11]

7. *Conversations dans le Loir-et-Cher*, p. 58.
8. *Alchimie du Verbe* in *Une Saison en Enfer*, p. 236.
9. *Conversations dans le Loir-et-Cher*, p. 58.
10. Ibid.
11. Ibid, pp. 58-59.

The image of water is fundamental to the works of both Rimbaud and Claudel. The first scenes of *Partage de Midi* and of *Le Soulier de Satin* take place on the high seas; and it is the water of the high seas that is particularly significant in poems like Rimbaud's *Le Bateau Ivre* and *L'Éternité: "C'est la mer allée/Avec le soleil"* ["It is the sea gone/With the sun"]. In the fourth of Claudel's *Cinq Grandes Odes,* the sea unites the bark with the earth, just as Rimbaud's "drunken boat" is associated with the universe through its voyage on the open seas. Nevertheless, there is an essential difference between Rimbaud's imagery of the sea and Claudel's: Rimbaud's seas and oceans lead him far away from European ports and separate him from them, whereas the Claudelian sea is always bound up with these ports: *"la mer qui atteint sa plénitude en silence à cette heure qui joint à l'Océan les ports humains pleins de navires attendants"* ["the sea which reaches its fullness in silence at that hour which joins to the Ocean human ports full of waiting ships"].[12] The sea, like the ports, is only one of many integral parts of the divine creation. Yet, immense and formidable, it is, for Claudel, a unifying factor, symbolic of the unity of the universe.

The fact that the color of the sea, blue, is "something anterior to the word" suggests a further association of it with God, as is seen by a comparison of the Claudel text with the beginning of the Gospel according to John: "In the beginning was the Word, and the Word was with God." Claudel also mentions that in the windows of Chartres, Mary, Mother of God, appears bathed in periwinkle blue: *"Marie, que l'on voit précisément dans une des grandes planches du bas apparaître dans une auréole de pervenche"* ["Mary, whom one sees, as a matter of fact, in one of the large lower plates, appearing in a halo of periwinkle blue"].[13] And finally, near the end of *Conversations dans le Loir-et-Cher,* he makes specific reference to God's blue quality: *"Ce n'est pas la mer qu'il va regarder, il va regarder Dieu, l'éternel, le bleu sombre"* ["It is not the sea that he is going to look at, he is going to look at God, the eternal, the dark blue"].[14]

Violet, on the other hand, represents for Claudel *"quelque chose d'incertain et de précaire"* ["something uncertain and precarious"].[15] It should most likely be interpreted as a balance between red and blue, between men's passions and God's benevolence, just as blue

---

12. *La Muse qui est la Grâce* from *Cinq Grandes Odes,* p. 115.
13. *Conversations dans le Loir-et-Cher,* p. 59.
14. *Conversations dans le Loir-et-Cher,* p. 165.
15. *Conversations dans le Loir-et-Cher,* p. 58.

is the balance between night and day. It represents not so much lack of faith as the uncertainty of the believer who is waiting for some outward sign of God, of the impenetrable, the unknown—which would not be inconsistent with Rimbaud's "violet beam of His Eyes." Furthermore, Claudel's angel is dressed in purple: *"cet ange qui s'avance vers nous dans sa simarre de pourpre"* ["that angel coming towards us in his purple chimer"].[16] Violet, then, like blue, is associated with the beginning, the all-enveloping, the omnipresent, the stabilizing force in life, the obscurity become visibility that evokes a passage from the Gospel according to John (8:12), "I am the light of the world. Whoever follows me will have the light of life and will never walk in darkness." A first relationship between Rimbaud's and Claudel's imagery in color can be established in the similarity between their uses of blue—*"O—bleu"* and *"Dieu . . . le bleu sombre"*—as a symbol of the mystery and presence of God.

The second color discussed in *Conversations dans le Loir-et-Cher* is red. Red is, first of all, "the color of fire"[17] —the consuming fire that represents passion: *"La figure la plus animale, regardez ce qu'elle devient quand le feu s'y met, quand la passion l'anime, quand elle arrive pour une raison ou une autre à une espèce de transparence"* ["Look at what the most brutal face becomes when it catches fire, when it is animated by passion, when it arrives for one reason or another at a kind of transparency"].[18] It is also the color of love and shame:

> *La rougeur de l'amour et celle de la honte*
> *Couvrant ma face d'où j'ai retiré mes mains*
> *Je me tiendrai debout, bravant les yeux humains,*
> *Comme un homme marqué de qui nul ne prend compte.*

> With the redness of love and of shame
> Covering my face from which I have withdrawn my hands
> I will hold myself erect, defying human eyes,
> Like a marked man of whom no one takes count.]
>
> (*VI* in *Vers d'Exil*)[19]

And it is the color of blood, since "blood purified by the air . . . is nothing if not liquid fire"—the color of spilled blood like Rimbaud's *"sang craché,"* as we see in *Derrière Eux* from *Poèmes de Guerre:*

16. *Conversations dans le Loir-et-Cher*, p. 64.
17. *Conversations dans le Loir-et-Cher*, p. 59.
18. *Conversations dans le Loir-et-Cher*, p. 69.
19. *VI* in *Vers d'Exil*, Vol. 1 of *Œuvres Complètes* (1950), p. 36.

*Plus douce encore à ses veines toutefois quand
il vient s'y mêler, s'il faut du sang,
L'âme rouge dans elle de ses fils et la libation
comme du lait et comme du vin
Du soldat qui pour la défendre est tombé, les
armes à la main.*

[Sweeter yet to her veins when it becomes mingled
there, if blood is needed,
The red soul in her of her sons and the libation
like blood and like wine
Of the soldier who has fallen to defend her, arms
in hand.] [20]

Red is also violence: *"rouge . . . quelque chose d'aigu et de violent"*
["red . . . something shrill, sharp, and violent"].[21] Finally, like the
"Loud, shrieking Redskins" from the first strophe of *Le Bateau Ivre*,
red is shouts; associated with sound as well as with liquid and fire,
it has the "flux" of Rimbaldian imagery, for Claudel sees or feels
correspondences, interchanges between various elements of his own
imagery, a certain "instability" or mobility, a constant flow and
movement:

*Sang, feu, cri, pointe, c'est le domaine du rouge, la couleur
de ce qui était dedans et qui sort! Tout ce qui est violence,
aveu, obstacle surmonté ou détruit, désir longuement recuit
ou médité, amour morose, colère contenue, menace, éclat,
manifestation. Non seulement le feu, la braise.*

[Blood, fire, shout, advance, this is the domain of red, the
color of what was inside and comes out! All that is violence,
admission, surmounted or destroyed obstacle, long-simmering
or meditated desire, gloomy love, pent-up anger, threat, ex-
plosion, demonstration. Not only fire, embers.]
(*Conversations dans le Loir-et-Cher*)[22]

This association of *"la braise,"* "embers," with violence and strong
desires, appears often in Rimbaud's works as in,

*Plus de lendemain,
Braises de satin,
Votre ardeur
Est le devoir.*

20. *Derrière Eux* in *Poèmes de Guerre*, Vol. 2 of *Œuvres Complètes* (1952),
p. 198.
21. *Conversations dans le Loir-et-Cher*, p. 58.
22. *Conversations dans le Loir-et-Cher*, p. 60.

[No more tomorrows,
Satin embers,
Your ardor
Is duty.]

(*L'Eternité* in *Une Saison en Enfer*)

In passages like the preceding ones, it becomes apparent that, in Claudel's poetry, references to apparently concrete objects, even while descriptive, become significant for their associations with ideas, and that objects must be considered not just in terms of their mass, but also of their color and of their abstract associations as well as of their contrasts in justaposition with each other within a particular passage. This is quite different from the "descriptions" of Parnassian poetry, in which the poem may be quite disassociated from the poet's inner self, existing as a reflection of plastic impressions, the success of its imagery dependent on its descriptive intensity. It is this essential difference that causes Claudel to say of *Connaissance de l'Est*— which gives the impression in certain instances of being a series of descriptive passages—that "it is not a collection of impressions, but of explanations, of definitions, of clarifications."[23] In this context, the color red, as in Rimbaud's poetry, serves for Claudel not so much to describe physical appearance as to communicate the inner reality of the object described or concepts that the poet identifies with it.

Included in the principal colors of Claudel's kaleidoscope is *vert*, green, which represents the germination, the beginning, and the imminent continuation of life, its potential; in effect, life itself: *"quelque chose qui commence et qui va exister à l'instant"* ["something which is beginning and which is going to exist presently"].[24] This "green" of terrestrial life is not to be confused with divine existence, the "blue" beginning and source of the universe, God, for it is *"la couleur des Dimanches vides de Saints"* ["the color of Saintless Sundays"],[25] the liturgical color used by the Catholic Church on Sundays when no saint is commemorated. Moreover, the various qualifications of green, *vert choux, vert salade, herbe, feuilles, légumes* [cabbage green, salad green, grass, leaves, vegetables],[26] demonstrate that it is the color of nature, the color of life, the spring, the coming into life: *"le végétal, quelque chose de vireux qui du fond de sa nativité arrive lentement à la couleur"* ["plantlife, something virose which, from the depths of its birth, slowly arrives at color"].[27]

23. *Les Sources de Paul Claudel*, pp. 141-142.
24. *Conversations dans le Loir-et-Cher*, p. 66.
25. *Conversations dans le Loir-et-Cher*, p. 66.
26. Ibid.
27. Ibid.

Even the shape of the first letter of *vert*, V, suggests to Claudel this opening-out, this blossoming into life, *"quelque chose qui pousse en divergeant"* ["something which divaricates as it grows"].[28] In finding meaning in the shapes of words, Claudel is appealing to the original concept of Chinese written characters, in which he was extremely interested from the time he took up his first diplomatic post in China and which he discusses in *La Poésie française et l'Extrême Orient:*

> *Le caractère chinois n'est autre chose que la traduction d'un être, d'une idée, et, comme je le voyais indiqué récemment dans un excellent article de M. Fenellosa, d'une action, disons un ensemble de ces caractères juxtaposés et séparés par le blanc, une espèce de volée, non plus de cygnes blancs, comme ceux dont vous parlait tout à l'heure mon confrère Li Oey, mais d'ailes noires, établissant dans l'invisible des points de repère. L'esprit n'est plus conduit, comme chez nous, du sujet à l'objet par la ligne continue de la syntaxe, par une chaîne ininterrompue de verbes, de prépositions et d'incidentes. Le poëme n'est pas livré tout fait, il se fait dans l'esprit du lecteur à qui l'on laisse le soin d'établir les rapports entre une série de positions déterminées.*

[The Chinese character is simply the translation of a being, of an idea, and, as I saw indicated recently in an excellent article by M. Fenellosa, of an action, let us say an ensemble of these characters juxtaposed and separated by white, a kind of flight, no longer of white swans, like those that my colleague Li Oey was telling you about a short while ago, but of black wings, establishing landmarks in the invisible. The mind is no longer led, as with us, by the continuous line of syntax, by the uninterrupted chain of verbs, of prepositions and parenthetical clauses. The poem is not delivered already made, it is created in the mind of the reader to whom is left the care of establishing the rapports between a series of determined positions.][29]

However such explanations may strike the philologist, this association of shapes of letters and words with semantics has roots in Western culture as well, and it was neither Rimbaud nor Claudel who first introduced it into Western literature. Dante, for example,

---

28. Ibid.
29. *La Poésie Française et l'Extrême Orient* in *Ecrits Divers*, Vol. 4 of *Œuvres Complètes* (1952), pp. 372-373.

says that there is a resemblance between the shape of the word *omo*
(un uomo) and the object it designates: two eyes separated by a nose,
the face of a man. The poetic possibilities of such associations are
virtually limitless, and Claudel was not one to discount the diverse
poetic aspects of things. After all, neither Claudel, nor Dante—nor
Rimbaud—was a philologist. Thus, for Claudel, the letter V appropriately begins the color *vert,* since, expanding upwards from a focal
point, it symbolizes a blossoming-out of nature.

The color mentioned more than any other throughout Claudel's
works is black. In the context of Chartres, black is the color of the
leading that separates the pancs of stained glass; it outlines form.
Although it represents the unknown, it is also the designator, the
common denominator; it contains all without revealing; it suggests
form without divulging detail: *"En effet nous ne voyons pas le noir,
nous en sommes simplement exclus, nous ne le comprenons que par
ses contours"* ["In effect, we do not see black, we are simply excluded from it, we understand it only by its contours"].[30] Claudel
is saying that while man does see the contours of God—nature, the
universe—he cannot see God Himself; he has before him only the
evidence of His existence, but not the actual vision; man is excluded
from His divinity, but not from an awareness of His mystery. While
blue symbolizes the spirit of God and His grace, black refers to the
mystery of God, which is "inexhaustible" and therefore ineffable.
Thus, though the Virgin Mary—her substance—appears bathed in
periwinkle blue, the mystery of Mary is suggested at Chartres by
black: *"de tout petits chrétiens sont prosternés devant la Vierge
Noire"* ["very small Christians lie prostrate before the Black Virgin"].[31]
We may understand that the Divine Being exists, but not the "why
and wherefore" of it. The "why and wherefore" is the mystery and
holds the whole together, just as the black leading of the stained-
glass windows holds them together. Black, then, the unknown, is
comparable to Rimbaud's *"golfes d'ombre"*; it is the impenetrable,
as in Ysé's remark about Mesa's eyes in *Partage de Midi: "il me regarde . . . de ses grands yeux noirs (on ne peut rien voir dans ses
yeux)"* ["he looks at me . . . with his big black eyes (you can see
nothing in his eyes)"].[32] (This reference to black eyes is all the more
curious, since, in Claudel's works, eyes are usually blue, as they
usually are in Rimbaud's poetry as well.) Black is also the obscurity
of night, the darkness of man's ignorance, which needs God's blue
to be illumined: *"avec le bleu, la matière de la nuit est pénétrée"*

30. *Conversations dans le Loir-et-Cher,* p. 58.
31. *Conversations dans le Loir-et-Cher,* p. 62.
32. *Partage de Midi,* p. 24.

["with blue, the matter of the night is penetrated"].[33] This final identification of black with night establishes the essential idea of obscurity and mystery, comparable to Rimbaud's symbolism.

One final color discussed in the first section of *Conversations dans le Loir-et-Cher,* and often referred to by Claudel throughout his prose and poetry, is *jaune,* yellow. Yellow is described as being "dry," *"le jaune est sec."*[34] But, it is the dryness of lucidity, not of aridity; the essence of enlightenment: *"Le jaune est l'esprit extrême, la lumière même quand de la matière il ne lui reste plus attaché qu'un peu de sable ou de pollen"* ["Yellow is intense spirit, light itself when the only matter still clinging to it is a bit of sand or pollen"].[35] It is the color of gold: *"le trésor de doubles pistoles dans un tonneau"* ["the treasure of doubloons in a barrel"].[36] Above all, this yellow, the color of gold, is truth, the lamp that lights up the darkness of a cave, *"la lampe qui brûle souterrainement au fond d'une cave (éclairant le front et l'énorme main de ce vieillard athlétique)"* ["the lamp which burns underground in the depths of a cave (illuminating the brow and the enormous hand of that athletic old man)"].[37] It is the golden truth of those who have found completion in liberation from terrestrial shackles, in the supreme serenity of death, united with God:

> *Une autre pensée est celle qu'exprime saint Grégoire quand il dit de nos chers défunts:* ils seront transparents comme le verre, ils seront splendides comme l'or ... *Splendides comme l'or, cela veut dire qu'ils rayonneront de toutes parts cette vérité qui les pénètre et qui les a libérés.*
>
> [Another thought is the one expressed by Saint Gregory when he said of our dear departed: *they will be transparent like glass, they will be resplendent like gold* ... Resplendent like gold, that means they will radiate from all over this truth which penetrates them and which has liberated them.]
>
> *(Contacts et Circonstances)*[38]

Although truth is here associated with "our dear departed," it does not stand alone and apart from mankind, for the revelation of it is dependent on man's passionate struggle through revolt as well as on

33. *Conversations dans le Loir-et-Cher,* p. 58.
34. *Conversations dans le Loir-et-Cher,* p. 62.
35. Ibid.
36. *Conversations dans le Loir-et-Cher,* p. 63.
37. Ibid.
38. *Contacts et Circonstances,* p. 221.

God's grace: *"le rouge n'est pas loin [du jaune] et le bleu est si néces-saire que c'est comme s'il était là"* ["red is not far [from yellow] and blue is so necessary that it is as though it were there"].[39] In this gold, in truth, lies the final justification of man's life; the ultimate goal, the culmination of a lifetime of "the red soul." The search for truth constitutes a *raison d'être* for man's existence, and the finding of it gives him spiritual substance:

> *Il faut beaucoup de temps, il faut une vie tout entière, pour qu'au fond du cœur de l'homme s'amasse une seule goutte d'or, le dur grain fait d'amidon et de gluten. C'est pour arriver à cet alcool et à ce sucre essentiel, à cette maturité, à ce jaunisse-ment de l'âme, à cette prière permanente, qu'il faut trouver le moyen de donner à l'homme la pratique et l'habitude de la paix et des choses immobiles.*

> [A great deal of time is needed, an entire life, to accumulate in the bottom of a man's heart one single drop of gold, the hard grain made of starch and gluten. It is so that he may arrive at this alcohol and this essential sugar, at this maturity, at this ripening of the soul, at this permanent prayer, that a means must be found to give man the practice and the habit of peace and of things immobile.][40]

It is this association of truth with gold that explains why gold is men-tioned so often in Claudel's work, even in the *Premiers Vers* in which innumerable references to gold appear in much the same context as Rimbaud uses them; for his works are an expression of his truth which, for him, is faith, God's grace, and God Himself.

Rimbaud and Claudel have this in common: gold—truth—is the ultimate goal. Although there is in Claudel's thinking, as in Rim-baud's, a certain questioning, since he wonders at one point where, "by what mystical route" he will be granted the discovery of gold,

> *Là-bas, dans cette fosse carée que la montagne enclôt d'un mur sauvage, l'air et l'eau brûlent d'un feu mystérieux: je vois un or si beau que la nature tout entière me semble une masse morte, et, au prix de la lumière même, la clarté qu'elle répand une nuit profonde. Désirable élixir! par quelle route mystique, où? me sera-t-il donné de participer à ton flot avare.*

---

39. *Conversations dans le Loir-et-Cher*, p. 63.
40. *Conversations dans le Loir-et-Cher*, pp. 129-130.

[Over there, in that square pit which the mountain encloses
with a wild wall, air and water burn with a mysterious fire:
I see a gold so beautiful that the whole of nature seems to me
to be a dead mass, and, compared with light itself, the bright-
ness given off by nature seems a dark night. Desirable elixir!
by what mystical route, where? will it be given me to share
in your miserly wave.]

(*Novembre* in *Connaissance de l'Est*)[41]

he nevertheless felt that he had realized that goal, that he had found
and embraced it when, like the bark in *La Muse qui est la Grâce,* he
bent down to the earth to adore its pantheistic wonders, virtually
worshiping the earth as a manifestation of God. Thus gold, although
it is envisioned by Rimbaud but does not figure in *Voyelles* because
it has no place in his physical reality and must remain an unattained
goal, has a prominent place in Claudel's *Conversations dans le Loir-
et-Cher.*

Of the colors in *Voyelles,* only one, white, is not discussed in
Conversations dans le Loir-et-Cher. There are, however, frequent
mentions of white in this work which make clear just what it represented for Claudel. On a first level and in a commonplace connota-
tion, white symbolizes purity: angels are white, *"ces deux anges
blancs à longs plis à côté d'un harmonium"* ["those two long-pleated
white angels beside a harmonium"] ;[42] white snowflakes are "little
pure mouths," as in,

C'est le psaume où l'on représente Dieu en hiver comme un
semeur qui puise à pleine main la neige dans son sac et qui la
répand dans l'air, sicut buccellas, ce sont de toutes petites
bouches pures qui nous couvrent la figure de baisers!

[It is the psalm in which God in winter is represented as a
sower who takes handfuls of snow from his sack and scatters
it in the air, *sicut buccellas,* little pure mouths that cover our
face with kisses.][43]

White symbolizes virginity: *"Tout en haut dans le ciel une blancheur
resplendissante—virginale—la supplication in excelsis—L'élévation—
Ce que la terre a à offrir de plus blanc et de plus pur"* ["Way up high
in the sky a resplendent whiteness—virginal—supplication *in excelsis—*

41. *Novembre* in *Connaissance de l'Est,* p. 60.
42. *Conversations dans le Loir-et-Cher,* p. 118.
43. Ibid.

the Elevation—the whitest and purest that the earth has to offer"].[44]
Whiteness, through association with purity and therefore with the
purity of God, also suggests eternity—once more the "inexhaustible,"
the limitless, mystery: *"L'Eternité dans ce coin en bas commence à
blanchir à cause de la génération du Verbe"* ["Eternity in this corner
below begins to whiten because of the generating power of the Word"].[45]
This last reference to "the Word" is a further confirmation that certain Biblical references are implied in Claudel's use of colors and in
the interpretation of them as seen in these texts, for, again, it can be
an allusion only to the opening passage of the Gospel according to
John: "In the beginning was the Word, and the Word was with God
and the word was God." As early as 1929, several years before writing *Conversations dans le Loir-et-Cher,* Claudel said, in an interview
with Frédéric Lefèvre, that the Bible was his main source of constant
reading. In fact, he was acquainted with the Bible long before that,
for his sister Camille had been given a Protestant Bible many years
earlier, while Claudel was still an adolescent, and he read it at the
time he underwent his dramatic conversion.

In other contexts, white does take on a different meaning from
this Biblical one, however. Reminiscent of Mallarmé, white represents latent poetry, unexpressed words, in fact, the very essence of
a poem, and in this sense is essential to what the poet writes; in *Positions et Propositions I,* Claudel speaks of "an idea isolated by white,"
and in the first of the *Cinq Grandes Odes,* he writes, *"O mon âme!
le poème n'est point fait de ces lettres que je plante comme des
clous, mais du blanc qui reste sur le papier"* ["O my soul! the poem
is not made of these letters which I put down like nails, but of the
white which remains on the paper"].[46] But there is a fundamental
difference between the concepts of these two poets: white means
sterility for Mallarmé, as in the image of the white swan in *Le vierge,
le vivace et le bel aujourd'hui,* or *"le vide papier que la blancheur
défend"* ["the empty paper that its whiteness protects"] from *Brise
Marine,* whereas it is fecund for Claudel. In a lecture given in Florence,
Italy, for *L'Exposition du Livre* in 1925, and published in *Positions
et Propositions I,* Claudel was quite specific as to the importance of
white in a poem:

> *La page consiste essentiellement en un certain rapport du bloc
> imprimé ou* justification, *et du blanc, ou* marge. *Ce rapport*

44. *Conversations dans le Loir-et-Cher,* p. 167.
45. *Conversations dans le Loir-et-Cher,* p. 58.
46. *Les Muses* from *Cinq Grandes Odes,* p. 55.

n'est pas purement matériel, il est l'image de ce que tout mouvement de la pensée, quand il est arrivé à se traduire par un bruit et une parole, laisse autour de lui d'inexprimé, mais non pas d'inerte, mais non pas d'incorporel, le silence environnant d'où cette voix est issue et qu'elle imprègne à son tour, quelque chose comme son champ magnétique.

[The page consists essentially of a certain relationship between the printed block or *justification*, and the white, or *margin*. The relationship is not just material, it is the image of what every movement of thought, when translated by a noise and a word, leaves around it unexpressed, but not inert, but not incorporeal, the surrounding silence out of which has come this voice and which, in its turn, leaves its own impression, something like its magnetic field.] [47]

For Claudel, then, color, and white in particular, is, along with sound, the sine qua non of poetry. For, as he also said, "An artist has his own taste; he needs, he waits for certain sounds, certain ideas, certain colors, and he bears a grudge against the colleague who does not furnish him any" (*Richard Wagner* in *Contacts et Circonstances*).[48]

Although these colors are the same as those observed in the stained-glass windows of Chartres, they also have a great deal in common with the colors that predominate in Rimbaud's poetry and that are seen in *Voyelles*. The fact that Claudel's images, like Rimbaud's, are drawn from nature and symbolize much the same *état d'âme* as Rimbaud's, reminds us of what Claudel expressed about his own system of colors and what Rimbaud himself might well have written: *"J'ai choisi ma teinte sur le comptoir de la Nature"* ["I have chosen my colors from Nature's counter"].[49] And the fact that many examples of these uses of color are found in *Connaissance de l'Est*, written comparatively soon after his first acquaintance with Rimbaud's works and long before *Conversations dans le Loir-et-Cher*, suggests that Claudel owes his concept of color as much to Rimbaud as to "nature's counter." The six colors predominant in Rimbaud's work (along with a variation in violet) are the same six peculiar to Claudel's; they symbolize to a great extent the same ideas for both Rimbaud and Claudel, and evoke the same associations of sensations and ideas. Not only does Claudel analyze them poetically in *Conversations dans le Loir-et-Cher* and use them consistently in other works, he also selects them

47. *Positions et Propositions I*, p. 72.
48. *Richard Wagner* in *Contacts et Circonstances*, p. 299.
49. *Conversations dans le Loir-et-Cher*, p. 159.

as those colors to be used in his ideal church, projected for Chicago:
"The colors will be red, blue, green, violet, white, black and gold"
(*Positions et Propositions II*).[50]

Of all these colors, the three most frequently mentioned in the
works of both Rimbaud and Claudel are gold, red, and black. Not
only are the frequency and the proportionate use of the colors much
the same, the kinds of contrasts are also strikingly similar. For example, both Rimbaud and Claudel contrast red and black. This in
itself is not unusual; one has to look no further than Stendhal's *Le
Rouge et le Noir*. What is unusual is the fact that Claudel uses almost exactly the same kind of image as Rimbaud in connection with
this color combination. In at least two places in *Connaissance de
l'Est*, he refers to contrasts of red and black in alluding to the earth,
to soil and rocks:

> *Voici la mer avec ses archipels et ses caps; par l'artifice de
> deux pierres, l'une noire, l'autre rouge et comme usée et
> poreuse, on a représenté deux îles accouplées par le point
> de vue . . .*

> [Here is the sea with its archipelagoes and capes; by means
> of two stones, one black, the other red and seemingly worn
> and porous, have been depicted two islands apparently paired
> off . . .]

> (*Çà et là*)[51]

> *La terre, telle que les tranchées que nous suivons en montrent
> les couches, est d'abord un mince humus noir comme du char-
> bon, puis du sable jaune, et enfin l'argile, rouge de soufre ou
> de cinabre.*

> [The earth, as the trenches we are following shows us its layers,
> is at first a thin, coal-black humus, then yellow sand, and final-
> ly sulphur-red or cinnabar-red clay.]

> (*L'Arche d'Or dans la Forêt*)[52]

Rimbaud uses a similar image in *Mauvais Sang* from *Une Saison en
Enfer*: "*la boue m'apparaissait soudainement rouge et noire*" ["the
mud seemed to me suddenly red and black"], and another in *Enfance*
from *Les Illuminations*: "*la boue est rouge ou noire*" ["the mud is red
or black"]. In Claudel's *Contacts et Circonstances*, the red glow of a

50. *Positions et Propositions II*, p. 299.
51. *Çà et là* in *Connaissance de l'Est*, pp. 117-118.
52. *L'Arche d'Or dans la Forêt* in *Connaissance de l'Est*, pp. 111-112.

city is contrasted with the black night sky: *"Déjà, la rambleur de Tokyo commence à rougeover dans le ciel noir"* ["Already the *'rambleur'* of Tokyo begins to redden in the black sky"].[53] And in Rimbaud's *Parade*, also from *Les Illuminations*, red is used in contrast with the black summer night: *"Des yeux hébétés à la façon de la nuit d'été, rouges et noirs"* ["Eyes deadened like the summer's night, red and black"]. Nor are these the only similarities; they are to be found in other combinations as well. Both Claudel and Rimbaud associate gold with nature, with the color green. In another example from *Une Saison en Enfer*, in *Alchimie du Verbe*, gold refers to the joy of existence enlightened through "green" nature, which is tantamount to saying that a kind of perfection is to be found in nature:

Enfin, ò bonheur, ò raison, j'écartais du ciel l'azur, qui est du noir, et je vécus, étincelle d'or de la lumière nature. De joie, je prenais une expression boufonne et égarée au possible.

[At last, O happiness, O reason, I removed from the sky the azure, that is black, and I lived, gold spark of *pure* light *in nature*. Out of sheer joy, I took an expression as clownish and strange as possible.]

Similarly, in *Conversations dans le Loir-et-Cher*, Claudel expresses the essence of joy that is to be found in "green gold," in the harvest of nature's autumnal gift to mankind: *"Alors qu'attendons-nous pour nous installer tout de suite dans la joie, pour coloniser la gloire de Dieu, pour nous mettre à table, pour nous installer en plein dans la moisson et l'or vert?"* ["So what are we waiting for to settle ourselves in joy, to colonize the glory of God, to sit down at the table, to install ourselves right in the harvest and the green gold?"].[54] This association of yellow—gold—with green is found also in *La Dérivation* from *Connaissance de l'Est*: *"Entre ces replis violets, voici l'eau peinte comme du reflet des cierges, voici l'ambre, voici le vert le plus doux, voici la couleur de l'or"* ["Between these fat violet folds, here is water painted like the reflection of tapers, here is amber, here is the softest green, here is the color of gold"].[55] And we encounter much the same kind of reference, nature coupled with gold, in *Rome* from *Poèmes de Guerre*: *"Glisse et pousse et ramifie de tous côtés au travers de l'Europe, feuille et or, qui se dilate et s'approfondit"* ["Slips and

53. *Contacts et Circonstances*, p. 319.
54. *Conversations dans le Loir-et-Cher*, p. 175.
55. *La Dérivation* in *Connaissance de l'Est*, p. 72.

pushes and branches out on all sides throughout Europe, leaf and gold, expanding and deepening"].[56]

The color combination in Rimbaud's works that recurs most frequently in Claudel's and that is perhaps the most striking in its similarity of usage in the works of both poets is red and gold: the passion and violence of the soul in contrast with the supreme truth and joy that is the poets' ultimate goal. Two especially interesting examples of this are to be found in *Les Illuminations:*

> *L'essaim des feuilles d'or entoure la maison du général. Ils sont dans le midi.—On suit la route rouge pour arriver à l'auberge vide. Le château est à vendre; les persiennes sont détachées.*

> [The swarm of golden leaves encircles the general's house. They are in the south.—You take the red road to get to the empty inn. The château is up for sale; the shutters are loose.]
>
> *(Enfance II)*

> *. . . enluminée comme les dix mois de la nuit rouge—(son cœur ambre et spunk),—pour ma seule prière muette*

> [. . . flushed, illuminated like the ten months of the red night— (her heart amber and spunk),—for my one silent prayer]
>
> *(Dévotion)*

During "the ten months of the red night," comparable to the "ten nights" of the "drunken boat's" unbridled "sail" [*"vogueurs"*], the poet's "amber and spunk" heart (amber is a gold-yellow color, and spunk burns with a yellow sparkle) is joyful; it recognizes the "golden fish" and is concerned with truth. Similarly, this contrast between red and gold, between violent passions and truth, is conspicuous in Claudel's works, particularly in *Connaissance de l'Est:*

> *Quoi! dans la plus mince flaque, dans la plus étroite ornière laissée au tournant de la route publique, il trouvera de quoi mirer son visage vermeil, et seule l'âme secrete de l'homme lui demeurera-t-elle si close qu'elle lui refuse sa ressemblance et du fond de ses ténèbres un peu d'or?*

> [What! in the smallest puddle, in the narrowest rut left in the bend of a public highway, he will find something in which to look at his vermilion face, and will the secret soul of man

56. *Rome* from *Poèmes de Guerre*, p. 209.

alone remain so closed that it refuses him his likeness and from the depths of its darkness a bit of gold?

(La Délivrance d'Amaterasu)[57]

(note that in connection with *"un beau petit enfant"* ["a beautiful little child"] who sees his reflection "in the smallest puddle"—like Rimbaud's "squatting child" near the "cold, black puddle" in *Le Bateau Ivre*—Claudel instructs us to "give our heart to the good sun!" to become, in effect, *"le fils du soleil"* ["the sun's son"] that Rimbaud refers to in *Vagabonds*)

Sur la rive où j'embarque, une femme lave son linge; la cuvette de laque vermillon où elle empile ses hardes a un rebord d'or qui éclate et fulmine au soleil de la solennité.

[On the bank from which I am embarking, a woman is washing her linen; the washbasin of vermilion lacquer in which she piles up her clothes has a border of gold that glitters and fulminates in the sun of solemnity.]

(Le Jour de la Fête-de-tous-les-Fleuves)[58]

Dans la lumière rose et dorée de l'automne, je vois toute la berge de ce canal dérobé à ma vue ...

[In the rose and gold autumn light, I see the whole bank of the canal that is hidden from my view ...]

(Heures dans le Jardin)[59]

Ce n'est point du rouge, et ce n'est point la couleur du soleil; c'est la fusion du sang dans l'or.

[It is not red, and it is not the color of the sun; it is the fusion of blood with gold!]

(La Descente)[60]

Je n'omets pas que le sang de cochon sert à fixer l'or.

[I am not neglecting the fact that pig's blood is used to fix gold.]

(Le Porc)[61]

---

57. *La Délivrance d'Amaterasu* in *Connaissance de l'Est*, p. 159.
58. *Le Jour de la Fête-de-tous-les Fleuves* in *Connaissance de l'Est*, p. 172.
59. *Heures dans le Jardin* from *Connaissance de l'Est*, p. 146.
60. *La Descente* from *Connaissance de l'Est*, pp. 90-91.
61. *Le Porc* from *Connaissance de l'Est*, p. 70.

(the red blood of the lowly pig—to be compared with the "red" of "penitent drunkenness" in Rimbaud's *Voyelles*—has its proper place in the universe, its connection with gold, with truth). The same kind of contrast appears in *Le Précieux Sang* from *Poèmes de Guerre:*

> *Si ce vin a quelque vertu,*
> *Et si notre sang est rouge, comme vous le dites,*
> *comment le savoir,*
> *Autrement que quand il est répandu?*
> *Si notre sang est vraiment précieux comme vous le*
> *dites, si vraiment il est comme de l'or,*
> *S'il sert, pourquoi le garder?*

> [If this wine has some virtue,
> And if our blood is red, as you say, how shall we
> know it,
> Except when it is spilled?
> If our blood is really *precious* as you say, if really
> it is like gold,
> If it serves, why keep it?] [62]

And in reference to Baudelaire's tormented soul in search of Christian truth through prayer, Claudel once again juxtaposes red and gold:

> *Parmi les volutes d'une affreuse fumée et de cet âcre soufre*
> *qui offusque le souffle et la vue, il a suffi qu'un instant l'or*
> *sanglant d'une prière désespérée illuminât la poésie du pauvre*
> *Baudelaire, pour que l'opaque littérature qui l'accompagne*
> *et le suit se désagrège, cette atteinte au point essentiel reçue*
> *d'une occulte décantation.*

> [Among the spiral curls of a ghastly smoke and of that acrid
> sulfur which is offensive to breathing and seeing, it was enough
> that the poetry of poor Baudelaire be illumined an instant by
> the bloody gold of a desperate prayer in order for the opaque
> literature that accompanies and follows him to disintegrate,
> this blow at the essential point received from an occult de-
> cantation.]

(Positions et Propositions II) [63]

Gold—Claudel's truth—though inspired and revealed by the spirit of God, is nevertheless closely associated with and even dependent on

62. *Le Précieux Sang* from *Poèmes de Guerre*, p. 208.
63. *Positions et Propositions II*, p. 276.

"red," man's passions, and therefore on Claudel himself—his works being in many respects an intellectual and spiritual autobiography.

This predominance of the same three colors—red, gold, and black—points to a similarity of poetic temperament in Rimbaud and Claudel. Both poets are virtually obsessed with the idea that truth is incompatible with the violence of men's passions, yet aware that one leads inexorably towards the other. Both are profoundly close to nature. Both indicate an awareness of God and an ineluctable involvement with Him. All of these themes are complemented by similar patterns of color in their works.

Imagery in sound

The term music, as applied to poetry, is best understood in the context of "aleatory music," which includes all manner of sound with or without rhythms; it refers specifically to the cumulative tonal effects and, at times, the rhythmic patterns created by certain vowels and consonants in juxtaposition, as in alliteration or assonance—often used as a complement to imagery or in contrast with it, and sometimes to evoke a mood. Certainly it is this kind of music that Verlaine found essential to poetry, *"De la musique avant toute chose"* ["Music before everything"] (*Art Poétique*), and it is this element in particular that makes poetry difficult if not impossible to translate. Even composers' attempts to set musical poems, as in the case of certain French art songs, tend to obscure the tonal effects intended by poets like Verlaine and Rimbaud—and perhaps Claudel, despite his having collaborated closely with Honegger on *Jeanne d'Arc au Bûcher.* Yet, although the music of poetry is not to be confused with traditional musical composition, both are involved with sound and therefore interrelated, as is suggested by references to musical instruments and words appropriate to traditional music throughout the poetry of Rimbaud and Claudel, and their prominent place in both poets' vision of the cosmos.

The importance of music in Rimbaud's aesthetic is clear from the outset. It is manifest not only in his combinations of sound and color in *Voyelles,* but, even earlier, in the *Lettre du Voyant* to Paul Demeny. His "hour of new literature" begins with a reference to Greek poetry, which he describes as having "verses and lyres" that "give rhythm to Action." He goes on to say that "afterwards, music and rhymes are games," implying that although music and rhyme are important in poetry, they have been neglected, in their essential meaning, by the poets who followed the Greeks, especially by the French poets. A scathing and sarcastic comment to the effect that critics, like the Romantics, "prove so well that the song is too seldom the work, that is to say the thought sung and understood by the singer" also points to the fact that Rimbaud has an acute awareness of the fundamental importance of music in poetry. Even the vocabulary and images in this letter are largely musical: "If copper comes out of its sleep a bugle, that is in no way its fault"; "I draw my bow across the strings"; and "Always full of *Number* and *Harmony,* these poems will be written to last" (both italicized terms apply to music; the italics are Rimbaud's). And he says, "my thought" becomes "a symphony," just as Claudel, in reference to the third of *Cinq Grandes Odes,* wrote to Gide: "I am happy that you like this Ode which represents, I think, something quite new in literature, and which is constructed, like a symphony, on different themes."[64] As a preface to the inclusion of *Mes Petites Amoureuses* in this letter to Demeny, Rimbaud writes, "please lend a sympathetic ear—I have the bow in hand, I begin." Furthermore, he refers to Verlaine, the poet's musician, as "a true poet." Finally, he finishes the letter "with a pious hymn."

The essential place of music in Rimbaud's poetry becomes all the more apparent upon examination of the poems themselves; of all of them, only a scant dozen lack a mention of music in one form or another. Lucretius's "harmony of the spheres" plays an important role in many of Rimbaud's poems, for he describes music as "a turning away from abysses and shock of ice floes against the stars" [*"virement des gouffres et choc des glaçons aux astres"*] (*Barbare*). Music evokes certain moods and qualifies the ideas that he is expressing. For example, a summer night is suggested by the soft rustling of the stars, *"Mes étoiles au ciel avaient un doux frou-frou"* ["My stars in the sky made a soft rustling sound"] (*Ma Bohème*); the day of final judgment is evoked in a classical image by a *"Clairon plein des strideurs étranges"* ["Bugle full of strange stridors"] (*Voyelles*); the devil, like the devil in Stravinsky's version of Ramuz's *L'Histoire du Soldat,* scrapes out harsh tones on a squeaky violin, *"Belzébuth enragé racle ses violons"* ["Beelzebub in a rage saws on his violins"] (*Bal des Pendus*); bells toll or tinkle, *"la sonnerie des bestiaux à l'écho des vals"* ["the ringing of cattle-bells to the echo of the valleys"] (*Fairy*), or are ominously silent, *"il y a une horloge qui ne sonne pas"* ["there is a

64. *Correspondance: Claudel et Gide,* p. 132. Letter written from the Consulat de France at Prague, 20 avril 1910.

church clock that doesn't strike"] (*Enfance*); even the fish sing,
"les poissons chantants" ["the singing fish"] (*Le Bateau Ivre*):
Rimbaud's sea fed by rivers full of song, *"le fleuve murmure / Un
chant plein de bonheur"* ["the river murmurs / A song full of happiness"] (*Soleil et Chair*), is no more silent than his sky. And if
eternity is "the sea gone with the sun" (*L'Eternité*), then it is a
cacaphonous eternity—or certainly polyphonic.

Claudel, too, places sound in a cosmic setting. In less joyous moments, he becomes aware of silence in nature, *"Le silence est profond et la campagne est vide"* ["The silence is deep and the countryside is empty"] (*X* from *Vers d'Exil*).[65] But he also knows it has
multifarious sounds, like those of the sea, of the earth, of the wind,
of birds singing in a deep wood: *"Bruit de la mer! bruit de la terre!
bruit du vent! / Murmure au bois profond, l'oiseau chante"* ["Sound
of the sea! sound of the earth! sound of the wind! / Murmur in the
deep wood, the bird is singing" (*V* from *Vers d'Exil*).[66] The heavens
dance to music:

> *Mais écoute, cœur! Fais silence cœur anxieux!*
> *—Quoi, mon oreille a droit à cela seul, paroles!*
> *Je prends en vain et je remange ces voix folles,*
> *Je bois l'eau vaine!—Clair branle des vastes cieux.*

[But listen, heart! Be silent, anxious heart!
—What, my ear has a right to that alone, words!
I take in vain and yet take still more of these foolish voices,
I drink the useless water!—Simple dance of vast skies.]
(*IX* from *Vers d'Exil*)[67]

Claudel compares the poet to a singer or a wind instrument:

> *Car le poëte pareil à un instrument où l'on souffle*
> *Entre sa cervelle et ses narines pour une conception*
> *pareille à l'acide conscience de l'odeur*
> *N'ouvre pas autrement que le petit oiseau son âme,*
> *Quand prêt à chanter de tout son corps il s'emplit d'air*
> *jusqu'à l'intérieur de tous ses os!*

[For the poet like an instrument into which one blows
    Between his brains and his nostrils for a conception
like the acid conscience of odor

---

65. *X* from *Vers d'Exil*, p. 44.
66. *V* from *Vers d'Exil*, p. 35.
67. *IX* from *Vers d'Exil*, p. 42.

Does not open his soul differently from a little bird,
When ready to sing with all his body he fills himself up
with air right into all of his bones!]
(Les Muses from Cinq Grandes Odes)[68]

(present-day "acid heads" have nothing on Claudel who needed no
artificial stimulants to inspire his visions and sensation). He hears the
sound of golden cities, perfection: *"ramage des grandes villes dorées"*
["song of the great gilded cities"] (*L'Esprit et l'Eau* from *Cinq Grandes
Odes*).[69] He compares the unity of the universe to that of an orchestra:

> *Comme la phrase qui prend aux cuivres*
> *Gagne les bois et progressivement envahit les*
> *profondeurs de l'orchestre,*
> *Et comme les éruptions du soleil*
> *Se répercutent sur la terre en crises d'eau et*
> *en raz de marée,*
> *Ainsi du plus grand Ange qui vous voit jusqu'au*
> *caillou de la route et d'un bout de votre création*
> *jusqu'à l'autre,*
> *Il ne cesse point continuité, non plus que de*
> *l'âme au corps.*

[Just as the phrase of music that begins in the brass section
Takes over the woodwinds and progressively invades the
depths of the orchestra,
And just as flare-ups of the sun
Have repercussions on the earth in droughts and tidal
waves
So from the greatest Angel who sees you to the least
pebble on the highway and from one end of your creation
to the other,
There is no interruption of continuity, no more than from
the soul to the body.]
(L'Esprit et l'Eau from Cinq Grandes Odes)[70]

The waters makes themselves hears, *"les sonnantes eaux de ce fleuve
armé"* ["the resounding waters of this armed river"] (*La Cantate à
trois voix*);[71] a bell rings out melancholy, *"la cloche mélancolique à
ma gauche quatre fois se mêle à la pure splendeur de Chuzenji"* ["the
melancholy bell at my left four times mingles with the pure splendor

68. *Les Muses* from *Cinq Grandes Odes*, pp. 56-57.
69. *L'Esprit et l'Eau* from *Cinq Grandes Odes*, p. 71.
70. *L'Esprit et l'Eau* from *Cinq Grandes Odes*, p. 79.
71. *La Cantate à trois voix*, Vol. 1 of *Œuvres Complètes* (1950), p. 183.

of Chuzenji"] (*Pauline Jaricot* from *Poésies Diverses*);[72] the stars implore the waters to receive them, *"L'eau recueille / L'étoile au ciel qui l'exhorte"* ["The water gathers / The star in the sky which is exhorting it"] (*Le Cygne*);[73] the poet hears the forest and the sea speaking to him:

> *Je ne veux que dormir près de toi en te donnant la main,*
> *Ecoutant la forêt, la mer, l'eau qui fuit, et l'autre qui revient toujours,*
> *Cette joie sacrée, cette tristesse immense, mélangée à ce bonheur ineffable.*

> [I only want to sleep next to you in giving you my hand,
> Listening to the forest, the sea, the water that runs away, and the other that always comes back,
> That sacred joy, that immense sadness, mixed with this ineffable happiness.]

> (*Le Soulier de Satin*)[74]

Nature speaks with the sound of human words: *"tous les vocables couchés aux pages de la nature ont pour elle une valeur propre, un sens indispensable"* ["all the vocables lying on the pages of nature have for her a particular value, an essential meaning"] (*Art Poétique*).[75] Music characterizes the unity of man in the universe:

> *La fonction de l'ouvrier est de fournir sans cesse aliment à cette musique infatigable, cependant qu'apres s'en être éloigné il rentre en foule à la reprise dans ce refrain qui fait trembler la terre . . . Le jour viendra peut-etre où toutes les œuvres de l'humanité s'accompliront ainsi à grand orchestre et où l'esprit soufflera sur les villes comme dans les replis d'un instrument gigantesque.*

> [The worker's function is to constantly furnish food for this tireless music, while, after having left it, he is returning among the crowd at the repeat in that refrain that makes the earth tremble . . . Perhaps the day will come when the works of humanity will be accomplished as with a full orchestra and

72. *Pauline Jaricot* from *Poésies Diverses*, Vol. 2 of *Œuvres Complètes* (1952), p. 404.
73. *Le Cygne* from *Poésies Diverses*, p. 411.
74. *Le Soulier de Satin*, p. 129.
75. *Art Poétique*, p. 22.

when the spirit will breathe on the cities as into the innermost
recesses of a gigantic instrument.]

(*Conversations dans le Loir-et-Cher*)[76]

Apart from such generalized cosmic sounds that qualify nature and
its sonorous communication with man or with the poet, both Rimbaud
and Claudel mention musical instruments—in particular, the violin,
trumpets, drums, and flutes. Bells are not included in our list since
the bells mentioned by both Rimbaud and Claudel are not those of
an orchestra, rather, they are church bells, like Claudel's *"les cloches
de Rome"* ["the bells of Rome"] (*Le Soulier de Satin*).[77] They are
percussive, are associated essentially with rhythm, and, although they
certainly have musical tones, they are not to be compared with caril-
lons.

Of all these instruments, the ones most frequently mentioned in
Rimbaud's works are flutes, drums, and trumpets.[78] This is particularly true of *Les Illuminations,* the first of the works that Claudel
became acquainted with during the spring and summer of 1886. In
these prose poems, Rimbaud makes numerous references to music
or to the production of music in general: *"l'éveil fraternel de toutes
les énergies chorales et orchestrales et leurs applications instantanées"*
["the fraternal awakening of all choral and orchestral energies and
their instantaneous application"] (*Solde*); the coming of the time,
a new era—perhaps the modern one (or is it only envisioned by the
poet?)—when "resounding and moving" suffering, both that which
is heard and that which is felt, will be abolished, *"l'abolition de
toutes souffrances sonores et mouvantes"* ["the abolition of all resounding and moving suffering"] (*Génie*); red-costumed foot soldiers
in a pipers' band crossing London Bridge, *"On distingue une veste
rouge, peut-être d'autres costumes et des instruments de musique"*
["You can make out a red jacket, perhaps other costumes and musical instruments"] (*Les Ponts*); the complex horrors of war ironically
referred to as being *"aussi simple qu'une phrase musicale"* ["simple
as a phrase of music"] (*Guerre*); a choir, music, soothes the soul,
quiets the nerves and fills the void of absence in young hearts, *"Un
chœur, pour calmer l'impuissance et l'absence! Un chœur de verres
de mélodies nocturnes . . . En effet les nerfs vont vite chasser"* ["A
choir, to calm impotence and absence! A choir of glasses of nocturnal
melodies . . . Sure enough nerves will quickly chase off"] (*Jeunesse*).

76. *Conversations dans le Loir-et-Cher,* p. 152.
77. *Le Soulier de Satin.*
78. *"Clairons,"* bugles, are also mentioned; but bugles and trumpets are essentially the same instrument.

Rimbaud is even more specific in other references, such as the concentration of harmony by banging on a drum, *"Un coup de ton doigt sur le tambour décharge tous les sons et commence la nouvelle harmonie"* ["Your finger tap on the drum releases all sounds and begins the new harmony"] (*A Une Raison*); a primitive pastoral scene in the countryside, isolated by flute and drum, as unreal—or as real— as the theater, *"Des scènes lyriques, accompagnées de flûte et de tambour"* ["Lyric scenes, accompanied by flute and drum"] (*Scènes*); the transformed poet duped by love "bugles and brandishes" his complaint, like the ass in *Midsummer Night's Dream, "je courus aux champs, âne, claironnant et brandissant mon grief"* ["I ran to the fields, ass, bugling and brandishing my complaint"] (*Bottom*). In *Une Saison en Enfer,* the two principal mentions of a musical instrument refer to drums: *"Cris, tambour, danse, danse, danse, danse!"* ["Shouts, drum, dance, dance, dance dance!"] (*Mauvais Sang*); and *"une école de tambours faite par des anges"* ["a school of drums made by angels"] (*Alchimie du Verbe*). The trumpets, often associated with the colors rose or red, evoke a feeling of violence or of excitement of some kind. The flutes are generally associated with a lyric, pastoral-like scene: serenity and tranquility. And drums underline the primitive elements.

Similarly, in Claudel's works, it is principally these three instruments that stand out. Scattered throughout his plays, various texts on art criticism, or simply commentaries on art, prose poems, and exegetic texts, we find references to flutes in connection with the greenness of nature, *"Tout à coup l'humanité est devenue distraite, à travers les saisons recommençantes elle a perçu la flûte neuve"* ["Suddenly humanity has become inattentive, through the seasons starting afresh it has pierced a new flute"] (*Le Soulier de Satin*),[79] or with gardens, *"Je me rappelle ce jardin noir et blanc qu'on eût dit composé par la flûte"* ["I remember that black and white garden that you would have said was composed by a flute"] (*L'Œil Ecoute*),[80] or with nascent love and the potential for expression, with a man's desire to shower the object of his affections with new expressions of ardor,

Cette flûte entre les doigts du gentilhomme amoureux de Rembrandt, mince tube pour la note contractée comme ce pertuis qui s'ouvre entre les lèvres du siffleur, quel meilleur instrument imaginer pour un toast à l'idéal dans une effervescence d'adjectifs?

79. *Le Soulier de Satin*, p. 154.
80. *L'Œil Ecoute*, p. 98.

[That flute between the fingers of the gentleman in love by
Rembrandt, thin tube for the note contracted like this tap-
hole that opens between the lips of the whistler, what better
instrument can you imagine for a toast to the ideal in an ef-
fervesence of adjectives?]

(*L'Œil Ecoute*)[81]

The poet is fascinated by the solitary piercing sound of the flute
disappearing in the distance, *"n'est-ce pas sa flûte que j'entends
aigrement s'éloigner dans l'étincelante averse?"* ["isn't it his flute
that I hear growing acrimoniously fainter in the glistening sudden
shower?"] (*Figures et Paraboles*),[82] by the possibility of a return
to the simplicity of the "fife and drum," the one representing pastoral existence and the other, rhythm, movement—and both being
primitive instruments, *"je regagne la pipe et le tambour"* ["I am
getting back to the pipe and the drum"] (*Art Poétique*).[83] Trumpets,
associated with red or rose, announce excitement and general activity,
*"Tout à la fois reprend âme, un sentiment de gaîté se mêle à ces yeux
de tous côtés qui s'ouvrent, et ce je ne sais quoi de rose qui s'allie
aux accents de la trompette!"* ["everything comes back to life at once,
a general feeling of gaiety mixes with those eyes that are beginning
to open, a certain rose something that harmonizes with the accents
of the trumpet!"] (*Figures et Paraboles*),[84] or startled surprise at a
contrast between red and blue:

*Mais ce qui m'avait fait tressaillir à distance, ce qui, pour moi,
faisait sonner comme une trompette cet ensemble assourdi,
c'était, je le comprenais à présent, là, ce petit point vermillon,
et, à côté, cet atome de bleu, un grain de sel et un grain de
poivre!*

But what had startled me at a distance, what, for me, made
that muffled ensemble resound like a trumpet, was, I understood it now, that little vermilion dot, right there, and, beside
it, that atom of blue, a grain of salt and a grain of pepper!]

(*L'Œil Ecoute*)[85]

Trumpets also awaken the dormant strength within man's soul and
herald his future accomplishments:

81. *L'Œil Ecoute*, pp. 52-53.
82. *Figures et Paraboles*, p. 180.
83. *Art Poétique*, p. 87.
84. *Figures et Paraboles*, p. 230.
85. *L'Œil Ecoute*, p. 15.

Il ne s'agit pas d'Abélard et d'Astralabius mais de ce puissant coup de trompette au fond de nous-mêmes qui a travaillé toute la civilisation chrétienne et qui a mis debout tant de saints et tant d'artistes, tant de théologiens, tant de trouveurs d'îles, tant de fondateurs d'ordres et de bâtisseurs de cathédrales!

[It doesn't concern Abélard and Astralabius, but, rather, that powerful trumpet call deep within ourselves that has obsessed the whole of Christian civilization and that has put so many saints and artists on their feet, so many theologians, so many discoverers of islands, so many founders of orders and builders of cathedrals!]

(Conversations dans le Loir-et-Cher)[86]

Drums isolate man in the solitary primitiveness of the desert and the intense sun, like Rimbaud's *"fils du soleil," "J'entends un son grave comme celui d'un tambour de bronze et cela est associé à une idée de désert et de grand soleil"* ["I hear a solemn sound like that of a bronze drum and that is associated with an idea of desert and of full sun"] *(Le Soulier de Satin)*,[87] and drums determine his capacity for vibrant existence, just as Rimbaud's drums "discharge all sounds and begin the new harmony," *"Le coup d'un maillet sur un tambour détermine un être sonore"* ["The tap of a mallet on a drum puts into action a sonorous being"] *(Art Poétique)*.[88]

In *Connaissance de l'Est,* in which echoes of Rimbaud reverberate in *Rêves* with its apparently disconnected paragraphs all related to an exhortation of nature, comparable to *Phrases* from *Les Illuminations,* as well as in *Ville la Nuit* which begins, *"Il pleut doucement"* ["It is raining gently"], like Rimbaud's *"il pleut doucement sur la ville"* ["it is raining gently on the town"] from *Bribes* or like *une poudre noire pleut doucement sur ma veillée"* ["a black powder is raining gently on my vigil"] also from *Phrases,* the musical allusions are for the most part restricted to flutes and drums. Silence is intensified by its contrast with the sound of a voice and the rhythmic beat of a drum, *"Rien ne parle, ni voix ni tambour"* ["Nothing is speaking, neither voice nor drum"] *(Le Temple de la Conscience)*.[89] Awareness of man's closeness to the earth, his primitiveness, the dust from which he is made, the element that supports life or in which life moves, is awakened by the throbbing of a distant drum, *"Le thème*

86. *Conversations dans le Loir-et-Cher,* pp. 120-121.
87. *Le Soulier de Satin,* p. 53.
88. *Art Poétique,* p. 62.
89. *Le Temple de la Conscience* from *Connaissance de l'Est,* p. 55.

de la Terre est exprimé par les détonations de ce distant tambour" ["The theme of the Earth is expressed by the detonations of that distant drum"] (*Heures dans le Jardin*).[90] Especially noteworthy is the lyric scene evoked and characterized by a flute and tom-tom, just as Rimbaud mentions "lyric scenes, accompanied by flute and drum":

> *Ou, donc, je jouerai de la flûte: je battrai le tam-tam, et la batelière qui, debout sur une jambe comme une cigogne, tandis que de l'autre genou elle tient son enfant attaché à sa mamelle, conduit son sampan à travers les eaux plates, croira que les dieux derrière le rideau tiré de la nue se jouent dans la cour de leur temple.*

> [Or, then, I will play the flute: I will beat the tam-tam, and the boatwoman who, standing on one leg like a stork while with the other knee she props her child up to her breast, steers her sampan across the flat waters, will believe that be-hind the drawn cloud curtain the gods are playing in the courtyard of their temple.]

(La Mer Supérieure)[91]

In *Le Jour de la Fête-de-tous-les-fleuves,* the vivid red and rose dawn associated with the trumpet is contrasted with the muted, somber black evening and the drum: *"l'Aurore sonne de la trompette . . . le Soir s'en va dans le tambour!"* ["the Dawn blows the trumpet . . . the Evening leaves with drums!"].[92] Here again, all of these sounds recall or awaken something elemental or primitive, and Claudel uses them to evoke a certain mood or image. They certainly have little to do with the many references to classical music that one finds scattered throughout Claudel's works. In his dramas, we find numer-ous mentions of orchestras; but the individual instruments referred to in his other poetry—especially in his early works, those most closely associated with his first acquaintance of Rimbaud—are the instruments referred to in *Les Illuminations* and *Une Saison en En-fer.*

For both Rimbaud and Claudel, the most important of all these is the drum, the instrument used mainly to mark rhythm. And, as is suggested by the preponderance of drums in their works, it is the rhythmic aspects of music that interest them in particular. In Rim-

90. *Heures dans le Jardin* from *Connaissance de l'Est,* p. 145.
91. *La Mer Supérieure* from *Connaissance de l'Est,* p. 53.
92. *Le Jour de la Fête-de-tous-les-fleuves* from *Connaissance de l'Est,* p. 171.

baud's works, the drum puts the universe in motion, as in *"Un coup de ton doigt sur le tambour décharge tous les sons et commence la nouvelle harmonie"* ["Your finger tap on the drum releases all sounds and begins the new harmony"] (*A Une Raison*). Rhythm is suggested in the association of colors with dance, *"Les couleurs propres de la vie se foncent, dansent, et se dégagent autour de la Vision, sur le chantier"* ["The very colors of life deepen, dance, and emerge around the Vision, on the worksite"] (*Being Beauteous*). Bells do not only sound, they move, like shuddering bellflowers, *"les clochettes mouvantes"* ["the swinging bellflowers"] (*Après le Déluge*). Rhythms— action, movement— take over a household, *"Les calculs de côté, l'inévitable descente du ciel et la visite des souvenirs et la séance des rythmes occupent la demeure, la tête et le monde de l'esprit"* ["Homework put aside, the inevitable descent from heaven and the visit of memories and the session of rhythms fill the dwelling, the head, and the world of the spirit"] (*Jeunesse*). Rimbaud says in *Alchimie du Verbe* that he had attempted to regulate not only the form but also "the movement of each consonant." And as we pointed out earlier, he refers to "number" as the essence of poetry—number being, of course, the basic principle of rhythm.

In *Figures et Paraboles,* Claudel too points out that the most important aspect of music is rhythm and its association with movement:

> *C'est ici que comme le Vieil Homère, ou dans tous les pays*
> *du monde ces amis déguenillés du Vent-qui-souffle, scaldes,*
> *bardes, rhapsodes, qui allaient d'une ville à l'autre, les yeux*
> *à demi fermés, pleins de visions et de paroles, en se grommelant*
> *à eux-mêmes de longues épopées confuses, je voudrais avoir*
> *sous la main l'instrument par excellence de leur profession,*
> *lyre, banjo, quelque chose pour d'une main crispée en tirer*
> *une ébauche de rythme—une poignée de cordes! quelque*
> *chose qui interrompe le discours pour lui donner un élan, une*
> *élasticité, un coup de fouet, et qui fasse monter des profon*
> *deurs de l'esprit de monstrueux paquets d'images et d'idées!*

[It is here that like Old Homer, or like, in every country in the world, those ragged friends of the Wind-which-blows, skalds, bard, rhapsodists, who went from city to city, their eyes half closed, full of visions and words, muttering to themselves long, confused epic poems, I would like to have in hand the instrument par excellence of their profession, lyre, banjo, something for a clenched hand to pull a first attempt at rhythm out of— a handful of cords! something which interrupts discourse to give it feeling, elasticity, a snap of a whip, and which makes monstrous packages of images and ideas come up out of the depths of the mind!] [93]

Elsewhere, he equates music with movement: *"Et partout où il y a du mouvement il y a de la musique"* ["And wherever there is movement there is music"] (*Conversations dans le Loir-et-Cher*).[94] This theme, as in the following three examples, is repeated over and over as a leitmotif of his basic concept that "poetry is doing," *"la poésie est de faire"* (*faire*, doing, is inseparable from movement): *"Mon idée . . . est que tout mouvement régulier est l'élément d'une musique"* ["My idea . . . is that every regular movement is the element of some musique"] (*Conversations dans le Loir-et-Cher*);[95] *"On peut dire que le son est la peinture du mouvement"* ["One can say that sound is the painting of movement"] (*Art Poétique*);[96] *"Le sens de l'ouïe est, en effet, éminemment le sens de ce qui passe, ce qu'on nomme la hauteur des sons, l'aigu, le grave, n'étant que l'indice de leur rapidité"* ["The sense of hearing is, in fact, eminently the sense of what is happening, what one calls the pitch of sounds, high or low, being only the indication of their rapidity"] (*Art Poétique*).[97] It becomes all the more obvious in certain of the rhythmic patterns that Rimbaud and Claudel use to create or to complement an image.[98]

In *Le Bateau Ivre*, for example, the boat's calm descent of the river, *"Comme je descendais des fleuves impassibles,"* is contrasted with its sudden liberation, *"Je ne me sentis plus guidé par les haleurs,"* not only by means of the choice of vocabulary and the contrast of the imperfect with the simple past tense, but even more by the rhythmic patterns established by the contrast of the mid open vowels of *"comme," "descendais," "fleuves,"* with the mid and high vowels of *"sentis," "plus," "guidé."* Its hurried flight towards the sea, the conjunction of the river's current with the sea's tides at the mouth of the river, and the sound of these choppy waters and waves against the side of the boat are evoked by a piling up of mid and high vowels and a second simple past tense: *"Dans les clapotements furieux des marées/. . . Je courus! Et les Péninsules démarrées/N'ont pas subi*

93. *Figures et Paraboles*, p. 200.
94. *Conversations dans le Loir-et-Cher*, p. 125.
95. *Conversations dans le Loir-et-Cher*, p. 149.
96. *Art Poétique*, p. 69.
97. *Art Poétique*, p. 69.
98. In the following discussion of sound and rhythmic patterns, the English translation of several of the French texts has been purposely omitted, since English here would obscure the point of our observations.

tohu-bohus plus triomphants." The final two nasalized mid open vowels of *"triomphants"* vibrate like extended undulations, like the swells that announce an arrival on the open sea. They also mark and underline the completeness of the break, the fullness of victory, as it were. In the fourth strophe, the image of a cork dancing on the waves, *"Plus léger qu'un bouchon j'ai dansé sur les flots,"* captures a bobbing movement in its use of successive high vowels, *"u," "é," "er,"* contrasted with mid and low open and nasalized vowels, *"bouchon," "flots,"* very similar to the effect achieved by Claudel in *La Muse qui est la Grâce,* in which he, too, uses the image of a boat waiting to be liberated.

In the first lines of this ode, Claudel's vocabulary and rhythm remind us of the sea. Technical words such as *marée* [tide], *syzygie* [syzygy], *ber* [cradle], and *tanguer* [pitch] create a marine impression; short words and phrases and high close vowels suggest, within the verse line itself, a choppy rhythm analagous to the movement of a pitching boat, *"Comme une barque . . . qui danse furieusement, et qui tape, et qui saque, et qui fonce, et qui encense, et qui culbute, le nez à son piquet,"* like a boat impatient to leave, tossed about at its mooring. Similar to Rimbaud's device, the use of a simple past tense to mark the arrival of the Amazon indicates a brusque movement, signaling departure, *"l'amazone qui bondit sur lui de côté et qui saisit brutalement les rênes avec un rire éclatant!"*[99] Finally, the bark which was held back only by its rope, *"qui ne tient plus qu'à sa corde"* ["which is now held only by its cord"] feels itself liberated and plows through the ocean swells triumphantly, *"je foule les eaux de la mer en triomphe!"* ["I ride roughshod over the waters in triumph!"] . [100] The cord has snapped: the revolt is complete and the bark is free to wander on the high seas in search of its truth. The words that describe the intensity of this movement are similar in both Rimbaud's poem and Claudel's ode: Rimbaud's *"furieux"* ["furious"] as in *"les clapotements furieux"* ["the furious rip-tides"], is to be compared with Claudel's *"furieusement"* ["furiously"]. Both poets describe the successful revolt of their boats as a triumph: Rimbaud's *"tohu-bohus . . . triomphants"* ["triumphant . . . hubbub"], is to be compared with *"en triomphe"* ["in triumph"] in Claudel's ode.

Both Rimbaud and Claudel use rhythmic patterns to evoke an impression of the movements of the sea as well as of the boat itself. Claudel makes us feel this movement by the irregular, seemingly un-

---

99. *La Muse qui est la Grâce* from *Cinq Grandes Odes,* p. 115.
100. *La Muse qui est la Grâce,* p. 117.

calculated rhythm of *versets* varying in length, comparable to the uneven and unequal waves that make a boat roll and pitch, almost engulfing it at times, and to waves reaching their apogee and breaking:

> −*O Muse, il sera temps de dormir un autre jour!*
> *Mais puisque cette grande nuit toute entière est à nous,*
> *Et que je suis un peu ivre en sorte qu'un autre*
> *mot parfois*
> *Vient à la place du vrai, à la façon que tu aimes,*
> *Laisse-moi avoir explication avec toi,*
> *Laisse-moi te refouler dans cette strophe,*
> *avant que tu ne reviennes sur moi comme une vague*
> *avec un cri félin!*[101]

Rimbaud evokes this sensation of the sea's waves and heavy swells by using elongated "stretched-out" sounds, as in *rouleurs éternels,"* in contrast to series of "taut" mid and high vowels, and he captures an image of the immensity of the swells by showing the impotence of man confronted by the sea, when he mentions the "victims" of these "eternal rollers": *"Plus léger qu'un bouchon j'ai dansé sur les flots/Qu'on appelle rouleurs éternels de victimes."* The movement of the sea is doubly emphasized; it is evoked not only by an immediate physical feeling, but also by everything that is associated with this movement and with its uncontrollable and destructive power. Similarly, it is the movement of the sea that snaps the cord holding Claudel's bark at its mooring and thus permits the boat to fly off on "golden sandals" towards its visions of truth and transcendent perfection.

All of this brings us to the matter of the origin of the Claudelian *verset,* which has been subject to a great deal of speculation. Henri Guillemin, for one, asserts that it has its origin in the chants that Claudel, as a child, listened to in the church at Villeneuve, a view that fits in very nicely with the concept of Claudel as a poet-mystic or a Christian poet. However, by the very nature of its contrasts in consonants and vowel tones and its marked variations in intonation, the Claudelian *verset* is strikingly different from the monotone of liturgical chants or the sparse modal Gregorian chants sung at high Mass. Another critic has suggested that the *verset* was at least partially inspired by Rimbaud's prose poems. Yet, in terms of the way in which imagery is developed, there is really little resemblance be-

101. *La Muse qui est la Grâce,* p. 117.

tween the two, and parallels of this nature cannot be satisfactorily drawn: the images of Rimbaud's prose poems are elliptical to the point of being often obscurely complex and condensed, whereas Claudel tends to draw out his images in a manner that borders on hyperbole. Furthermore, in contrast with Rimbaud who seldom uses the word *comme* and who prefers to reconstruct a vision in such a way that it takes on a life of its own, is valid within itself and stands alone, unassisted by attenuating comparisons, Claudel makes free and excessive use of *comme,* though there are a few exceptions, notably in *Cinq Grandes Odes* and *La Cantate à trois voix,* in which the poet's voice is assimilated in the imagery and the poet transformed, much as Rimbaud is in *Le Bateau Ivre,* to become one with his imagery.

Claudel himself does not discuss the origin of the *verset,* as such. He did say in an interview with Guillemin, however, that Rimbaud revealed "modulation" to him, "the phrase with its summit somewhere and its final resolution and these interior echoes of strong syllables of which the memory keeps some trace."[102] His use of a musical term, modulation, to describe the relationship between his own poetic lines and Rimbaud's, indicates once again the importance he places on the sonorous qualities of his poetry and expresses succintly his concept of the interdependence of rhythm and tonal qualities as expressed in an impressionistic explication of two sentences from *Une Saison en Enfer* that he used to demonstrate this aspect of poetry in general:

> *Et nous arrivons à l'épanouissement total de la langue française développant enfin toutes les ressources de le sonorité comme un Guarnerius sous l'archet d'un maître. Voici une phrase d'Arthur Rimbaud,—mais il n'y aurait qu'à puiser dans cet assemblage de merveilles qu'est la* Saison en Enfer:
> > Et par une route de dangers ma faiblesse me menait aux confins du monde et de la Cimmérie, patrie de l'ombre et des tourbillons.
> *Je n'ose profaner ce texte superbe par des accentuations scolastiques et je laisse au lecteur le plaisir d'en découvrir toutes les beautés de consonances, d'allitération, de mouvements et de dessin. C'est fini! c'est en l'air! cela ne tient à rien! ce n'est plus porté que par la musique, c'est comme un beau cygne qui vole les ailes étendues dans un milieu élyséen!*

102. Claudel quoted by Henri Guillemin, *Claudel et son art d'écrire* (Paris: Gallimard, 1956), p. 45.

*Je ne résiste pas au bonheur de citer cet autre vers beaucoup
plus simple, mais si grand et si pathétique:*
    Sur la mer que j'aimais comme si elle eût dû me laver
de souillure, je voyais se lever la croix consolatrice.
Avec quel art est préparée l'apparition amère et viride de
souillure *qui répand sa lueur sur les eaux ténébreuses et fris-
sonnantes! Par une inspiration géniale l'impression épiphanique
de la Croix, dont le nom même est comme élargi et rompu
dans la cavité d'un ïambe, est reportée* en avant *sur cette âcre
et unique syllabe en* ure *suivant une mouillée. Et les deux mots
en reflet de* laver *et* lever.

[And we arrive at the total blossoming out of the French language developing at last all the resources of sonority like a
Guarnerius under the bow of a master. Here is one of Arthur
Rimbaud's sentences,—but you have only to choose at random
in that collection of marvels, *Une Saison en Enfer:*
    *Et par une route de dangers ma faiblesse me menait aux
confins du monde et de la Cimmérie, patrie de l'ombre
et des tourbillons.*
I hardly dare profane this superb text with scholastic accentu-
ations and I leave to the reader the pleasure of discovering in it
all the beauties of consonants, alliteration, movement and design. It's finished! it's in the air. it's supported by nothing! it
is carried along by music alone, it is like a beautiful swan flying with its wings stretched out in an Elysian sphere!
    I cannot resist the pleasure of quoting another much more
simple line of verse, but so great and so moving:
    *Sur la mer que j'aimais comme si elle eût dû me laver
d'une souillure, je voyais se lever la croix consolatrice.*
With what art has been prepared the bitter, green *viride* appearance of *souillure* which spreads its glow on the dark,
shivering waters! Through a brilliant inspiration, the epiphanic
impression of the Cross, the very name of which seems enlarged and broken in the hollow of an iambus, is carried
forward on the single, pungent syllable *ure* following a pala-
talized consonant. And the two words reflecting each other,
laver and *lever.*]

                             (*Positions et Propositions I*)[103]

103. *Positions et Propositions I,* pp. 47-48. Later, in this same passage, Claudel
stresses the importance of complementary rhythm and tonal qualities: "... *la
césure variable et les différences de distance et de hauteur qui séparent les som-
mets phonétiques suffisent à créer pour chaque phrase un dessin sensible à notre
œil auditif en même temps que le jeu des consonnes et de la syntaxe associé à
celui des timbres indique la tension et le mouvement de l'idée.*"

It is primarily this sort of combination of rhythm and vowel tones that represents the extent of the influence of Rimbaud on Claudel's *verset*. Moreover, the musical device of high close vowels used with increasing frequency within a verse line, followed by mid and low close vowels to create an opening-up effect that builds up in a crescendo to broad, full open vowels which are then suddenly interrupted by a quick-tempoed final cadence, a device of which two especially effective examples are to be found in *Phrases* from *Les Illuminations,*

> *J'ai tendu des cordes de clocher à clocher; des guirlandes de fenêtre à fenêtre; des chaînes d'or d'étoile à étoile, et je danse.*
>
> *Avivant un agréable goût d'encre de Chine, une poudre noire pleut doucement sur ma veillée.—Je baisse les feux du lustre, je me jette sur le lit, et, tourné du côté de l'ombre, je vous vois, mes filles! mes reines!*

is remarkably similar to that used in a series of *versets* like the following from *La Muse qui est la Grâce:*

> *Ce que les gens ont fait autour de moi avec le canon qui ouvre les vieux Empires,*
> *Avec le canot démontable qui remonte l'Aruwhimi, avec l'expédition polaire qui prend des observations magnétiques.*
> *Avec les batteries de hauts fourneaux qui digèrent le minerai, avec les frénétiques villes haletantes et tricotantes, (et ça et là une anse bleue de la rivière dans la campagne solennelle),*
> *Avec les ports tout bordés intérieurement de pinces et d'antennes et le transatlantique qui signale au loin dans le brouillard,*
> *Avec la locomotive qu'on attelle à son convoi, et le canal qui se remplit quand la fille de l'Ingénieur en chef du bout de son doigt sur le coup-de-poing fait sauter à la fois la double digue,*
> *Je le ferai avec un poëme qui ne sera plus l'aventure d'Ulysse parmi les Lestrygons et les Cyclopes, mais la connaissance de la Terre,*
> *Le grand poëme de l'homme enfin par delà les causes secondes réconcilié aux forces éternelles,*
> *La grande Voie triomphale au travers de la Terre réconcilée pour que l'homme soustrait au hasard s'y avance!*[104]

---

104. *La Muse qui est la Grâce* from *Cinq Grandes Odes,* pp. 119-120.

The same device is found in many of Claudel's dramatic works in which the tonal effect is of such consequence that lines fairly cry out to be read aloud, as in this passage from *Le Soulier de Satin:*

> *Elle me baigne et je n'y puis goûter! c'est un rayon qui me perce, c'est un glaive qui me divise, c'est le fer rouge effroyablement appliqué sur le nerf même de la vie, c'est l'effervescence de la source qui s'empare de tous mes éléments pour les dissoudre et les recomposer, c'est le néant à chaque moment où je sombre et Dieu sur ma bouche qui me ressuscite, et supérieure à toutes les délices, ah! c'est la traction impitoyable de la soif, l'abomination de cette soif affreuse qui m'ouvre et me crucifie!*[105]

Although the development of these passages is slower paced than Rimbaud's, the tonal similarities are too markedly present to be purely coincidental. This is not to suggest that Claudel made an analytical study of Rimbaud's style in an attempt to classify and re-create his poetic devices; rather, it was a matter of having become so intimately acquainted with Rimbaud's poetry as to have assimilated unconsciously his metrical, tonal, and rhythmic cadences. Yet at the same time, he was aware of these tonal effects, and, in mentioning the "modulation" in Rimbaud's poems and his own, he himself set the precedent for drawing such parallels.

In *Le Promeneur* from *Connaissance de l'Est,* Claudel reflects upon two of the essential elements of music, harmony and melody, stating that he understands "the harmony of the world" while wondering when he will discover "its melody."[106] This has nothing to do with music as such, but it does point to the importance of musical imagery in his global as well as his poetic concepts which are essentailly one and the same thing: the world is a poem, and it is through poetry that he will create a new world or reflect the creation, give it meaning and order for those who find only chaos in it:

> *... toutes choses me sont nécessaires ...*
> *Elles ne sont pas faites pour moi, leur ordre n'est pas avec moi, mais avec la parole qui les a créées ...*
> *Ce que les gens ont fait autour de moi avec le canon qui ouvre les Empires ...*
> *Je le ferai avec un poëme ...*

105. *Le Soulier de Satin*, pp. 193-194.
106. *Le Promeneur* from *Connaissance de l'Est*, p. 116.

[. . . all things are indispensable to me . . .
They are not made for me, their order is not with me, but
with the word that created them . . .[107]
What people have done around me with the canon which
opens Empires . . .
I will do with a poem . . .]

(*La Muse qui est la Grâce*)[108]

To continue Claudel's own sort of musical comparison, then, it is
his juxtaposition of vowel tones that forms his melodies, the harmony
and the rhythmic qualities being inherent in the "fundamental iambus,"
in the accents, the "natural" caesuras of his poetic lines, the Claudelian
"souffle," "breath," that governs his *"vers libre,"* "free verse," and
what Samson calls his "musical prose." And if "the consonant is the
essential element of diction," it is because it limits and accentuates
the vowel tones, just as harmony and rhythmic patterns limit, accentuate, or direct the development of melody. Claudel himself makes
this sort of comparison of vowels and consonants in a letter to Samson:

*Pour un musicien, tout consiste somme toute dans la voyelle,
la note n'est qu'une voyelle glorifiée. Pour l'écrivain, au con-
traire, et surtout pour l'écrivain dramatique, l'élément essentiel
de la diction est la consonne. La voyelle est la matière, la consonne est la forme, la matrice du mot, et aussi l'engin pro-
pulsateur dont la voyelle avec tout son charme n'est que le
projectile . . . Qui ne voit que dans ce vers:
Et moi je lui tendais les mains pour l'embrasser l'élément
dynamique affirmé par les redoublements de consonnes est
l'essentiel et l'élément mélodique des voyelles secondaire?*

[For a musician, everything consists finally of vowels, a note
being nothing more than a glorified vowel. On the other hand,
for a writer, and especially for a playwright, the essential element of diction is the consonant. The vowel is matter, the
consonant is form, the matrix of the word, and also the pro-
pelling device of which the vowel, with all its charm, is only
the projectile . . . Who does not see that in this line of verse:
Et moi je lui tendais les mains pour l'embrasser the dynamic
element supported by the doubling of the consonants in the

107. *La Muse qui est la Grâce*, p. 127.
108. *La Muse qui est la Grâce*, p. 119.

essential one and the melodic element of the vowels only secondary?][109]

Since consonants are equivalent to rhythm and movement and vowels to color as well as to "glorified notes" for Claudel,[110] we must bear in mind that it was first Rimbaud who, having invented "the color of the vowels," had tried to regulate "the movement of each consonant" in an attempt to emphasize both the visual and the auditive aspects of poetry. Moreover, in his long digressions on the musical aspects of poetry, written after he had access to such documents as *La Lettre du Voyant* to Paul Demeny, Claudel has expounded at length essentially on the basic principles proposed by Rimbaud.

109. Quoted from a letter written by Claudel to Samson, in 1944, *Paul Claudel Poète Musicien*, p. 80.
110. For Claudel's implication that for him too vowels have color, see p. 117 of this text.

8.
Conclusion

In the course of reviewing the broad scope of Claudel's works, which
lend themselves to the kind of "critical editions" in which are seen
"the books of great writers garnished with the notes of some schoolmaster, like heads of game riddled with pieces of lead from the shot-
gun that brought them down,"[1] it gradually becomes apparent that
his literary evolution, from the rudimentary formation of the *verset*
to the complex aspects of his religious thinking, was subject to a vast
number of influences in varying degrees. It cannot be said that any
single individual brought to his works a definitive form or a specific
metaphysic, philosophy, or theology; rather, like his personal opinions,
Claudel's literary production was essentially eclectic. Apparent con-
tradictions in many of his works serve to corroborate this point of
view, and the varied subjects of his discussions along with the diverse
considerations he gives to them and the poetic forms with which he
envelops them, as well as his diffuse prose, are so all-inclusive and
massive as to be like a pipe organ played at full diapason with all the
stops pulled out.

Claudel's theme of "universality" in the sphere of his thematic development also applies to his aethetic precepts. In his concept of
poetic rapports, for example, a fundamental interest in the symbolic
and mystical aspects of Baudelaire's correspondence is manifest.
Mallarmé's concretized hermeticism, expressed in the symbolism
of white sterility, has evolved into Claudel's discovery of a fecund
rapport between the printed text and the secrets hidden in the blank
margins of a page, waiting to be brought to life through imaginative
associations; Claudel's is the whiteness that speaks louder than words.
Verlaine's preoccupation with musicality is reflected in the sonorous
aspects of Claudel's concepts. Bossuet's rich rhetoric and religious
dogmatism find their way into Claudel's Catholic orthodoxy and
fanaticism as well as his theologic imagery. Even Pascal, whose works

1. *Journal,* 1920.

were long considered by Claudel as bordering on heresy (though he eventually conceded that whereas Pascal was not necessarily influential on or even germane to the thought of a devout believer in the Catholic faith, he could very well be instrumental in convincing doubters), is reflected in the Claudelian placing of man in a context in which he is necessarily humble in his awareness of the Creation's vast complexity yet indomitably proud of his contribution to its completeness. Shakespeare's penchant for the global and massive aspects of theater, his rich flourish of imagery, his view of characters strutting across a stage and of the world as a magnificent stage for man's actions are all to be found in Claudel's cosmic perspective, in which the world is a setting for his dramas in a curiously baroque way. References to Greek and Roman mythology point to the pagan spirit that lay behind many of Claudel's images—if by pagan we mean a passion for the earth and its evocations of sensuality. Nor can we neglect the Biblical phrases and allusions that testify to Claudel's constant reading of Scripture, the *versets* that owe at least a partial debt to the lyric poetry of the Old Testament.

The source of each of these influences, except, of course, for the Bible, has been subject to severe criticism from Claudel. However, he did recognize the role that they played in his poetic evolution. This is not to say that his works are merely pastiches or clever combinations of source materials, any more than are Rimbaud's. But Claudel's originality does not lie in Catholicism—others before him were deeply involved with Catholic Christian beliefs and inspiration— nor in his orthodoxy, nor in his sense of sacrifice through divinely inspired or saintly love, nor even in his theological views and proselytizing. Rather, it lies, at least partly, in the paganistic spirit and lyric cosmic song that exist simultaneously with the devoutly religious feeling expressed in his tenacity to Catholic dogma. In order to understand this apparent duality in the man and his works, another element must be taken into consideration, an element that acts as the focal point of Claudel's works and that is really their unifying factor, their one fundamental constant.

More than anything else—more than a reflection of Claudel's eclecticism, more than a contribution to literature or even to proselytizing, more than a dramatization of man's invincible role in the universe— Claudel's works as a whole constitute an act, an act of faith. And since they reveal the wide, panoramic scope of his thought and experience, an understanding of them is contingent on a consideration of certain biographical details, for they also reveal, in a literal sense, his native country, the Tardenois region where he was born, the countries in which he was a diplomat, and the people with whom he came into contact. And they are witness to a subjective examination and analysis, an interiorization, that is in great part the basis for Claudel's lyrically poetic soul; for his works also reflect his passions, his hatreds, his soaring lyricism, his essential belief in mystery, his need to resolve, and his resolution of, what Camus has called the absurd: man's search for spiritual absolutes in a relative world, the dichotomy between spiritual needs and physical realities—a resolution that he arrived at, or to which he was awakened, through reading Rimbaud. If other writers found their "proper" place in Claudel's works, Rimbaud's spirit formed the basis for it—Rimbaud's spirit in tandem with Claudel's. Claudel's works, then, like his life, are an act of faith in his resolution of that dichotomy; they are an act of faith not only in God, but also in man.

In Rimbaud's poetry, especially in *Les Illuminations* and *Une Saison en Enfer,* Claudel found a reflection of himself, as well as a kind of intellectual solitude and spiritual inspiration. As C.A.Hackett has said, Rimbaud's works are above all a poetization of the child's confidence in his own omnipotence; but they are also an expression of adolescent dreams, frustrations, hopes, fantasies, the uncertain adolescent search for some definitive answers to broad indefinite questions, and a revolt against that uncertainty and against the conformity of bourgeois society and conventionality. It was because of this adolescent revolt that, as a youth, Claudel discovered in the sensitive, revolt-prone poet from Charleville, an *âme sœur*—an event unprecedented in French literature, with the possible exception of Montaigne and La Boétie—who inspired in him the realization that his doubts and questioning were not solitary, that he was indeed not alone in his inability to accept what he called Renan's "materialistic determinism." There can be no doubt that the young Claudel was fundamentally dissatisfied with the smugness of the nineteenth century and the pat answers that theories of evolution were attempting, or seemed to him to be attempting, to find for irrational mysteries. Endowed with an expansive imagination, Claudel could not accept science as the be-all and end-all of existence; in Rimbaud, he discovered the same reaction. As a correlation to this, Rimbaud presented Claudel with a broad, all-inclusive cosmic view of the universe: he also showed him the poetic possibilities of a close association with nature, which Claudel turned into pantheistic adoration. Thus it was principally—and first of all—the thematic content of Rimbaud's poetry, deeply imbued with a fantastic vision of man's spiritual communication with the unknown, that appealed to Claudel. Rimbaud's initial

importance was that he crystallized for Claudel his own basic temperament. Beyond this, Rimbaud's poetry acted as a catalyst that pre-
cipitated Claudel's materialistic doubts and brought with it a profound
awareness, or at least prepared him for an awareness of God's munificence as reflected in His creation. It was, for Claudel, *"cette minute
d'éveil"* ["this moment of awakening"] to which Rimbaud refers
at the end of *L'Impossible* in *Une Saison en Enfer,* and which Claudel
vividly evokes in the sixth *cahier* of his *Journal.*[2] It prepared him for
his conversion.

This similarity of temperament is apparent throughout Claudel's
works, from the first of the plays written after the initial Rimbaldian
experience, *Tête d'or,* to the most comprehensive of his dramatic
creations, *Le Soulier de Satin.* It is also found in the religiously inspired evocations of *Cinq Grandes Odes* as well as in his meditations
on literature, art, and music. It permeates the whole of Claudel's
thinking and explains why many of his themes are similar and even
exactly parallel to those in Rimbaud's poetry. Beginning with the
revolt against "the human condition" reflected in *Tête d'or,* the
Claudelian heroes and their women are set in a context which is unmistakably Rimbaldian: an identification of man's innocence and
purity with the past, a nostalgic longing for *le festin ancien* and a desire to regain the lost paradise or to transcend reality in order to
establish a new spiritual order in which love will be "reinvented";
the placing of woman outside of the domain of this new transcendence
and separated from the willful Nietzschean-Rimbaldian adventurer-
conqueror who, through his love of nature and his need to depart,
is actually "another fancier of the high road," as Claudel said Rimbaud was; heroes who must leave the "sullied cities" of Western
civilization and push towards the Orient and the splendors of exotic
existence, their lives governed by the dominance of the sun, which
represents power and strength as well as the isolation and solitude
of this unusual strength; the night that, as a balance to the sun, brings
the peace of a promise and the black of a mystery to be discovered,
the hope of eventual realization of one's goals. All of these themes
are in some way involved with a religious awareness, but they are
also developed in an aura of what is virtually a paganistic worship
of nature. For all his pious Catholicism, Claudel was basically an

2. *Journal,* Tome I, Cahier 6, November 1931, p. 976. *"'Ne pouvez-vous rester
éveillés une heure avec moi?' Il entend éveillés à Dieu, éveillés à la vie réelle. Cf.
Rimbaud: 'C'est cette petite minute d'éveil... Si je restais éveillé à partir de
ce moment-ci.' Veillez et priez. La prière dans la connaissance."*

unbridled spirit, and his religion acts as a self-imposed brake to this ferociousness, just as the religious element often seems imposed on his heroes.

However, Rimbaud's presence in Claudel's works is more than a reflection of temperament and of thematic parallels. The *poète-voyou*'s influence also involves aesthetic doctrine and, to a certain degree, style, technique, and form. *Connaissance de l'Est,* for example, in which we find unmistakable echoes of Rimbaud in the contrasts of color complemented by musical overtones, in the kinds of musical instruments mentioned, in the way the principal images—the sea, the night, and the sun—are developed through an opening-up process, in the device of striking contrasts between the vulgar and the sublime, between the exotic beauty of the Orient and the "filth" of the West and its encroachment on the simplicity and pristine beauty of nature, is essentially a Claudelian rendition of *Les Illuminations.* We also find a similarity of attitude in the concept of poetry as a means to an end rather than as an end in itself, the idea that poetry is a re-creation of the universe, or, at least, a reflection of the mysterious, intangible *au-delà*, the world beyond, the "unknown" of which visions are awakened through poetry. A similarity of stylistic approach is particularly noticeable in the specific colors associated with vowels and in the "movement" of consonants; the interrelationship of these elements and the symbolic values assigned to them by Claudel all reflect an attitude first proposed by Rimbaud. They are all elements which both poets commented on and developed in their pronouncements about poetic theory and aesthetic doctrine. Yet, despite what appear to be intellectual considerations of poetic theory, a reading of their works brings us to the realization that theirs is not an intellectual poetry such as we find in the works of other French poets like Mallarmé or Valéry, or in the efforts of English-language poets sensitive to French symbolism, like T. S. Eliot. Rather, it is a poetry based primarily on a direct appeal to the reader's visual and sonorous sensitivity, in an *élan* of hermetic lyrical inspiration—especially for Rimbaud—and excluding virtually all classical literary conceits. We discover evidence of both poets' application of these ideas to poetry through the colored rhythmic polyphony of their works. As concerns Claudel, they are especially apparent in the dialogues and in the words spoken by the poet Cœuvre in *La Ville,* and are further supported by the activities of heroes like Rodrigue. None of these similarities, however, when considered separately, indicates anything more than a coincidental evolution of ideas or forms. But when considered in the aggregate they present formidable and all but irrefutable evidence that Rimbaud's influence was indeed all that Claudel said it was.

Claudel himself never discussed the specific aspects of the Rimbaldian influence on his works, except to say that Rimbaud's "modulation" was essential. He felt that the "extreme value of Arthur Rimbaud's works immediately strikes every reader in whom a certain sense of divine poetry exists or sleeps, but to join their elements is delicate, and to specify them is profane." In fact, he evolved an image of Rimbaud that was certainly opposed in many of its facets to what has long been accepted as basic to Rimbaud's character. He did not see, or, rather, refused to see the sordid, sadistic, homosexual, iconoclastic *enfant terrible* in Rimbaud, and he was unrelenting in his opinion. This dogmatic viewpoint as it applied to Rimbaud was parallel to his religious fanaticism: having arrived at his conversion, he never compromised with it. He saw in religion the revelation of love in its relation to God, quite separate from any physical involvement; it was essentially cerebral and spiritual. And if he accepted and liked "men of action"—as Louis Chaigne says he did—if his Rodrigue, his Pierre de Craon, and his Tête d'Or are his real-life as well as his dramatic heroes, they were acceptable only insofar as they related to contemplative Catholic Christianity. This was also his view of Rimbaud, for even his acceptance of Rimbaud depended in part on Rimbaud's eventual conversion to Catholicism. Yet, if he evolved his own "myth of Rimbaud," there are, as in all myths, many elements of truth in Claudel's vision: the revolt, the anger, the sensitivity, the love of nature. And certainly even Claudel did not consider Rimbaud's works a definitive statement of theological beliefs, but rather a philosophical and metaphysical question mark reflecting the spiritual agony of a deeply sensitive young man.

One must necessarily wonder why Claudel held on to this dogmatism and fanaticism so tenaciously, why he clung so desperately to his religion and to his myth of Rimbaud. In all likelihood, we must interpret this as a kind of fear, parallel to the panic he saw in Rodin's statue of Victor Hugo. Realizing his own penchant for belligerence, for violence, ferociousness, and pride—all the excesses he discovered in Rimbaud—his religion and fanaticism were really a desperate clinging to some stability that would deliver him from the chaos that characterized Rimbaud's life and even the final hours before his death. Claudel could not accept for himself a totally adventurous kind of life, being too deeply imbued with what he himself recognized as *un esprit fonctionnaire*, a functionary spirit. Thus his faith was the balance between the reason of normal human existence and the madness of his sister Camille—as well as Rimbaud's ferocious spirit, just as the single underlying theme that gives unity to the whole of Rimbaud's themes, the one haunting aspect of his works, is a need for faith in God, his admission in himself of a "religious spirit."[3] Rimbaud's works are really a questioning to which the answer is suggested but never totally offered, and which Claudel brought to what was for him its logical conclusion. Claudel answers what Rimbaud questions; Claudel completes. In this sense, there is a profound unity between Rimbaud's and Claudel's works. Having discovered the Rimbaldian themes, the techniques, the poetic attitudes and doctrines, Claudel amplifies and brings them to the spiritual, metaphysical, theological, and philosophical conclusions that liberate him from the burden of doubt. In accepting his servitude to God, he has found the complete freedom of his soul that allows him to investigate the poetic possibilities posed by the universe: *"Je suis l'Inspecteur de la Création, le Vérificateur de la chose présente; la solidité de ce monde est la matière de ma béatitude!"* ["I am the Inspector of the Creation, the Verifier of things present; the solidity of this world is the substance of my bliss!"] (*Le Promeneur* in *Connaissance de l'Est*).

It may be said that Rimbaud, in attempting to become equal with the angels, had fallen into a Pascalian trap: *qui veut faire l'ange fait la bête,* he who wishes to be an angel becomes a beast—a fool. It remained for Claudel to take this "beast" and turn him into a "prince," just as Beauty had done for the Beast when, having experienced the profusion of fantasmagoric scenes in the enchanted castle, she realized that she liked him better than she liked other men who, with their false, corrupt, thankless hearts, were far more monstrous than he, and that she could not live without him. It was this prince who became the genie for Claudel, in a projection of his own spiritual and poetic aspirations. Through his love of Rimbaud, his having believed

---

3. Claudel was extremely close to his older sister Camille, and it was he who placed her in an institution for the insane after she was discovered living in paranoic solitude in her apartment in Paris. Her mental derangement, the result of her break with Rodin after having lived with him for several years as his disciple-mistress, was a source of deep bitterness and anguish for Claudel.

him on his word—albeit a "word" qualified by his own interpretation of it—his acceptance of him as not only a spiritual or thematic
but also a stylistic mentor, through his cult of Rimbaud, Claudel
has placed him at last among the angels—certainly little lower than
them. Rimbaud's influence is no longer the figment of some poetic
imagination but a reality as evident and as true, for Claudel, as the
mystery of God's Creation. In turning himself towards the earth in
order to glorify it poetically, Claudel has realized Rimbaud's quest
to discover "truth in one soul and one body."

Bibliography

Only works referred to in *The Prince and the Genie* are listed.

Baudelaire, Charles. *Les Fleurs du Mal.* Paris: Editions Garniers Fiereo, 1961.
Chaigne, Louis. *Vie de Paul Claudel.* Mame, 1961.
Chisholm, A. R. *The Art of Arthur Rimbaud.* London: MacMillan & Co., 1930.
Claudel, Paul. *Journal.* Paris: Bibliothèque de la Pléiade, Gallimard, 1968 (Tome I), 1969 (Tome II).
———. "Letter to H. F. Stewart," *Bulletin de la Société Paul Claudel,* 18 (1965).
———. *Œuvres Complètes.* 26 vols. Paris: Gallimard, 1950-67.
    Vol. 1 (1950): *Premiers Vers; Vers d'Exil; Cinq Grandes Odes; Processionnal pour saluer le siècle nouveau; La Cantate à trois voix; Corona Benignitatis Anni Dei.*
    Vol. 2 (1952): *La Messe là-bas; Feuilles de Saints; Poèmes de Guerre; Visages Radieux; Poésies Diverses.*
    Vol. 3 (1952): *Connaissance de l'Est; L'Oiseau Noir dans le Soleil Levant.*
    Vol. 4 (1952): *Sous le signe du dragon; Cent Phrases pour éventails; Petits Poëmes d'après le chinois; Autres Poëmes d'après le chinois; Dodoitzu; Ecrits divers.*
    Vol. 5 (1953): *Art Poétique; Figures et Paraboles; Quelques Planches du Bestiaire Spirituel; Le Symbolisme de la Salette.*
    Vol. 6 (1953): *Dédicace; L'Endormie; Fragment d'un drame; Tête d'Or.*
    Vol. 7 (1954): *La Ville; La Jeune Fille Violaine.*
    Vol. 8 (1954): *L'Echange; Le Repos du septième jour; Agamemnon; Les Choéphores; Les Euménides.*
    Vol. 9 (1955): *L'Annonce Faite à Marie.*
    Vol. 10 (1956): *L'Otage; Le Pain Dur; Le Père humilié.*
    Vol. 11 (1957): *Partage de Midi.*
    Vol. 12 (1958): *Le Soulier de Satin.*
    Vol. 13 (1958): *Protée; La Nuit de Noël 1914; L'Ours et la lune; l'Homme et son désir; La Sagesse ou la parabole du festin; Sous le rempart d'Athènes.*
    Vol. 14 (1958): *Le Livre de Christophe Colomb; Jeanne d'Arc au bûcher; L'Histoire de Tobie et de Sara; La Lune à la recherche d'elle-même; Le Jet de pierre; Le Ravissement de Scapin.*
    Vol. 15 (1959): *Positions et Propositions I; Positions et Propositions II.*
    Vol. 16 (1959): *Conversations dans le Loir-et-Cher; Contacts et Circonstances.*
    Vol. 17 (1960): *L'Œil Ecoute; Autres Textes sur l'art.*
    Vol. 18 (1961): *Accompagnements; Discours et Remerciements.*
    Vol. 19 (1962): *Les Aventures de Sophie; Un Poète regarde la croix.*
    Vol. 20 (1963): *L'Epée et le Miroir; Présence et Prophétie.*

Vol. 21 (1963): *Du Sens Figuré de l'Ecriture; Introduction à l'Apocalypse; Le Livre de Job; La Rose et le Rosaire; J'aime la Bible.*
Vol. 22 (1963): *Cantique des Cantiques.*
Vol. 23 (1964): *Seigneur, apprenez-nous à prier; Emmaüs.*
Vol. 24 (1965): *L'Evangile d'Isaie; Trois Figures saintes pour le temps actuel.*
Vol. 25 (1965): *Paul Claudel Interroge l'Apocalypse; Autres Textes Religieux.*
Vol. 26 (1967): *Au milieu des vitraux de l'Apocalypse.*
Correspondance: André Suarès et Paul Claudel. Paris: Gallimard, 1951.
Correspondance: Jacques Rivière et Paul Claudel 1907-1914, Paris: Librairie Plon, 1926.
Correspondance: Paul Claudel et André Gide 1899-1926. Paris: Gallimard, 1949.
Correspondance: Paul Claudel—Francis Jammes, Gabriel Frizeau 1897-1938. Paris: Gallimard, 1952.
Dhôtel, André. *Rimbaud et la révolte moderne.* Paris: Gallimard, 1952.
Etiemble, René. "D'André Suarès: la ténébreuse affaire Claudel-Rimbaud," *Le Monde,* November 16, 1968.
——. *Le Mythe de Rimbaud.* Paris: Gallimard, 1952.
Faurisson, Robert. Interpretation of *Voyelles, Bizarre,* spec. no., 4th quarter (1961).
Fowlie, Wallace. *Paul Claudel.* New York: Hillary House, 1957.
Frohock, W. M. *Rimbaud's Poetic Practice.* Cambridge, Mass.: Harvard University Press, 1963.
Galperine, Charles. Review of *Regards sur le théâtre de Claudel* by Gabriel Marcel, *Bulletin de la Société Paul Claudel,* 18 (1965).
Gengoux, Jacques. *La Pensée Poétique de Rimbaud.* Paris: Librairie Nizet, 1950.
Gide, André. *Journal: 1889-1912.* Rio de Janeiro: Americo-Edit., 1943.
Guillemin, Henri. "Claudel et Rimbaud," *Le Monde,* July 14-20, 1955.
——. *Claudel et son art d'écrire.* Paris: Gallimard, 1956.
——. *Le "Converti" Paul Claudel.* Paris: Gallimard, 1968.
Hackett, C. A. *Le Lyrisme de Rimbaud.* Paris: Librairie Bazet et Bastard, 1938.
——. *Rimbaud.* New York: Hillary House, 1957.
Lasserre, Pierre. *Les Chapelles Littéraires.* Paris: Librairie Garnier Frères, 1920.
Lefèvre, Frédéric. *Les Sources de Paul Claudel.* Paris: Librairie Lemercier, 1928.
Méléra, Marguerite-Yerta. "Les Voyages d'Arthur Rimbaud," *La Revue Universelle,* 35, no. 18 (December 15, 1928).
Mondor, Henri. *Claudel Plus Intime.* Paris: Gallimard, 1960.
Montaigne. *Essais.* Paris: Bibliotèque de la Pléiade, Gallimard, 1950.
Rimbaud, Jean-Arthur. *Œuvres.* Paris: Mercure de France, 1949.
——. *Œuvres.* Paris: Editions Garniers Frères, 1960.
——. *Œuvres Complètes.* Paris: Bibliotèque de la Pléiade, Gallimard, 1954.
Rivière, Jacques. *Rimbaud.* Paris: Editions Emile-Paul Frères.
Samson, Joseph. *Paul Claudel Poète Musicien.* Paris: Editions du Milieu du Monde, 1957.
Sausy, Lucien. "Le Text exact des *Voyelles,*" *Les Nouvelles Littéraires,* September 2, 1933.

Starkie, Enid. *Arthur Rimbaud.* New York: New Directions, 1961.

Van Hoorn, Herman Jan Willem. *Poésie et Mystique.* Paris: Librairie Minard, 1957.

Verlaine, Paul. *Œuvres Poétiques Complètes.* Paris: Bibliotèque de la Pléiade, Gallimard, 1957.

Index

his life